Selected Papers
on Computer Science

CSLI LECTURE NOTES NUMBER 59

Selected Papers on Computer Science

Donald E. Knuth

CSLI Publications

Copyright ©1996
Center for the Study of Language and Information
Leland Stanford Junior University
Printed in the United States
19 18 17 16 15   9 8 7 6 5

Library of Congress Cataloging-in-Publication Data

```
Knuth, Donald Ervin, 1938-
   Selected papers on computer science / Donald E. Knuth
   xii,276 p. 23 cm. -- (CSLI lecture notes ; no. 59)
   Includes bibliographical references and index.
   ISBN 978-1-881526-91-9 (paperback :  alk. paper) --
   ISBN 978-1-881526-92-6 (hardback :  alk. paper)
   1. Computer science. I. Title. II. Series.
QA76.6.K537  1996
004.1'1--dc20                              96-11382
                                               CIP
```

Internet page
   http://www-cs-faculty.stanford.edu/~knuth/cs.html
contains further information and links to related books.

to George Forsythe (1917–1972)
whose inspiring leadership
shaped the field

Contents

Preface

This book assembles under one roof all of the things I've written about computer science for people who aren't necessarily specialists in the subject — for scientists and mathematicians in general, and for educated people in all fields. I'm grateful for this opportunity to put the materials into a consistent format, and to correct errors in the original publications that have come to my attention. If any of this work deserves to be remembered, it is now in the form that I most wish people to remember it.

Scientists always find it easiest to write for colleagues who share their own subspecialty. But George Forsythe told me in 1970 that I should be prepared to explain things to a wider group of people — at least once or twice during my life — even though it is somewhat scary to talk to people you don't know very well. I kept his advice in mind during the next years and tried my best to fulfill this responsibility whenever suitable opportunities arose. Writing such papers has proved to be a pleasant task, and quite instructive, because it has given me a chance to reflect on what I've been doing and to see things in a broader perspective. Therefore I hope the reader will learn at least a fraction of what I've learned while preparing the expository material in this book.

Chapter 0 gives a brief definition of Computer Science together with the related notions of algorithms and programs. Then Chapter 1 discusses the relationship between Computer Science and the branch of science that is its nearest neighbor: Mathematics. Synergy between Computer Science and Mathematics is explored further in Chapter 2, which tells the story of how we are learning to cope with fundamental limitations of time and space, as computers get faster and more powerful yet do not keep up with our growing expectations.

Algorithms are the life-blood of Computer Science, so Chapter 3 is a general introduction to algorithms: what they are, what they're good for, how they are studied and compared. The similarities and differences between "algorithmic thinking" and "mathematical thinking" are highlighted in Chapter 4, which tries to understand modes of thought by analyzing a randomly chosen sample of works by prominent mathematicians. Chapter 5, "Algorithmic Themes," was written for the 100th birthday of the American Mathematical Society; it gives an overview of some interesting topics that belong to both Computer Science and Mathematics.

When I try to characterize my own life's work, I think of it primarily as an attempt to balance theoretical studies with practical achievements. Therefore I have often chosen the title "Theory and Practice" when I've been asked to speak on special occasions. The texts of four such talks appear in Chapters 6–9. Chapter 6, never before published, was the speech I gave when I was appointed to Stanford's first endowed chair in Computer Science (1977); Chapter 7 was a keynote speech delivered to the European Association for Theoretical Computer Science in the ancient Greek theater of Epidaurus (1985); Chapter 8, previously unpublished, was an after-dinner talk at the 40th birthday party for ENIAC, the first electronic computer (1986); Chapter 9 was the opening address of the 11th World Congress of the International Federation of Information Processing (1989). The philosophical flavor of these speeches carries over into Chapter 10, "Are Toy Problems Useful?", which discusses the relevance of work that may seem at first to be purely recreational.

The remaining chapters are devoted to topics in the *history* of Computer Science. Chapter 11 goes back thousands of years to the ancient origins of algorithms in middle-Eastern cultures. Then Chapter 12 skips to modern times (1945), with a detailed analysis of the first computer program written by John von Neumann, one of computing's key pioneers. Chapter 13 is about the IBM 650, the first computer to be installed in more than 1000 centers around the world. That machine was near and dear to my heart, because I spent many pleasant evenings with it during 1957–1960. Chapters 14 and 15 are brief and somewhat autobiographical. Finally, Chapter 16 is an obituary of George Forsythe, the inspiring leader who was chiefly responsible for the establishment of Computer Science as an academic discipline.

I have made minor adjustments to the texts, but by and large these chapters remain essentially as I originally wrote them. The bibliographies have been put into a consistent format, and many of the illustrations have been improved by redrawing them with METAPOST. Additional references have been added where appropriate, and I've also added supplementary material describing recent progress on problems that were unsolved when I had first discussed them. The most extensive amendments appear in Chapters 4 and 11.

I'm extremely grateful to Stanford's Center for the Study of Language and Information (CSLI) for the opportunity to publish this book and for their expertise in preparing everything the way I like to see it. In particular, Michael Inman prepared electronic forms of many files that had originally been typed by my secretary, Phyllis Winkler; Tony Gee collected and organized the materials in a timely manner; Copenhaver Cumpston designed the cover; and Dikran Karagueuzian initiated and supervised the entire project. Sun Microsystems provided me with a computer on which I was able to do the final editing and polishing.

This is the second in a series of books that CSLI plans to publish containing archival forms of the papers I have written. The first volume, *Literate Programming*, appeared in 1992. Six additional volumes are in preparation containing selected papers on Analysis of Algorithms, Computer Languages, Design of Algorithms, Digital Typography, Discrete Mathematics, Fun and Games.

Donald E. Knuth
Stanford, California
December 1995

Acknowledgments

"Algorithm and Program; Information and Data" originally appeared in *Communications of the ACM* **9**, Number 9 (June 1966), p. 654, as a letter to the editor. Copyright ©1966 by ACM Press. Reprinted by permission. Copyrights and Permissions courtesy Association for Computing Machinery, Inc.

"Computer Programming and Computer Science" originally appeared in *The Academic Press Dictionary of Science and Technology* (1992), p. 490. Copyright ©1992 by Academic Press, a subsidiary of Harcourt, Brace & Co. Reprinted by permission.

"Computer Science and its Relation to Mathematics" originally appeared in *American Mathematical Monthly* **81**, Number 4 (December 1974), pp. 323–343. Copyright ©1974 by Mathematical Association of America. Reprinted by permission.

"Mathematics and Computer Science: Coping with Finiteness" originally appeared in *Science* **194**, Number 4271 (December 17, 1976), pp. 1235–1242. Copyright ©1976 by American Association for the Advancement of Science. Reprinted by permission.

"Algorithms" originally appeared in *Scientific American* **236**, Number 4 (April 1977), pp. 63–80. The illustrations have been redrawn by Donald E. Knuth using METAPOST. Copyright ©1977 by Scientific American. Reprinted by permission.

Algorithms, Programs, and Computer Science

Let's begin by trying to understand some basic terms.

1. Algorithm and Program; Information and Data

*[Originally published in Communications of the ACM **9** (1966), 654.]*

EDITOR:

The letter by Dr. Huber defines "algorithm" in terms of programming languages. I would like to take a slightly different point of view, in which algorithms are concepts that have existence apart from any programming language. To me the word *algorithm* denotes an abstract method for computing some output from some input, while a *program* is an embodiment of a computational method in some language. I can write several different programs for the same algorithm (e.g., in ALGOL 60 and in PL/I, assuming that those languages are given an unambiguous interpretation).

Of course if I am pinned down and asked to explain more precisely what I mean by these remarks, I am forced to admit that I don't know any way to define any particular algorithm except in a programming language. Perhaps the set of all concepts should be regarded as a formal language of some sort. But I believe that algorithms were present long before Turing *et al.* formulated them, just as the concept of the number "two" was in existence long before the writers of first grade textbooks and other mathematical logicians gave it a certain precise definition.

By "computation" I mean essentially the same thing as what many people nowadays call "data processing," "symbol manipulation," or more generally "information processing."

There seems to be confusion between the words *information* and *data* much like that between *algorithm* and *program*. When a scientist conducts an experiment in which some quantity is being measured, we

1

have four things present, each of which is often called "information": (a) the true value of the quantity; (b) the approximation to this true value that is actually obtained by the measuring device; (c) a representation of the value (b) in some formal language; and (d) the concepts learned by the scientist by a study of the measurements. The word "data" is most appropriately applied to (c), and the word "information" when used in a technical sense should be further qualified by stating what kind of information is meant.

2. Computer Programming and Computer Science

[Originally published in the Academic Press Dictionary of Science and Technology (1992).]

A computer program is a representation of an algorithm in some well-defined language. Algorithms are abstract computational procedures for transforming information; programs are their concrete embodiments.

The world's first programmer may have been Lord Byron's daughter, A. Ada Lovelace, who worked with Charles Babbage to formulate precise instructions for the calculation of Bernoulli numbers on Babbage's unfinished Analytical Engine in 1843. The total number of people who now consider programming to be part of their profession has risen to more than 5 million in the United States alone, and there are perhaps 50 million people worldwide who regularly write programs of one kind or another.

The best programs are written so that computing machines can perform them quickly and so that human beings can understand them clearly. A programmer is ideally an essayist who works with traditional aesthetic and literary forms as well as mathematical concepts, to communicate the way that an algorithm works and to convince a reader that the results will be correct. Programs often need to be modified, because requirements and equipment change. Programs often need to be combined with other programs. Success at these endeavors is directly linked to the effectiveness of a programmer's expository skills.

Many subtle techniques are known by which programs can be made to run considerably faster than would be possible with a naïve approach. The quantitative theory of program efficiency is often called the analysis of algorithms. This field of study has many important subfields, including numerical analysis (the study of algorithms for scientific computation); complexity theory (the study of the best possible ways to solve given problems using given hardware); symbolic computation (the study of algorithms for manipulating algebraic formulas); computational geometry (the study of algorithms that deal with lines, surfaces, and volumes); combinatorial optimization (the study of algorithms for selecting the best of many possible alternatives); information retrieval and database theory (the study of algorithms for storing and retrieving large collections of facts); and the study of data structures (techniques of representing the relationships between discrete items of information).

Computer programming and the analysis of algorithms are, in turn, subfields of a considerably larger discipline called computer science, which deals with all of the complex phenomena surrounding computers. Computer science is known as "informatics" in French, German, and several other languages, but American researchers have been reluctant to embrace that term because it seems to place undue emphasis on the stuff that computers manipulate rather than on the processes of manipulation themselves.

Computer science answers the question "What can be automated?" Its principal subfields, besides the analysis of algorithms, presently include software engineering (the study of languages and methodologies for programming, of operating systems for controlling computer resources, and of utility programs tailored to significant applications like accounting or desktop publishing); graphics and visualization (the development of tools for analysis and synthesis of images); computer architecture and communication (the design of machines and of networks to connect them); artificial intelligence (the development of tools for accumulating, applying, and reasoning about knowledge); human-machine interaction (the study of interfaces between people and computers); robotics (the development of mobile machines with sensors); and interdisciplinary connections with virtually every other branch of science, technology, medicine, and the humanities.

Chapter 1

Computer Science and its Relation to Mathematics

*[Originally published in American Scientist **61** (1973), 707–713; and in The American Mathematical Monthly **81** (1974), 323–343, with additional material that is included here.]*

A new discipline called Computer Science has recently arrived on the scene at most of the world's universities. The present article gives a personal view of how this subject interacts with Mathematics, by discussing the similarities and differences between the two fields, and by examining some of the ways in which they help each other. A typical nontrivial problem is worked out in order to illustrate these interactions.

What is Computer Science?

Since Computer Science is relatively new, I must begin by explaining what it is all about. At least, my wife tells me that she has to explain it whenever anyone asks her what I do, and I suppose most people today have a somewhat different perception of the field than mine. In fact, no two computer scientists will probably give the same definition; this is not surprising, since it is just as hard to find two mathematicians who give the same definition of Mathematics. Fortunately it has been fashionable in recent years to have an "identity crisis," so computer scientists have been right in style.

My favorite way to describe computer science is to say that it is the study of algorithms. An algorithm is a precisely-defined sequence of rules telling how to produce specified output information from given input information in a finite number of steps. A particular representation of an algorithm is called a program, just as we use the word "data" to stand for a particular representation of "information" [16]. Perhaps the most significant discovery generated by the advent of computers will

5

turn out to be that algorithms, as objects of study, are extraordinarily rich in interesting properties; and furthermore, that an algorithmic point of view is a useful way to organize knowledge in general. G. E. Forsythe has observed that "the question 'What can be automated?' is one of the most inspiring philosophical and practical questions of contemporary civilization" [8].

From these remarks we might conclude that Computer Science should have existed long before the advent of computers. In a sense, it did; the subject is deeply rooted in history. For example, I recently found it interesting to study ancient documents, learning to what extent the Babylonians of 3500 years ago were computer scientists [18]. But computers are really necessary before we can learn much about the general properties of algorithms; human beings are not precise enough nor fast enough to carry out any but the simplest procedures. Therefore the potential richness of algorithmic studies was not fully realized until general-purpose computing machines became available.

I should point out that computing machines (and algorithms) do not only compute with *numbers*. They can deal with information of any kind, once it is represented in a precise way. We used to say that a sequence of symbols, such as a name, is represented inside a computer as if it were a number; but it is really more correct to say that a number is represented inside a computer as a sequence of symbols.

The French word for computer science is *Informatique*; the German is *Informatik*; in Danish, the word is *Datalogi* [23]. All of these terms wisely imply that computer science deals with many things besides the solution to numerical equations. However, these names emphasize the "stuff" that algorithms manipulate (the information or data), instead of the algorithms themselves. The Norwegians at the University of Oslo have chosen a somewhat more appropriate designation for computer science, namely *Databehandling*; its English equivalent, "Data Processing" has unfortunately been used in America only in connection with business applications, while "Information Processing" tends to connote library applications. Several people have suggested the term "Computing Science" as superior to "Computer Science."

The search for a perfect name is somewhat pointless, of course, since the underlying concepts are much more important than the name. Yet we cannot help noticing that these other names for computer science all de-emphasize the role of computing machines themselves, apparently in order to make the field more legitimate and respectable. Many people's opinion of a computing machine is, at best, that it is a necessary evil: a difficult tool to be used if other methods fail. Why should we give so much emphasis to teaching how to use computers, if they are merely valuable tools like (say) electron microscopes?

Computer scientists, knowing that computers are more exciting than mere tools, instinctively underplay the machine aspect when they are defending their new discipline. However, it is not necessary to be so self-conscious about machines; this has aptly been pointed out by Newell, Perlis, and Simon [24], who define computer science simply as the study of computers, just as botany is the study of plants, astronomy the study of stars, and so on. The phenomena surrounding computers are immensely varied and complex, requiring description and explanation; and, like electricity, these phenomena belong both to engineering and to science.

When I say that computer science is the study of algorithms, I am singling out only one of the "phenomena surrounding computers," so computer science actually includes more. I have emphasized algorithms because they are really the central core of the subject, the common denominator that underlies and unifies the different branches. It might happen that technology someday settles down, so that in say 25 years computing machines will be changing very little. There are no indications of such a stable technology in the near future, quite the contrary, but I believe that the study of algorithms will remain challenging and important even if the other phenomena of computers might someday be fully explored. The reader interested in further discussions of the nature of computer science is referred to [19], [30], and [32], in addition to the references cited above.

Is Computer Science Part of Mathematics?

Certainly there are diverse phenomena about computers that are now being actively studied by computer scientists, phenomena that are hardly mathematical. But if we restrict our attention to the study of algorithms, isn't this merely a branch of mathematics? After all, algorithms were studied primarily by mathematicians, if by anyone, before the days of computing machines. Therefore one could argue that this central aspect of computer science is really part of mathematics.

However, I believe that a similar argument can be made for the proposition that mathematics is a part of computer science! Thus, by the definition of set equality, the subjects would be proved equal; or at least, by the Schröder-Bernstein theorem, they would be equipotent. My own feeling is that neither of these set inclusions is valid. It is always difficult to establish precise boundary lines between disciplines (compare, for example, the subjects of "physical chemistry" and "chemical physics"); but it is possible to distinguish essentially different points of view between mathematics and computer science.

The following true story is perhaps the best way to explain the distinction I have in mind. Some years ago I had just learned a mathematical theorem from which it followed that any two $n \times n$ matrices A and B of integers have a "greatest common right divisor" D. This means that D is a right divisor of A and of B, i.e., $A = A'D$ and $B = B'D$ for some integer matrices A' and B', and that every common right divisor of A and B is a right divisor of D. So I wondered how to calculate the greatest common right divisor of two given matrices. A few days later I happened to be attending a conference where I met the mathematician H. B. Mann, and I felt that he would know how to solve this problem. I asked him, and he did indeed know the correct answer; but it was a mathematician's answer, not a computer scientist's answer! He said, "Let $\mathfrak{R}$ be the ring of $n \times n$ integer matrices; in this ring, the sum of two principal left ideals is principal, so let D be such that

$$\mathfrak{R}A + \mathfrak{R}B = \mathfrak{R}D.$$

Then D is the greatest common right divisor of A and B." This formula is certainly the simplest possible one; we need only eight symbols to write it down. And it relies on rigorously-proved theorems of mathematical algebra. But from the standpoint of a computer scientist, it is worthless, since it involves constructing the infinite sets $\mathfrak{R}A$ and $\mathfrak{R}B$, taking their sum, then searching through infinitely many matrices D until finding one for which this sum matches the infinite set $\mathfrak{R}D$. I could not determine the greatest common right divisor of $\left(\begin{smallmatrix} 1 & 2 \\ 3 & 4 \end{smallmatrix}\right)$ and $\left(\begin{smallmatrix} 4 & 3 \\ 2 & 1 \end{smallmatrix}\right)$ by doing such infinite operations. (Incidentally, I eventually found a computer scientist's answer to this question in a book by E. Cahen, 1914; see [17, exercise 4.6.1–19].)

One of my mathematical friends told me he would be willing to recognize computer science as a worthwhile field of study, as soon as it contains 1000 deep theorems. This criterion should obviously be changed to include algorithms as well as theorems, say 500 deep theorems and 500 deep algorithms. But even so it is clear that computer science today does not measure up to such a test, if "deep" means that a brilliant person would need many months to discover the theorem or the algorithm. Computer science is still too young for this; I can claim youth as a handicap. We still do not know the best way to describe algorithms, to understand them or to prove them correct, to invent them, or to analyze their behavior, although considerable progress is being made on all these fronts. The potential for "1000 deep results" is there, but only perhaps 50 have been discovered up to the present time (1974).*

In order to describe the mutual impact of computer science and mathematics on each other, and their relative roles, I'm therefore looking somewhat to the future, to the time when computer science is a bit more mature and sure of itself. Recent trends have made it possible to envision a day when computer science and mathematics will both exist as respected disciplines, serving analogous but different roles in a person's education. To quote George Forsythe again, "The most valuable acquisitions in a scientific or technical education are the general-purpose mental tools which remain serviceable for a lifetime. I rate natural language and mathematics as the most important of these tools, and computer science as a third" [9].

Like mathematics, computer science will be a subject that is considered basic to a general education. Like mathematics and other sciences, computer science will continue to be vaguely divided into two areas, which might be called "theoretical" and "applied." Like mathematics, computer science will be somewhat different from the other sciences, in that it deals with artificial laws that can be proved, instead of natural laws that are never known with certainty. Thus, the two subjects will be like each other in many ways. The difference is in the subject matter and the approach — mathematics dealing more or less with theorems, infinite processes, static relationships, and computer science dealing more or less with algorithms, finitary constructions, dynamic relationships.

Many computer scientists have been doing mathematics, but many more mathematicians have been doing computer science in disguise. I have been impressed by numerous instances of mathematical theories that are really about particular algorithms; these theories are typically formulated in mathematical terms that are much more cumbersome and less natural than the equivalent algorithmic formulation today's computer scientists would use. For example, most of the content of a 35-page paper by Abraham Wald can be presented in about two pages when it is recast into algorithmic terms [17, Section 3.5D]; and numerous other examples can be given. But that is a subject for another paper.

Educational Side Effects

A person well-trained in computer science knows how to deal with algorithms: how to construct them, manipulate them, understand them,

---

* I now believe that the 1000 mark was passed about 1980. And Volume 1000 of Springer's *Lecture Notes in Computer Science* was published in 1995.

analyze them. This knowledge is preparation for much more than writing good computer programs; it is a general-purpose mental tool that will be a definite aid to the understanding of other subjects, whether they be chemistry, linguistics, or music, etc. The reason for this may be understood in the following way: It has often been said that a person does not really understand something until after teaching it to someone else. Actually a person does not *really* understand something until after teaching it to a *computer*, i.e., expressing it as an algorithm. "The automatic computer really *forces* that precision of thinking which is alleged to be a product of any study of mathematics" [7]. An attempt to formalize things as algorithms leads to a much deeper understanding than if we simply try to comprehend things in the traditional way.

Linguists thought that they understood languages, until they tried to explain languages to computers; they soon discovered how much more remains to be learned. Many people have set up computer models of things, and have discovered that they learned more while setting up the model than while actually looking at the output of the eventual program.

In the late 1940s, when UNIVAC was the first large-scale computer to be marketed commercially, a total of three customers signed up to buy one: the U.S. Census Bureau, the Prudential Life Insurance Company, and the A. C. Nielsen Company of television rating fame. When the Nielsen people, together with UNIVAC's technical representatives, analyzed their operations carefully enough to see how to computerize everything, they discovered how to save so much time and money that they didn't need a computer after all [14]!

For three years I taught a sophomore course in abstract algebra for mathematics majors at Caltech, and the most difficult topic was always the study of "Jordan canonical forms" for matrices. The third year I tried a new approach, by looking at the subject algorithmically, and suddenly it became quite clear. The same thing happened with the discussion of finite groups defined by generators and relations, and in another course with the reduction theory of binary quadratic forms. By presenting the subject in terms of algorithms, the purpose and meaning of the mathematical theorems became transparent.

Later, while writing a book on computer arithmetic [17], I found that virtually every theorem in elementary number theory arises in a natural, motivated way in connection with the problem of making computers do high-speed numerical calculations. Therefore I believe that the traditional courses in elementary number theory might well be changed to adopt this point of view, adding a practical motivation to the already beautiful theory.

These examples and many more have convinced me of the pedagogic value of an algorithmic approach; such an approach promotes the understanding of concepts of all kinds. I believe that students who are properly trained in computer science are learning things that will implicitly help them cope with many other subjects. Therefore there soon will be good reason to claim that undergraduate computer science majors have received a good general education, just as we now believe this of undergraduate math majors. On the other hand, the present-day undergraduate courses in computer science are not yet fulfilling this goal; at least, I find that many beginning graduate students with an undergraduate degree in computer science have been more narrowly educated than I would like. Computer scientists are working to correct this present deficiency, which I believe is probably due to an overemphasis on computer languages instead of algorithms.

Some Interactions

Computer science has been affecting mathematics in many ways, and I shall try to list the good ones here. In the first place, of course, computers can be used to compute, and they have frequently been applied in mathematical research when hand computations are too difficult; they generate data that suggests or demolishes conjectures. For example, Gauss said [11] that he first thought of the prime number theorem by looking at a table of the primes less than one million. In my own Ph.D. thesis, I was able to resolve a conjecture concerning infinitely many cases by looking closely at computer calculations of the smallest case [15]. An example of another kind is Marshall Hall's recent progress in the determination of all simple groups of orders up to one million. Secondly, there are obvious connections between computer science and mathematics in the areas of numerical analysis [31], logic, and number theory; I need not dwell on these here, since they are so widely known. However, I should mention especially the work of D. H. Lehmer, who has combined computing with classical mathematics in several remarkable ways; for example, he has proved that every set of six consecutive integers > 285 contains a multiple of a prime > 41.

Another impact of computer science has been an increased emphasis on constructions in all branches of mathematics. Replacing existence proofs by algorithms that construct mathematical objects has often led to improvements in an abstract theory. For example, E. C. Dade and H. Zassenhaus remarked, at the close of a paper written in 1963, "This concept of genus has already proved of importance in the theory of modules over orders. So a mathematical idea introduced solely with a view to computability has turned out to have an intrinsic theoretical value of its own." Furthermore, as mentioned above, the constructive algorithmic approach often has pedagogic value.

Another way in which the algorithmic approach affects mathematical theories is in the construction of one-to-one correspondences. Quite often there have been indirect proofs that certain types of mathematical objects are equinumerous; then a direct construction of a one-to-one correspondence shows that in fact even more is true.

Discrete mathematics, especially combinatorial theory, has been given an added boost by the rise of computer science, in addition to all the other fields in which discrete mathematics is currently being extensively applied.

For references to these influences of computing on mathematics, and for many more examples, the reader is referred to the following sampling of books, each of which contains quite a few relevant papers: [1], [2], [4], [5], [22], [26], [28]. Peter Lax's article [21] discusses the effect that computing has had on mathematical physics.

But actually, in my opinion, the most important impact of computer science on mathematics is somewhat different from all of the above. To me, the most significant thing is that the study of algorithms themselves has opened up a fertile vein of interesting new mathematical problems; it provides a breath of life for many areas of mathematics that had been suffering from a lack of new ideas. Charles Babbage, one of the "fathers" of computing machines, predicted this already in 1864: "As soon as an Analytical Engine [i.e., a general-purpose computer] exists, it will necessarily guide the future course of the science. Whenever any result is sought by its aid, the question will then arise — By what course of calculation can these results be arrived at by the machine in the shortest time?" [3]. And again, George Forsythe in 1958: "The use of practically any computing technique itself raises a number of mathematical problems. There is thus a very considerable impact of computation on mathematics itself, and this may be expected to influence mathematical research to an increasing degree" [10]. Garrett Birkhoff [4, p. 2] has observed that such influences are not a new phenomenon, they were already significant in the early Greek development of mathematics. I have found that a great many intriguing mathematical problems arise when we try to analyze an algorithm quantitatively, to see how fast it will run on a computer; a typical example of such a problem is worked out below. Another family of extremely interesting problems concerns the search for best possible algorithms in a given class; see, for example, the recent survey by Reingold [27]. One of the first mathematical theories to be inspired by computer science is the theory of languages, which by now includes many beautiful results; see [12] and [13]. The excitement of these new theories is the reason I became a computer scientist.

Conversely, mathematics obviously has a profound influence on computer science; nearly every branch of mathematical knowledge has been brought to bear somewhere. I recently worked on a problem dealing with discrete objects called "binary trees," which arise frequently in computer representations of things, and the solution to the problem involved the complex gamma function times the square of Riemann's zeta function [6]. Thus the results of classical mathematics often turn out to be useful in rather amazing places.

The most surprising thing to me, in my own experiences with applications of mathematics to computer science, has been the fact that so much of the mathematics has been of a particular discrete type, examples of which are discussed below. Such mathematics was almost entirely absent from my own training, although I had a reasonably good undergraduate and graduate education in mathematics. Nearly all of my encounters with such techniques during my student days occurred when working problems from the *American Mathematical Monthly*. I have naturally been wondering whether or not the traditional curriculum — the calculus courses, etc. — should be revised in order to include more of these discrete mathematical manipulations, or whether computer science is exceptional in its frequent application of them.

A Detailed Example

In order to clarify some of the vague generalizations and assertions made above, I believe it is best to discuss a typical computer-science problem in some depth. The particular example I have chosen is the one that first led me personally to realize that computer algorithms suggest interesting mathematical problems. This happened in 1962, when I was a graduate student in mathematics; computer programming was a hobby of mine, and a part time job, but I had never really ever worn my mathematician's cloak and my computing cap at the same time. A friend of mine remarked that "some good mathematicians at IBM" had been unable to determine how fast a certain well-known computer method works, and I thought it might be an interesting problem to look at.

Here is the problem: Many computer applications involve the retrieval of information by its "name"; for example, we might imagine a Russian-English dictionary, in which we want to look up a Russian word in order to find its English equivalent. A standard computer method called *hashing* retrieves information by its name as follows. A rather large number, m, of memory positions within the machine is used to hold the names; let us call these positions T_1, T_2, ..., T_m. Each of these positions is big enough to contain one name. The number m is always larger than the total number of names present; therefore at least one of the T_i is empty. The names are distributed among the T_i's in a certain way described below, designed to facilitate retrieval. Another set of memory positions E_1, E_2, ..., E_m is used for the information corresponding to the names; thus if T_i is not empty, E_i contains the information corresponding to the name stored in T_i.

The ideal way to retrieve information using such a table would be to take a given name x, and to compute some function $f(x)$, which lies between 1 and m; then the name x could be placed in position $T_{f(x)}$, and the corresponding information in $E_{f(x)}$. Such a function $f(x)$ would make the retrieval problem trivial, if $f(x)$ were easy to compute and if $f(x) \neq f(y)$ for all distinct names $x \neq y$. In practice, however, these latter two requirements are hardly ever satisfied simultaneously; if $f(x)$ is easy to compute, we have $f(x) = f(y)$ for some distinct names. Furthermore, we don't usually know in advance just which names will occur in the table, and the function f must be chosen to work for all names in a very large set U of potential names, where U has many more than m elements. For example, if U contains all sequences of seven letters, there are $26^7 = 8{,}031{,}810{,}176$ potential names; it is inevitable that $f(x) = f(y)$ will occur.

Therefore we try to choose a function $f(x)$, from U into the set of locations $\{1, 2, \ldots, m\}$, so that $f(x) = f(y)$ will occur with the approximate probability $1/m$, when x and y are distinct names. Such a function f is called a *hash function*. In practice, $f(x)$ is often computed by regarding x as a number and taking its remainder modulo m, plus one; the number m in this case is usually chosen to be prime, since this can be shown to give better results for the sets of names that generally arise in practice. When $f(x) = f(y)$ for distinct x and y, a "collision" is said to occur; collisions are resolved by searching through positions numbered $f(x) + 1, f(x) + 2$, etc.

The following algorithm expresses exactly how a hash function $f(x)$ can be used to retrieve the information corresponding to a given name x in U. The algorithm makes use of a variable i that takes on integer values.

STEP 1. Set the value of i equal to $f(x)$.

STEP 2. If memory position T_i contains the given name x, stop; the derived information is located in memory position E_i.

STEP 3. If memory position T_i is empty, stop; the given name x is not present.

STEP 4. Increase the value of i by one. (Or, if i was equal to m, set i equal to one.) Return to step 2.

We still haven't said how the names get into $T_1, \ldots, T_m$ in the first place; but that is really not difficult. We start with all the T_i empty. Then to insert a new name x, we look for x using the algorithm stated; it will stop in step 3 because x is not there. Then we set T_i equal to x, and put the corresponding information in E_i. From now on, we will be able to retrieve this information, whenever the name x is given, since the algorithm will find position T_i by repeating the actions that took it to position T_i when x was inserted.

The mathematical problem is to determine how much searching we should expect to make, on the average; how many times must step 2 be repeated before x is found?

This same problem can be stated in other ways, for example in terms of a modified game of "musical chairs." Consider a set of m empty chairs arranged in a circle. A person appears at a random spot just outside the circle, and dashes in a clockwise direction to the first available chair. This is repeated m times, until all chairs are full. How far, on the average, does the nth person have to run before finding a seat? For example, let $m = 10$ and suppose there are ten players: $A, B, C, D, E, F, G, H, I, J$. To get a random sequence, let us assume that the players successively start looking for their seats beginning at chairs numbered according to the first digits of π, namely 3, 1, 4, 1, 5, 9, 2, 6, 5, 3. Figure 1 on the next page shows the situation after the first six have been seated. (Thus player A takes chair 3, then player B takes chair 1, ..., player F takes chair 9.) Now player G starts at chair number 2, and eventually sits down in number 6. Finally, players H, I, and J will go into chairs 7, 8, and 10. In this example, the distances traveled by the ten players are respectively 0, 0, 0, 1, 0, 0, 4, 1, 3, 7.

It is not trivial to analyze this problem, because congestion tends to occur; one or more long runs of consecutive occupied chairs will usually be present. In order to see why this is true, let's consider Figure 1 again, supposing that the next player G starts in a random place; then G will land in chair number 6 with probability 0.6, but in chair number 7 with probability only 0.1. Long runs tend to get even longer. Therefore we cannot simply assume that the configuration of occupied vs. empty chairs is random at each stage; the piling-up phenomenon must be reckoned with.

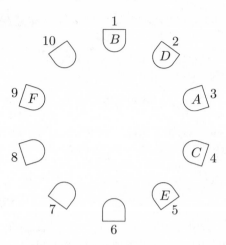

FIGURE 1.

A "musical chairs" game, which corresponds to an important computer method.

Let the starting places of the m players be $a_1 a_2 \ldots a_m$; we shall call this a *hash sequence*. For example, the hash sequence above is 3 1 4 1 5 9 2 6 5 3. Assuming that each of the m^m possible hash sequences is equally likely, our problem is to determine the average distance traveled by the nth player, for each n, in units of "chairs passed." Let us call this distance $d(m, n)$. Obviously $d(m, 1) = 0$, since the first player always finds an unoccupied place; furthermore $d(m, 2) = 1/m$, since the second player has to go at most one space, and the extra step is necessary only if both players start at the same spot. It is also easy to see that $d(m, m) = (0 + 1 + \cdots + (m - 1))/m = \frac{1}{2}(m - 1)$, since all chairs but one will be occupied when the last player starts out. Unfortunately the in-between values of $d(m, n)$ are more complicated.

Let $u_k(m, n)$ be the number of partial hash sequences $a_1 a_2 \ldots a_n$ such that chair k will be unoccupied after the first n players are seated. This quantity is easy to determine, by cyclic symmetry, since chair k is just as likely to be occupied as any other particular chair; in other words, $u_1(m, n) = u_2(m, n) = \cdots = u_m(m, n)$. Let $u(m, n)$ be this common value. Furthermore, $mu(m, n) = u_1(m, n) + u_2(m, n) + \cdots + u_m(m, n) = (m - n) m^n$, since each of the m^n partial hash sequences $a_1 a_2 \ldots a_n$ leaves $m - n$ chairs empty, and contributes 1 to exactly $m - n$ of the numbers $u_k(m, n)$. Therefore

$$u_k(m, n) = (m - n) m^{n-1}.$$

Let $v(m, n, k)$ be the number of partial hash sequences $a_1 a_2 \ldots a_n$ such that, after the n players are seated, chairs 1 through k will be occupied, while chairs m and $k + 1$ will not. This number is slightly harder to determine, but not really difficult. If we look at the numbers a_i that are $\leq k + 1$ in such a partial hash sequence, and if we cross out the other numbers, the k values that are left form one of the sequences enumerated by $u(k + 1, k)$. Furthermore the $n - k$ values crossed out form one of the sequences enumerated by $u(m - 1 - k, n - k)$, if we subtract $k + 1$ from each of them. Conversely, if we take any partial hash sequence $a_1 \ldots a_k$ enumerated by $u(k + 1, k)$, and another one $b_1 \ldots b_{n-k}$ enumerated by $u(m - 1 - k, n - k)$, and if we intermix $a_1 \ldots a_k$ with $(b_1 + k + 1) \ldots (b_{n-k} + k + 1)$ in any of the $\binom{n}{k}$ possible ways, we obtain one of the sequences enumerated by $v(m, n, k)$. (The binomial coefficient

$$\binom{n}{k} = \frac{n!}{k! \, (n - k)!}$$

denotes the number of ways to choose k positions out of n.) For example, let $m = 10, n = 6, k = 3$; one of the partial hash sequences enumerated by $v(10, 6, 3)$ is 2 7 1 8 2 8. This sequence splits into $a_1 a_2 a_3 = 2\ 1\ 2$ and $(b_1 + 4)(b_2 + 4)(b_3 + 4) = 7\ 8\ 8$, intermixed in the pattern $ababab$. From each of the $u(4, 3) = 16$ sequences $a_1 a_2 a_3$ that fill positions $\{1, 2, 3\}$, together with each of the $u(6, 3) = 108$ sequences $(b_1 + 4)(b_2 + 4)(b_3 + 4)$ that fill three of positions $\{5, 6, 7, 8, 9\}$, we obtain $\binom{6}{3} = 20$ sequences that fill positions $\{1, 2, 3\}$ and that leave positions 4 and 10 unoccupied, by intermixing the a's and b's in all possible ways.

The construction just described shows that

$$v(m, n, k) = \binom{n}{k} u(k + 1, k) \, u(m - k - 1, n - k);$$

hence our formula for $u(m, n)$ tells us that

$$v(m, n, k) = \binom{n}{k} (k + 1)^{k-1} (m - n - 1)(m - k - 1)^{n-k-1}.$$

This is not a simple formula. But it is correct, so we cannot do any better. If $k = n = m - 1$, the last two factors in the formula give $0/0$, which should be interpreted as 1 in this case.

Now we are ready to compute the desired average distance $d(m, n)$. The nth player must move k steps if and only if the preceding partial hash sequence $a_1 \ldots a_{n-1}$ has made chairs a_n through $a_n + k - 1$ occupied and chair $a_n + k$ empty. The number of such partial hash sequences is

$$v(m, n-1, k) + v(m, n-1, k+1) + v(m, n-1, k+2) + \cdots,$$

since circular symmetry shows that $v(m, n-1, k+r)$ is the number of partial hash sequences $a_1 \ldots a_{n-1}$ leaving chairs $a_n + k$ and $a_n - r - 1$ empty while the $k + r$ chairs between them are filled. Therefore the probability $p_k(m, n)$ that the nth player goes exactly k steps is

$$p_k(m, n) = \sum_{r \geq k} v(m, n-1, r)/m^{n-1};$$

and the average distance is

$$d(m, n) = \sum_{k \geq 0} k p_k(m, n)$$

$$= (m - n)\, m^{1-n} \sum_{r \geq k \geq 0} k \binom{n-1}{r} (r+1)^{r-1} (m - r - 1)^{n-r-2}$$

$$= \frac{(m - n)\, m^{1-n}}{2} \sum_{r \geq 0} r \binom{n-1}{r} (r+1)^r (m - r - 1)^{n-r-2}.$$

At this point, a person with a typical mathematical upbringing will probably stop, or resort to asymptotic approximation; the answer is a horrible-looking summation. Yet, if more attention were paid during our mathematical training to finite sums, instead of concentrating so heavily on integrals, we would instinctively recognize that a sum like this can be considerably simplified. When I first looked at this sum, I had never seen one like it before; but I suspected that something could be done to it, since the sum over k of $p_k(m, n)$ must be 1. Later I learned about the extensive literature of such sums. I don't wish to go into the details here, but I do want to point out that such sums arise repeatedly in the study of algorithms. By now I have seen literally hundreds of examples in which finite sums involving binomial coefficients and related functions appear in connection with computer science studies; so I have introduced a course called "Concrete Mathematics" at Stanford University, in which this kind of mathematics is taught.

Let $\delta(m, n)$ be the average number of chairs skipped past by the first n players:

$$\delta(m, n) = (d(m, 1) + d(m, 2) + \cdots + d(m, n))/n.$$

This corresponds to the average amount of time needed for the hashing algorithm to find an item when n items have been stored. The value of $d(m, n)$ derived above can be simplified to obtain the following formulas:

$$d(m,n) = \frac{1}{2}\left(2\frac{n-1}{m} + 3\frac{n-1}{m}\frac{n-2}{m} + 4\frac{n-1}{m}\frac{n-2}{m}\frac{n-3}{m} + \cdots\right),$$

$$\delta(m,n) = \frac{1}{2}\left(\frac{n-1}{m} + \frac{n-1}{m}\frac{n-2}{m} + \frac{n-1}{m}\frac{n-2}{m}\frac{n-3}{m} + \cdots\right).$$

These formulas can be used to see the behavior for large m and n. For example, if $\alpha = n/m$ is the ratio of filled positions to the total number of positions, and if we hold α fixed while m approaches infinity, then $\delta(m, \alpha m)$ increases to the limiting value $\frac{1}{2}\alpha/(1 - \alpha)$.

The formula for $\delta(m, n)$ also tells us another surprising thing:

$$\delta(m,n) = \frac{n-1}{2m} + \frac{n-1}{m}\delta(m, n-1).$$

If somebody could discover a simple trick by which this simple relation could be proved directly, it would lead to a much more elegant analysis of the hashing algorithm and it might provide further insights. Unfortunately, I have been unable to think of any direct way to prove this relation.

When $n = m$ (i.e., when all players are seated and all chairs are occupied), the average distance traveled per player is

$$\delta(m,m) = \frac{1}{2}\left(\frac{m-1}{m} + \frac{m-1}{m}\frac{m-2}{m} + \frac{m-1}{m}\frac{m-2}{m}\frac{m-3}{m} + \cdots\right).$$

It is interesting to study this function, which can be shown to have the approximate value

$$\delta(m,m) \approx \sqrt{\frac{\pi m}{8}} - \frac{2}{3}$$

for large m. Thus, the number π, which entered Figure 1 so artificially, is actually present naturally in the problem as well! Such asymptotic calculations, combined with discrete summations as above, are typical of what arises when we study algorithms; classical mathematical analysis and discrete mathematics both play important roles.

Extensions

We have now solved the musical chairs problem, so the analysis of hashing is complete. But many more problems are suggested by this one. For example, what happens if each of the hash table positions T_i is able to hold two names instead of one, i.e., if we allow two people per chair in the musical chairs game? Nobody has yet found the exact formulas for this case, although some approximate formulas are known.

We might also ask what happens if each player in the musical chairs game starts *simultaneously* to look for a free chair (still always moving clockwise), starting at independently random points. The answer is that each player will move past $\delta(m, n)$ chairs on the average, where $\delta(m, n)$ is the same as above. This follows from an interesting theorem of W. W. Peterson [25], who was the first to study the properties of the hashing problem described above. Peterson proved that the total displacement of the n players, for any partial hash sequence $a_1 a_2 \ldots a_n$, is independent of the order of the a_i's; thus, 3 1 4 1 5 9 2 leads to the same total displacement as 1 1 2 3 4 5 9 and 2 9 5 1 4 1 3. His theorem shows that the average time $\delta(m, n)$ per player is the same for all arrangements of the a_i, and therefore it is also unchanged when all players start simultaneously.

On the other hand, the average amount of time required until all n players are seated has not been determined, to my knowledge, for the simultaneous case. In fact, I just thought of this problem while writing the present paper. New problems flow out of computer science studies at a great rate!

We might also ask what happens if the players can choose to go either clockwise or counterclockwise, whichever is shorter. In the non-simultaneous case, the analysis above can be extended without difficulty to show that each player will then have to go about half as far. (We require everyone to go all the way around the circle to the nearest seat, not taking a short cut through the middle.)

Another variant of the hashing problem arises when we change the cyclic order of probing, in order to counteract the "piling up" phenomenon. This interesting variation is of practical importance, since the congestion caused by long stretches of occupied positions tends to slow things down considerably when the memory gets full. Since the analysis of this practical problem is largely unresolved, and since it has several interesting mathematical aspects, I shall discuss it in detail in the remainder of this article.

A generalized hashing technique that for technical reasons is called *single hashing* is defined by any $m \times m$ matrix Q of integers for which

(i) Each row contains all the numbers from 1 to m in some order;

(ii) The first column contains the numbers from 1 to m in order.

The other columns are unrestricted. For example, one such matrix for $m = 4$, selected more or less at random, is

$$Q_1 = \begin{pmatrix} 1 & 3 & 2 & 4 \\ 2 & 1 & 3 & 4 \\ 3 & 4 & 1 & 2 \\ 4 & 3 & 2 & 1 \end{pmatrix}.$$

The idea is to use a hash function $f(x)$ to select a row of Q and then to probe the memory positions in the order dictated by that row. The same algorithm for searching the memory is used as before, except that step 4 becomes

STEP 4′. Advance i to the next value in row $f(x)$ of the matrix, and return to step 2.

Thus, the cyclic hashing scheme described earlier is a special case of single hashing, using a cyclic matrix like

$$Q_2 = \begin{pmatrix} 1 & 2 & 3 & 4 \\ 2 & 3 & 4 & 1 \\ 3 & 4 & 1 & 2 \\ 4 & 1 & 2 & 3 \end{pmatrix}.$$

In the musical chair analogy, the players no longer are required to move clockwise; different players will in general visit the chairs in different sequences. However, if two players start in the same place, they must both follow the same chair-visiting sequence. This latter condition will produce a slight congestion, which is noticeable but not nearly as significant as in the cyclic case.

As before, we can define the measures $d'(m, n)$ and $\delta'(m, n)$, corresponding to the number of times step 4′ is performed. The central problem is to find matrices Q that are *best possible*, in the sense that $\delta'(m, m)$ is minimized. This problem is not really a practical one, since the matrix with smallest $\delta'(m, m)$ might require a great deal of computation per execution of step 4′. Yet it is very interesting to establish absolute limits on how good a single-hashing method could possibly be, as a yardstick by which to measure particular cases.

One of the most difficult problems in algorithmic analysis that I have had the pleasure of solving is the determination of $d'(m, n)$ for single hashing when the matrix Q is chosen at random, i.e., to find the value of $d'(m, n)$ averaged over all $(m - 1)!^m$ possible matrices Q. The resulting formula is

$$
d'_r(m, n) = m - \frac{m - n + 1}{m - n + 2}\left(1 + \right.
$$

$$
\left(m + \sum_{j=1}^{n-1} \frac{1 - 1/(m+2-j)}{m \prod_{i=1}^{j}(1 - 1/(m(m+2-i)))}\right) \prod_{j=1}^{n-1}\left(1 - \frac{1}{m(m+2-j)}\right)\left.\right).
$$

This one I do not know how to simplify at the present time. However, it is possible to study the asymptotic behavior of $d'_r(m, n)$, and to show that

$$
\delta'_r(m, m) \approx \ln m + \gamma - 1.5
$$

for large m, plus a correction term of order $(\log m)/m$. (Here $\gamma \approx$ .577216 is Euler's constant.) This order of growth is substantially better than the cyclic method, where $\delta(m, m)$ grows like the square root of m; and we know that some single-hashing matrices must have an even lower value for $\delta'(m, m)$ than this average value $\delta'_r(m, m)$. Table 1 shows the exact values of $\delta(m, m)$ and $\delta'_r(m, m)$ for comparatively small values of m; note that cyclic hashing is superior for $m \leq 11$, but it eventually becomes much worse.

Proofs of the statements above, together with additional facts about hashing, appear in [20].

No satisfactory lower bounds for the value of $\delta'(m, m)$ in the best single-hashing scheme are known, although I believe that none will have $\delta'(m, m)$ lower than

$$
\left(1 + \frac{1}{m}\right)\left(1 + \frac{1}{2} + \cdots + \frac{1}{m}\right) - 2;
$$

this is the value that arises in the musical chairs game if each player follows a random path independently of all the others. J. D. Ullman [29] has given a more general conjecture from which this statement would follow. If Ullman's conjecture is true, then a *random Q* comes within $\frac{1}{2}$ of the best possible value, and a large number of matrices will therefore yield values near the optimum. Therefore it is an interesting practical problem to construct a family of matrices for various m, having provably good behavior near the optimum, and also with the property that they are easy to compute in step 4'.

m	$\delta(m,m)$	$\delta'_r(m,m)$
1	0.0000	0.0000
2	0.2500	0.2500
3	0.4444	0.4630
4	0.6094	0.6426
5	0.7552	0.7973
6	0.8873	0.9330
7	1.0091	1.0538
8	1.1225	1.1626
9	1.2292	1.2615
10	1.3301	1.3523
11	1.4262	1.4360
12	1.5180	1.5138
15	1.7729	1.7183
20	2.1468	1.9911
50	3.7716	2.9037
100	5.6050	3.6135
1000	19.1516	5.9658
10000	61.9996	8.2839

TABLE 1. Cyclic hashing versus random single hashing.

It does not appear to be easy to compute $\delta'(m,m)$ for a given matrix M. The best method I know requires on the order of $m \cdot 2^m$ steps, so I have been able to experiment on this problem only for small values of m. (Incidentally, such experiments represent an application of computer science to solve a mathematical problem suggested by computer science.) Here is a way to compute $\delta'(m,m)$ for a given matrix $Q = (q_{ij})$: If A is any subset of $\{1, 2, \ldots, m\}$, let $|A|$ denote the number of elements in A, and let $p(A)$ be the probability that the first $|A|$ players occupy the chairs designated by A. Then it is not difficult to show that

$$p(A) = \frac{1}{m} \sum_{(i,j) \in s(A)} p(A - \{q_{ij}\})$$

when A is nonempty, where $s(A)$ is the set of all pairs (i, j) such that $q_{ik} \in A$ for $1 \leq k \leq j$; consequently

$$d'(m, n) = \frac{1}{m} \sum_{|A|=n-1} p(A) \, |s(A)|,$$

$$\delta'(m, n) = \frac{1}{mn} \sum_{|A|<n} p(A) \, |s(A)|.$$

For example, in the 4×4 matrix Q_1 considered earlier, we have

A	$p(A)$	$|s(A)|$	A	$p(A)$	$|s(A)|$
$\emptyset$	1	0	$\{4\}$	1/4	1
$\{1\}$	1/4	1	$\{1,4\}$	2/16	2
$\{2\}$	1/4	1	$\{2,4\}$	2/16	2
$\{1,2\}$	3/16	3	$\{1,2,4\}$	9/64	4
$\{3\}$	1/4	1	$\{3,4\}$	4/16	4
$\{1,3\}$	3/16	3	$\{1,3,4\}$	20/64	7
$\{2,3\}$	2/16	2	$\{2,3,4\}$	16/64	6
$\{1,2,3\}$	19/64	7	$\{1,2,3,4\}$	1	16

The first three chairs occupied will most probably be $\{1,3,4\}$; the set of chairs $\{1,2,4\}$ is much less likely. The "score" $\delta'(m,m)$ for this matrix comes to $653/1024$, which in this case is worse than the score $624/1024$ for cyclic hashing. In fact, cyclic hashing turns out to be the *best* single hashing scheme when $m = 4$.

When $m = 5$, the best single hashing scheme turns out to be obtained from the matrix

$$Q_5 = \begin{pmatrix} 1 & 2 & 4 & 5 & 3 \\ 2 & 3 & 5 & 1 & 4 \\ 3 & 4 & 1 & 2 & 5 \\ 4 & 5 & 2 & 3 & 1 \\ 5 & 1 & 3 & 4 & 2 \end{pmatrix}$$

whose score is 0.7440, compared to 0.7552 for cyclic hashing. Note that Q_5 is very much like cyclic hashing, since cyclic symmetry is present: each row is obtained from the preceding row by adding 1 modulo 5, therefore the probing pattern is essentially the same for all rows. We may call this *generalized cyclic hashing*; it is a special case of practical importance, because it requires knowing only one row of Q instead of remembering all m^2 entries.

When $m > 5$, an exhaustive search for the best single hashing scheme would be too difficult to do by machine, unless some new breakthrough is made in the theory. Therefore I have resorted to "heuristic" search procedures. For all $m \leq 11$, the best single hashing matrices I have been able to find actually have turned out to be generalized cyclic hashing schemes, and I am tempted to conjecture that this will be true in general. It would be extremely nice if this conjecture were true, since it would follow that the potentially expensive generality of a non-cyclic scheme would never be useful. However, the evidence for my guess is comparatively weak; it is simply that (i) the conjecture holds for $m \leq 5$; (ii) I have seen no counterexamples in experiments for $m \leq 11$; (iii) the best generalized cyclic hashing schemes for $m \leq 9$ are "locally optimum" single hashing schemes, in the sense that all possible interchanges of two elements in any row of the matrix lead to a matrix that is no better; (iv) the latter statement is *not* true for the standard (ungeneralized) cyclic hashing scheme, so the fact that it holds for the best ones may be significant.

Even if this conjecture is false, the practical significance of generalized cyclic hashing makes it a suitable object for further study, especially in view of its additional mathematical structure. One immediate consequence of the cyclic property is that $p(A) = p(A + k)$ for all sets A, in the formulas above for computing $d'(m, n)$, where "$A + k$" means the set obtained from A by adding k to each element, modulo m. This observation makes the calculation of scores almost m times faster. Another, not quite so obvious property, is the fact that the generalized cyclic hashing scheme generated by the permutation $q_1 q_2 \ldots q_m$ has the same score as that generated by the "reflected" permutation $q_1' q_2' \ldots q_m'$ where $q_j' = m + 1 - q_j$. (It is convenient to say that a generalized cyclic hashing scheme is "generated" by any of its rows.) This equivalence under reflection can be proved by showing that $p(A)$ is equal to $p'(m + 1 - A)$. Indeed, if c is any integer relatively prime to m and if $q_1' q_2' \ldots q_m'$ is a permutation with $q_j' \equiv cq_j \pmod{m}$, then $p(A)$ is equal to $p'(cA)$.

I programmed a computer to find the scores for all generalized cyclic hashing schemes when m is small, and the results of this computation suggested that further simplifications might also be valid:

(i) The sequences $q_1 q_2 q_3 \ldots q_m$ and $q_2 q_1 q_3 \ldots q_m$ generate equally good generalized cyclic hashing schemes.

(ii) The sequences $q_1 \ldots q_{m-2} q_{m-1} q_m$ and $q_1 \ldots q_{m-2} q_m q_{m-1}$ generate equally good generalized cyclic hashing schemes.

(iii) The sequences $(j - q_1) \ldots (j - q_k) q_{k+1} \ldots q_m$ and $q_{m-2} q_m q_{m-1}$ generate equally good generalized cyclic hashing schemes, if they both are permutations; here j is any constant, and arithmetic is done modulo m.

Conjectures (i) and (ii) are equivalent to the cases $k = 2$ and $k = m-2$ of conjecture (iii), and the case $k = m$ is known to be true. In fact, (ii) turns out to be true, basically because $d(m, m)$ is always equal to $\frac{1}{2}(m - 1)$. But (i) is false when $q_1 \ldots q_m = 1\ 2\ 5\ 4\ 3\ 6$; so (iii) is also false. However, my mistaken conjectures did suggest an interesting purely mathematical question, namely to determine how many inequivalent permutations of m objects there are, when $q_1 \ldots q_m$ is postulated to be equivalent to $(\varepsilon q_1 + j) \ldots (\varepsilon q_k + j) q_{k+1} \ldots q_m$, for $\varepsilon = \pm 1$ and $1 \le j, k \le m$ (whenever these are both permutations, modulo m). We might call these *necklace permutations*, by analogy with another well-known combinatorial problem, since they represent the number of different orders in which a person could change the beads of a necklace from all white to all black, ignoring the operation of rotating and/or flipping the necklace over whenever such an operation preserves the current black/white pattern. The total number of different necklace permutations for $1 \le m \le 10$ is 1, 1, 1, 2, 4, 14, 57, 347, 2375, 20752, respectively, and I wonder what can be said for general m.

Returning to the hashing problem, the theorems mentioned above make it possible to study all of the generalized cyclic hashing schemes for $m \le 9$, by computer; and the following turn out to be the best:

best permutation	$\delta'_{\min}(m, m)$	$\delta'_{\text{ave}}(m, m)$
1 2 3 4	0.6094	0.6146
1 2 4 5 3	0.7440	0.7515
1 2 5 3 4 6	0.8650	0.8819
1 4 2 3 6 5 7	0.9713	0.9866
1 3 4 8 7 2 6 5	1.0676	1.0919
1 5 2 3 8 4 6 7 9	1.1568	1.1780

The right-hand column gives the average $\delta'(m, m)$ over all $m!$ schemes. For $m = 10$ and 11 the best permutations I have found so far are 1 2 8 6 4 9 3 10 7 5 and 1 3 6 2 7 10 9 11 4 5 8, with respective scores of 1.2362 and 1.3103. The *worst* such schemes for $m \le 9$ are

worst permutation	$\delta'_{\max}(m, m)$
1 3 2 4	0.6250
1 2 3 4 5	0.7552
1 3 5 2 4 6	0.9132
1 2 3 4 5 6 7	1.0091
1 5 3 7 2 4 6 8	1.1719
1 4 7 2 5 8 3 6 9	1.2638

(This table suggests that the form of the worst cyclic scheme might be obtainable in a simple way from the prime factors of m. Indeed, subsequent calculations have shown that the worst cases when $m = 10$, 11, and 12 occur for the respective permutations 1 3 5 7 9 2 4 6 8 10, 1 2 3 4 5 6 7 8 9 10 11, and 1 5 9 3 7 11 2 6 10 4 8 12.)

Finally, I have tried to find the worst possible Q matrices, without the cyclic constraint. Such matrices can be very bad indeed; the worst I know, for any m, occur when $q_{ij} < q_{i(j+1)}$ for all $j \geq 2$, e.g.,

$$\begin{pmatrix} 1 & 2 & 3 & 4 & 5 \\ 2 & 1 & 3 & 4 & 5 \\ 3 & 1 & 2 & 4 & 5 \\ 4 & 1 & 2 & 3 & 5 \\ 5 & 1 & 2 & 3 & 4 \end{pmatrix}$$

when $m = 5$. Using discrete mathematical techniques like those illustrated above, it is not difficult to prove that the score for such matrices is

$$\delta'(m, m) = \left(m + 3 + \frac{2}{m} \right) \left(1 + \frac{1}{m} \right)^m - 2.5m - 7 - \frac{2.5}{m},$$

which is approximately $(e-2.5)m+2.5e-7$ when m is large. We certainly would not want to retrieve information in this way, and perhaps it is the worst possible single hashing scheme.

We have seen that the mathematical analysis of generalized hashing leads to interesting computational problems, which in turn lead to interesting mathematical problems. Thus, the example of hashing illustrates the typical interplay between computer science and mathematics.

I wish to thank Garrett Birkhoff for his comments on the first draft of this paper.

References

[1] American Mathematical Society and Mathematical Association of America, co-sponsors of conference, *The Influence of Computing on Mathematical Research and Education*, August 1973.

[2] A. O. L. Atkin and B. J. Birch, editors, *Computers in Number Theory* (New York: Academic Press, 1971).

[3] Charles Babbage, *Passages from the Life of a Philosopher* (London, 1864). Reprinted in *Charles Babbage and His Calculating Engines*, by Philip and Emily Morrison (New York: Dover, 1961); esp. p. 69.

[4] Garrett Birkhoff and Marshall Hall, Jr., editors, *Computers in Algebra and Number Theory*, SIAM-AMS Proceedings **4** (American Mathematical Society, 1971).

[5] R. F. Churchhouse and J.-C. Herz, editors, *Computers in Mathematical Research* (Amsterdam: North-Holland, 1968).

[6] N. G. de Bruijn, Donald E. Knuth, and S. O. Rice, "The average height of planted plane trees," in *Graph Theory and Computing*, ed. by Ronald C. Read (New York: Academic Press, 1972), 15–22.

[7] George E. Forsythe, "The role of numerical analysis in an undergraduate program," *American Mathematical Monthly* **66** (1959), 651–662.

[8] _____, "Computer Science and Education," *Information Processing 68* (Amsterdam: North-Holland, 1969), 1025–1039.

[9] _____, "What to do till the computer scientist comes," *American Mathematical Monthly* **75** (1968), 454–462.

[10] _____ and Paul C. Rosenbloom, *Numerical Analysis and Partial Differential Equations*, Surveys in Applied Mathematics **5** (New York: Wiley, 1958).

[11] C. F. Gauss, Letter to J. F. Encke, *Werke* **2**, 444–447.

[12] Seymour Ginsburg, *The Mathematical Theory of Context Free Languages* (New York: McGraw–Hill, 1966).

[13] _____, Sheila Greibach, and John Hopcroft, *Studies in Abstract Families of Languages*, American Mathematical Society Memoirs **87** (1969), 51 pp.

[14] F. E. Holberton and J. W. Mauchly, personal communication.

[15] Donald E. Knuth, "A class of projective planes," *Transactions of the American Mathematical Society* **115** (1965), 541–549.

[16] _____, "Algorithm and program; information and data," *Communications of the ACM* **9** (1966), 654. [Reprinted in Chapter 0 of the present volume.]

[17] _____, *Seminumerical Algorithms*, Vol. 2 of *The Art of Computer Programming* (Reading, Massachusetts: Addison–Wesley, 1969), 624 pp.

[18] _____, "Ancient Babylonian algorithms," *Communications of the ACM* **15** (1972), 671–677. [Reprinted as Chapter 11 of the present volume.]

[19] _____, "George Forsythe and the development of Computer Science," *Communications of the ACM* **15** (1972), 721–726. [Reprinted as Chapter 16 of the present volume.]

[20] _____, *Sorting and Searching* (Reading, Massachusetts: Addison–Wesley, 1973), 722 pp.

[21] Peter D. Lax, "The impact of computers on mathematics," in *Computers and Their Role in the Physical Sciences*, edited by S. Fernbach and A. H. Taub (New York: Gordon & Breach, 1970), 219–226.

[22] John Leech, editor, *Computational Problems in Abstract Algebra* (Long Island City: Pergamon, 1970).

[23] Peter Naur, " 'Datalogy', the science of data and data processes, and its place in education," *Information Processing 68* (Amsterdam: North-Holland, 1969), 1383–1387.

[24] Allen Newell, Alan J. Perlis, and Herbert A. Simon, "Computer Science," *Science* **157** (1967), 1373–1374.

[25] W. W. Peterson, "Addressing for random-access storage," *IBM Journal of Research and Development* **1** (1957), 130–146.

[26] Proceedings of Symposia in Applied Mathematics, Volume 15, *Experimental Arithmetic, High-Speed Computing, and Mathematics* (Providence, Rhode Island: American Mathematical Society, 1963).

[27] E. Reingold, "Establishing lower bounds on algorithms — A survey," *AFIPS Conference Proceedings* **40** (1972), 471–481.

[28] *Computers and Computing*, Herbert Ellsworth Slaught Memorial Papers No. 10, a supplement to *American Mathematical Monthly* **72** (February 1965), 156 pp.

[29] J. D. Ullman, "A note on the efficiency of hashing functions," *Journal of the Association for Computing Machinery* **19** (1972), 569–575.

[30] Peter Wegner, "Three computer cultures," *Advances in Computers* **10** (1970), 7–78.

[31] J. H. Wilkinson, "Some comments from a numerical analyst," *Journal of the Association for Computing Machinery* **18** (1971), 137–147. Reprinted in *ACM Turing Award Lectures* (New York: ACM Press, 1987), 243–256.

Additional Reference

[32] Peter J. Denning, "What is computer science?" *American Scientist* **73**, 1 (January–February 1985), 16–19.

Chapter 2

Mathematics and Computer Science: Coping with Finiteness

Advances in our ability to compute are bringing us substantially closer to ultimate limitations.

*[Originally published in Science **194** (1976), 1235–1242.]*

A well-known book entitled *One, Two, Three ... Infinity* was published by George Gamow about 30 years ago [1], and he began by telling a story about two Hungarian noblemen. It seems that the two gentlemen were out riding, and one suggested to the other that they play a game: Who can name the largest number. "Good," said the second man, "you go first." After several minutes of intense concentration, the first nobleman announced the largest number he could think of: "Three." Now it was the other man's turn, and he thought furiously, but after about a quarter of an hour he gave up. "You win," he said.

In this article I will try to assess how much further we have come, by discussing how well we can now deal with large quantities. Although we have certainly narrowed the gap between three and infinity, recent results indicate that we never will actually be able to go very far in practice. My purpose is to explore relationships between the finite and the infinite, in the light of these developments.

Some Large Finite Numbers

Since the time of Greek philosophy, scholars have prided themselves on their ability to understand something about infinity; and it has become traditional in some circles to regard finite things as essentially trivial, too limited to be of any interest. It is hard to debunk such a notion, since there are no accepted standards for demonstrating that something is interesting, especially when something finite is compared with something

31

transcendent. Yet I believe that the climate of thought is changing, since finite processes are proving to be such fascinating objects of study.

In the first place, it is important to understand that finite numbers can be extremely large. Let us start with some very familiar and fairly small numbers: The value of $x \, n$ is $x + x + \cdots + x$, the sum of n copies of x. Similarly we can define a number I shall write as $x \uparrow n$, which means the product $xx \ldots x$ of n copies of x. For example, $10 \uparrow 10 = 10 \cdot 10 \cdot 10 \cdot 10 \cdot 10 \cdot 10 \cdot 10 \cdot 10 \cdot 10 \cdot 10 = 10{,}000{,}000{,}000$ is 10 billion; this is usually written 10^{10}, but it will be clear in a minute why I prefer to use an upward arrow. In fact, the next step uses two arrows

$$x \uparrow\uparrow n = x \uparrow (x \uparrow (\cdots (x \uparrow x) \cdots)),$$

where we repeatedly form powers from n copies of x. For example,

$$10 \uparrow\uparrow 10 = 10^{10^{10^{10^{10^{10^{10^{10^{10^{10}}}}}}}}}$$

$$= 1 \text{ followed by } 10^{10^{10^{10^{10^{10^{10^{10^{10}}}}}}}} \text{ zeros.}$$

This is a pretty big number; at least, if a monkey sits at a typewriter and types at random, the average number of trials before he types perfectly the entire text of Shakespeare's *Hamlet* would be much, much less than this: It is merely a 1 followed by about 40,000 zeros. The general rule is

$$x \; \overbrace{\uparrow\uparrow \ldots \uparrow}^{k \text{ arrows}} \; n = \underbrace{x \overbrace{\uparrow \ldots \uparrow}^{k-1} (x \overbrace{\uparrow \ldots \uparrow}^{k-1} (\cdots (x \overbrace{\uparrow \ldots \uparrow}^{k-1} x) \cdots))}_{n \text{ occurrences of } x}.$$

Thus, one arrow is defined in terms of none, two in terms of one, three in terms of two, and so on.

In order to see how these arrow functions behave, let us look at a very small example,

$$10 \uparrow\uparrow\uparrow\uparrow 3 \,.$$

This is equal to

$$10 \uparrow\uparrow\uparrow (10 \uparrow\uparrow\uparrow 10) \,,$$

so we should first evaluate $10 \uparrow\uparrow\uparrow 10$. The latter is

$$10 \uparrow\uparrow (10 \uparrow\uparrow (10 \uparrow\uparrow (10 \uparrow\uparrow (10 \uparrow\uparrow (10 \uparrow\uparrow (10 \uparrow\uparrow (10 \uparrow\uparrow (10 \uparrow\uparrow 10)))))))) $$

and that is

$$10 \uparrow\uparrow (10 \uparrow\uparrow (10 \uparrow\uparrow (10 \uparrow\uparrow (10 \uparrow\uparrow (10 \uparrow\uparrow (10 \uparrow\uparrow 10^{10^{10^{10^{10^{10^{10^{10^{10^{10}}}}}}}}}))))))$$

$$= 10 \uparrow\uparrow (10 \uparrow\uparrow (10 \uparrow\uparrow (10 \uparrow\uparrow (10 \uparrow\uparrow (10 \uparrow\uparrow (10 \uparrow\uparrow 10^{10^{\cdot^{\cdot^{\cdot^{10}}}}}))))))$$

where the stack of 10's is $10 \uparrow\uparrow 10$ levels tall. We take the huge number at the right of this formula, which I cannot even write down without using the arrow notation, and repeat the double-arrow operation, getting an even huger number, and then we must do the same thing again and again. Let us call the final result ℋ. (It is such an immense number, we cannot use just an ordinary letter for it.)

Of course we are not done yet, we have only evaluated $10 \uparrow\uparrow\uparrow 10$; to complete the job we need to stick this gigantic number into the formula for $10 \uparrow\uparrow\uparrow\uparrow 3$, namely

$$10 \uparrow\uparrow\uparrow\uparrow 3 = 10 \uparrow\uparrow\uparrow ℋ = \underbrace{10 \uparrow\uparrow (10 \uparrow\uparrow (10 \uparrow\uparrow \cdots \uparrow\uparrow (10 \uparrow\uparrow 10) \cdots))}_{ℋ \text{ times}}.$$

The three dots "$\cdots$" here suppress a lot of detail—maybe I should have used four dots. At any rate it seems to me that the magnitude of this number $10 \uparrow\uparrow\uparrow\uparrow 3$ is so large as to be beyond human comprehension.

On the other hand, it is very small as finite numbers go. We might have used ℋ arrows instead of just four, but even that would not get us much further—almost all finite numbers are larger than this. I think such examples help open our eyes to the fact that some numbers are very large even if they are merely finite. Thus, mathematicians who stick mostly to working with finite numbers are not really limiting themselves too severely.

Realistic Numbers

This discussion has set the stage for the next point I want to make, namely that our total resources are not actually very large. Let us try to see how big the known universe is. Archimedes began such an investigation many years ago, in his famous discussion of the number of grains of sand that would completely fill the earth and sky; he did not have the benefit of modern astronomy, but his estimate was qualitatively the same as what we would say today. The distance to the farthest observable galaxies is thought to be at most about 10 billion light years.

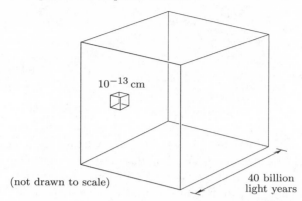

10^{-13} cm

(not drawn to scale)

40 billion
light years

FIGURE 1. The known universe fits inside this box.

On the other hand, the fundamental nucleons that make up matter are about 10^{-12} centimeter in diameter. In order to get a generous upper bound on the size of the universe, let us imagine a cube that is 40 billion light years on each side, and fill it with tiny cubes that are smaller than protons and neutrons, say 10^{-13} cm on each side (see Fig. 1). The total number of little cubes comes to less than 10^{125}. We might say that this is an "astronomically large" number, but actually it has only 125 digits.

Instead of talking only about large numbers of objects, let us also consider the time dimension. Here the numbers never even reach 50 digits; for example, if we take as a unit the amount of time that light rays take to travel 10^{-13} cm, the total number of time units since the dawn of the universe is only one fourth the number of little cubes along a single edge of the big cube in Fig. 1, assuming that the universe is 10 billion years old.

Coming down to earth, it is instructive to consider typical transportation speeds.

Snail	0.006	miles/hour
Man walking	4	miles/hour
U.S. automobile	55	miles/hour
Jet plane	600	miles/hour
Supersonic jet	1200	miles/hour

I would never think of walking from California to Boston, but the plane flight is only 150 times faster. Compare this to the situation with respect to the following computation speeds, given 10-digit numbers.

Man (pencil and paper)	0.2/sec
Man (abacus)	1/sec
Mechanical calculator	4/sec
Medium-speed computer	200,000/sec
Fast computer	200,000,000/sec

A medium-fast computer can add 1 million times faster than we can, and the fastest machines are 1000 times faster yet. Such a ratio of speeds is unprecedented in history: Consider how much a mere factor of 10 in speed, provided by the automobile, has changed our lives, and note that computers have increased our calculation speeds by at least six orders of magnitude. That is more than the ratio of the fastest airplane velocity to a snail's pace.

I do not mean to claim that computers do everything a million times faster than people can; mere mortals like us can do some things much better. For example, you and I can easily recognize the face of a friend who has recently grown a moustache. For tasks like filing, a computer may be only ten or so times faster than a good secretary. But when it comes to arithmetic, computers appear to be almost infinitely fast compared with people.

As a result, we have begun to think about computational problems that used to be unthinkable. Our appetite for calculation has caused us to deal with finite numbers much larger than those we considered before, and this has opened up a rich vein of challenging problems, just as exciting as the problems about infinity that have inspired mathematicians for so many centuries.

Of course, computers are not infinitely fast, and our expectations have become inflated even faster than our computational capabilities. We are forced to realize that there are limits beyond which we cannot go. The numbers we can deal with are not only finite, they are very finite, and we do not have the time or space to solve certain problems even with the aid of the fastest computers. Thus, the theme of this article is coping with finiteness: What useful things can we say about these finite limitations? How have people learned to deal with the situation?

Advances in Technology and Techniques

During the last 15 years computer designers have made computing machines about 1000 times faster. Mathematicians and computer scientists have also discovered a variety of new techniques by which many problems can now be solved enormously faster than they could before. I will present several examples of this; the first one, which is somehow symbolic of our advances in arithmetic ability, is the following factorization of a very large number, completed in 1970 by Morrison and Brillhart [2]:

$$340,282,366,920,938,463,463,374,607,431,768,211,457$$
$$= 5,704,689,200,685,129,054,721 \times 59,649,589,127,497,217.$$

The point, of course, is not simply to compute the exact 39-digit product of these two large numbers; that multiplication is trivial and takes only a few millionths of a second. The problem is to start with the big 39-digit number and to discover its prime factors. (The big number is $2^{128} + 1$, and its factors are of use, for example, in the design of codes of a type used for space communications.) The number of microseconds per year is only 31,556,952,000,000, a 14-digit number, so even if we could test 1 million factors every second it would take about 2000 years to discover the smaller factor. The factorization actually took about 90 minutes of computer time; it was achieved by a combination of sophisticated methods representing a culmination of mathematical developments that began about 160 years earlier.

Latin Squares

Now let us look at another kind of example. Here is a so-called latin square of order 8, an arrangement of eight numbers in eight rows and eight columns so that each number appears in each row and each column.

```
1 2 3 4 5 6 7 8
2 1 4 3 6 5 8 7
3 4 1 2 7 8 5 6
4 3 2 1 8 7 6 5
5 6 7 8 1 2 3 4
6 5 8 7 2 1 4 3
7 8 5 6 3 4 1 2
8 7 6 5 4 3 2 1
```

On top of this square we can overlay another latin square of order 8, using italic numbers; again there is one italic digit of every kind in every row and in every column.

1 *1*	2 *2*	3 *3*	4 *4*	5 *5*	6 *6*	7 *7*	8 *8*
2 *3*	1 *4*	4 *1*	3 *2*	6 *7*	5 *8*	8 *5*	7 *6*
3 *5*	4 *6*	1 *7*	2 *8*	7 *1*	8 *2*	5 *3*	6 *4*
4 *7*	3 *8*	2 *5*	1 *6*	8 *3*	7 *4*	6 *1*	5 *2*
5 *4*	6 *3*	7 *2*	8 *1*	1 *8*	2 *7*	3 *6*	4 *5*
6 *2*	5 *1*	8 *4*	7 *3*	2 *6*	1 *5*	4 *8*	3 *7*
7 *8*	8 *7*	5 *6*	6 *5*	3 *4*	4 *3*	1 *2*	2 *1*
8 *6*	7 *5*	6 *8*	5 *7*	4 *2*	3 *1*	2 *4*	1 *3*

These two latin squares are called orthogonal, since the superposition shows that every pair of roman and italic numbers occurs exactly once. Thus we have roman 1 with italic *1* (in the upper left corner), roman 1 with italic *2* (near the lower right corner), and so on; all 8 × 8 possibilities appear. Latin squares and orthogonal latin squares are commonly used in the design of statistical experiments and for such things as crop rotation.

The great 18th-century mathematician Euler showed how to construct pairs of orthogonal latin squares of all sizes except for order 2, 6, 10, 14, 18, and so on, and he stated his belief that orthogonal latin squares of these missing orders do not exist [3]. It is easy to verify this for order 2; and in 1900, an exhaustive analysis by a French mathematician [4] showed that orthogonal latin squares of order 6 are indeed impossible. During the next several years, mathematicians in France, Germany, and America each asserted [5] that Euler was right in the remaining cases 10, 14, 18, ...; but unfortunately their "proofs" had serious flaws, so the question was still not settled.

Finally computers were invented, and an attempt was made to test Euler's conjecture in the smallest remaining case, order 10. A group of mathematicians at the University of California at Los Angeles (UCLA) decided in 1952 to search for latin squares orthogonal to the following 10 × 10 example:

0	1	2	3	4	5	6	7	8	9
1	8	3	2	5	4	7	6	9	0
2	9	5	6	3	0	8	4	7	1
3	7	0	9	8	6	1	5	2	4
4	6	7	5	2	9	0	8	1	3
5	0	9	4	7	8	3	1	6	2
6	5	4	7	1	3	2	9	0	8
7	4	1	8	0	2	9	3	5	6
8	3	6	0	9	1	5	2	4	7
9	2	8	1	6	7	4	0	3	5

This particular square was selected more or less at random, using a procedure analogous to one discussed in the next example below; the probability of generating it [6] turns out to be about 10^{-26}, so I imagine that there are extremely many 10×10 latin squares, something like 10^{26} at least. However, the computer at UCLA ran for many hours trying to find an orthogonal mate for this square; finally, having produced no answers, it was shut off [7]. This failure was consistent with Euler's conjecture that no mates exist, but the investigators realized that several hundred more years of calculation would be required to show this exhaustively — and then they would have to try to find mates for the other 10^{26} or so initial squares.

The method used in their experiment was to look for a mate by filling in the entries row by row, one entry at a time in all possible ways, without violating the definition of orthogonal latin squares. Furthermore, they used the fact that the leftmost column of the orthogonal mate can be assumed to contain the digits 0 to 9 in order. Five years later E. T. Parker [8] discovered a far better way to look for orthogonal mates. His idea, which can in fact be traced to Euler's original paper [3], was to find all ways to put ten 0's into an orthogonal mate for a particular square; this means finding one entry in each row and each column so that no two entries contain the same digit. This is a much easier problem, and it turned out that there were roughly 100 ways to do it, using any cell in the first column. The remaining problem is to combine a solution for the 0's with a solution for the 1's and a solution for the 2's, and so forth; again this is comparatively simple. Parker was able to deduce that there is exactly one latin square orthogonal to the one studied at UCLA, namely the italic digits in the following array:

$$
\begin{array}{cccccccccc}
0\,0 & 1\,2 & 2\,8 & 3\,5 & 4\,9 & 5\,4 & 6\,7 & 7\,3 & 8\,6 & 9\,1 \\
1\,1 & 8\,7 & 3\,4 & 2\,9 & 5\,3 & 4\,6 & 7\,5 & 6\,0 & 9\,2 & 0\,8 \\
2\,2 & 9\,5 & 5\,6 & 6\,4 & 3\,8 & 0\,7 & 8\,0 & 4\,1 & 7\,9 & 1\,3 \\
3\,3 & 7\,6 & 0\,9 & 9\,0 & 8\,4 & 6\,5 & 1\,8 & 5\,2 & 2\,1 & 4\,7 \\
4\,4 & 6\,8 & 7\,1 & 5\,7 & 2\,5 & 9\,3 & 0\,6 & 8\,9 & 1\,0 & 3\,2 \\
5\,5 & 0\,1 & 9\,7 & 4\,8 & 7\,0 & 8\,2 & 3\,9 & 1\,4 & 6\,3 & 2\,6 \\
6\,6 & 5\,9 & 4\,0 & 7\,2 & 1\,7 & 3\,1 & 2\,3 & 9\,8 & 0\,4 & 8\,5 \\
7\,7 & 4\,3 & 1\,5 & 8\,1 & 0\,2 & 2\,0 & 9\,4 & 3\,6 & 5\,8 & 6\,9 \\
8\,8 & 3\,0 & 6\,2 & 0\,3 & 9\,6 & 1\,9 & 5\,1 & 2\,7 & 4\,5 & 7\,4 \\
9\,9 & 2\,4 & 8\,3 & 1\,6 & 6\,1 & 7\,8 & 4\,2 & 0\,5 & 3\,7 & 5\,0 \\
\end{array}
$$

The total time for his program to be completed, on a slow computer in 1959, was less than 1 minute.

This example, together with the previous example about factoring, illustrates an important point: We should never expect that the first way we try to do something on a computer is the best way. Good programming is much more subtle than that; chances are that an expert can find a method that will go considerably faster than that of a novice, especially in combinatorial problems where there have been significant advances in techniques during recent years. By analyzing Parker's method statistically, I estimate that his approach runs about 100 billion times faster than the original method used by the extremely competent mathematicians who studied this problem at UCLA; that is 11 orders of magnitude faster, because of a better idea.

By now many sets of orthogonal latin squares of order 10 have been found, and orthogonal pairs are known to exist for all orders greater than 6. But computers were of little help in discovering these facts; the constructions were discovered by hand (by Parker, Bose, and Shrikhande), generalizing from patterns observed in the smaller cases [9]. For order 14 the problem is so much larger that even Parker's method would no longer be fast enough to search for all orthogonal mates by computer. This illustrates another point about combinatorial problems: The computation time often increases greatly when the size of the input to the problem has gone up only slightly.

Counting the Paths on a Grid

The next examples are all based on a single diagram, namely a grid of 121 points and 100 squares; it is the diagram we would obtain if we drew boxes around the elements of a 10×10 latin square. (Incidentally, there are many possible examples that illustrate the points I wish to make, so it was necessary for me to find some way to narrow down the selection. Since a 10×10 array fits nicely on a page, I have decided to stick mostly to examples that are based somehow on this one diagram.)

First let us consider how many ways there are to go along the lines of such a grid from the lower left corner to the upper right corner, without touching the same point twice. Problems like this have been studied by chemists and physicists concerned with the behavior of large molecules [10]; it seems to be a difficult problem, and no way is known to calculate the exact number of such paths on a large grid in a reasonable amount of time. However, it is possible to obtain approximate solutions that are correct with high probability.

The idea is to construct a "random" path from the starting point to the finishing point. First we must go up or to the right; by flipping a coin or rolling some dice we might decide to go right. Again there

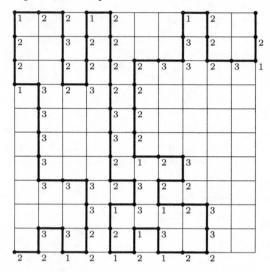

FIGURE 2. A "random" path from the lower left corner to the
upper right corner of a 10 × 10 array of squares.

are two choices, and half the time we will go up. From here there are
three possibilities, and we may choose from these at random, say to the
right. And so on. Figure 2 shows the first random path I generated in
this way. At each choice point of Fig. 2, I have written the number of
alternatives present when the path got that far. For example, the 1's at
the edges mean that there was only one way to go, since the other way
either was already occupied or led into a blind alley.

The probability that this particular path would be obtained by such
a random procedure is the product of all the individual probabilities at
each choice point, namely

$$\frac{1}{2} \cdot \frac{1}{2} \cdot \frac{1}{3} \cdot \frac{1}{3} \cdot \ldots \cdot \frac{1}{3} \cdot \frac{1}{1} \cdot \frac{1}{2} = 2^{-34} 3^{-24}$$

$$= 1/4{,}852{,}102{,}490{,}441{,}335{,}701{,}504,$$

about one chance in 5×10^{21}. So I am pretty sure that you have never
seen this particular path before, and I doubt if I will ever generate it
again.

In a similar vein, it is interesting to note that the great Mozart
wrote a considerable amount of music that has never yet been performed.
In one of his more playful moments, he specified 11 possibilities for
each of the 16 bars of a waltz [11]; the idea was that people from the

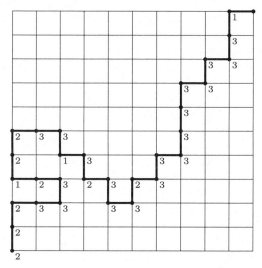

FIGURE 3. A second path, which would be obtained
with probability $2^{-8}3^{-19} \approx 3 \times 10^{-12}$.

audience should roll dice 16 times, obtaining a sequence of 16 numbers between 2 and 12 inclusive, and the performers would play the 16 bars corresponding to these respective rolls. The total number of ways to play Mozart's dice waltz is $2 \times 11^{14} = 759{,}499{,}667{,}166{,}482$ [12]; so it is safe to say that fewer than one out of every million of Mozart's melodies will ever be heard by human ear.

Actually I have a phonograph record that contains 36 randomly selected waltzes from Mozart's scheme [13], and after hearing the fifth or sixth one I began to feel that the rest all sounded about the same. We might suspect that a similar thing will happen in this random path problem: All random paths from lower left to upper right might tend to look approximately like the first few.

Figure 3 shows the second path I generated by making random choices. Notice that this one has quite a different character, and the strange thing is that the probability of obtaining it is more than ten orders of magnitude larger than we saw in Figure 2. But still the probability is "negligibly small."

The third path I generated in this way decided to get into a corner and to hug the edge. The fourth one had its own twist; and the fifth was reminiscent of the first. These paths are shown in Fig. 4. Of course I am displaying here each path exactly as I obtained it, not suppressing any that were uninteresting or unexpected, because the experiment must be unbiased.

The difference between this game and Mozart's dice music is that we know of no way to generate a truly random path, in the sense that each path should occur with the same probability. Although we have seen that each path occurs with extremely small probability, virtually zero, the actual probabilities differ from each other by many orders of magnitude.

If we want to estimate the total number of possible paths, solely on the basis of these data, a theorem of statistics tells us that the best estimate is obtained by using the average value of the reciprocals of the probabilities observed. Thus, although three of these five paths had probabilities around 10^{-11}, suggesting that there are about 10^{11} possible paths, the much lower probabilities in the other two cases imply that it is much better to guess that there are about 10^{22} paths in all. Based on the five experiments I have described, the best estimate of the average length of path will be about 70; and the best estimate of the chance that the point in the middle occurs somewhere on the path is that it almost always occurs, even though three-fifths of the experiments said the opposite. When large numbers like this are involved, we get into paradoxical situations, where the rules of statistics tell us that the best estimates are made by throwing away most of our data.

As you might expect, five experiments are not enough to determine the answers reliably. But by using a computer to generate several thousand random paths in the same way, I am fairly confident that the total number of possible paths from lower left to upper right is $(1.6 \pm 0.3) \times 10^{24}$, and that the average length of path is 92 ± 5. Conflicting evidence was obtained about the chance of hitting the center, but it seems that 81 ± 10 percent of all paths do hit the center point. Of course, I have only generated an extremely small fraction of these paths, so I cannot really be sure; perhaps nobody will ever know the true answer.*

The Shortest Paths

For the next examples we will add weights to the lines in the grid. The basic diagram is shown in Fig. 5, where a random digit has been placed beside each line; these digits may be thought of as the lengths of roads between adjacent points of intersection. Thus, there are three roads of length 4 on the bottom line, and the upper part of the diagram

---

*See the addendum at the end of this chapter.

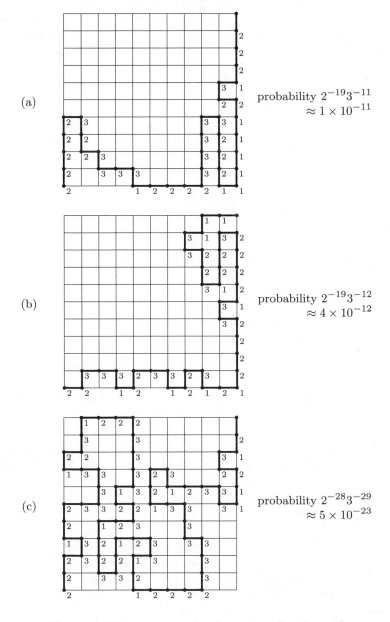

(a)   probability $2^{-19}3^{-11}$
       $\approx 1 \times 10^{-11}$

(b)   probability $2^{-19}3^{-12}$
       $\approx 4 \times 10^{-12}$

(c)   probability $2^{-28}3^{-29}$
       $\approx 5 \times 10^{-23}$

FIGURE 4. Three more randomly generated paths, with
their associated probabilities.

contains three adjacent roads of length 0. Actually I must admit that
the sequences of numbers are not completely arbitrary; for example, the
reader might recognize 1.414213562... in the top line as the square root
of 2, and π appears down the second column. For our purposes these
digits will be random enough.

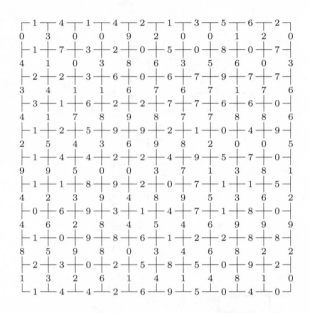

FIGURE 5. Network to be used in subsequent examples,
based on 22 mathematical constants.

The first problem we might ask about such a network of roads is:
What is the shortest route from the lower left corner to the upper right
corner? We have estimated that there are some 10^{24} possible paths,
altogether, and we might want to know which of these is shortest, using
the given lengths.

Fortunately we do not have to try all possible paths to find the
shortest; there is a simple method due to Dijkstra [14] that can be used
to solve this problem by hand in less than half an hour. The answer
(see Fig. 6) is a curious sort of path, which might very well be missed
if one does not use a systematic method; it is the only way to go from
southwest to northeast in a path of length 43.

The idea underlying Dijkstra's method is remarkably simple. Suppose that at some stage we have found all positions at distance 20 or

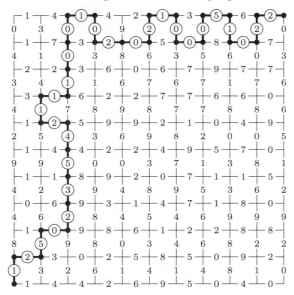

FIGURE 6. The shortest route from lower left to
upper right in the network of Figure 5.

less, say, from the southwest corner. By looking at the roads connecting
these points to the others it will be easy to see which points will be
at distance 21, and so on. You can imagine a fluid spreading over the
diagram at the rate of one unit of length per minute.

Connecting Points in a Network

The next problem is somewhat harder. Suppose we want to construct
electrical connections between all four of the corner points in Fig. 5:
What is the shortest electrical hookup joining these four points, using
only the lines and distances shown? Such a collection of wires is usually
called a Steiner tree [15], and Fig. 7 shows an optimal one.

The number of possible Steiner trees connecting the four corners
is much larger than the number of paths, but still I am sure that the
tree of Figure 7 is as short as possible. In this case I do not know
how to compute the shortest tree by hand, but a properly programmed
computer can do it in a few seconds.

We say that we have a "good" algorithm for some problem if the
time to solve it increases only as a polynomial in the size of the inputs;
in other words, if doubling the size of the problem increases the solution

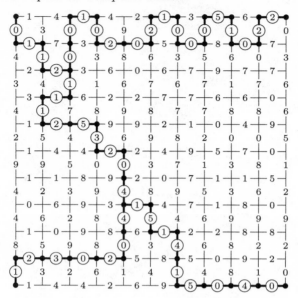

FIGURE 7. A shortest way to connect the four corners.

time by at most a constant factor. There is a good algorithm to find Steiner trees connecting up to five points; it takes roughly n^3 steps, where n is the total number of points in the network of roads [16]. But if we want to connect larger numbers of points by Steiner trees, the computation rapidly gets larger; and when the number of points to be connected is, say, as large as $n/10$, no good algorithm is known.

On the other hand, when our job is to find the shortest way to connect up all n of the points in the network, a good algorithm is available, again one that is so good it can be performed by hand in half an hour.

A minimal connection of all points in a network is called a spanning tree, and in the particular network we are considering it is possible to prove that the total number of possible spanning trees is really huge, more than 4×10^{52}. In fact, the exact number [17] is 40,325,021, 721,404,118,513,276,859,513,497,679,249,183,623,593,590,784.

Yet we can find the best one, in a remarkably easy way discovered by J. B. Kruskal [18]: Simply consider all the lines one by one in order of increasing length, starting with the shortest, then the next shortest, and so on. In case of ties between lines of the same length, use any desired order. The rule is to include each line in the spanning tree if and only if it connects at least two points that are not connected by a path of previously selected lines. This is called a "greedy algorithm" because it is based on the idea of trying the best conceivable possibilities first. Such a policy does not always solve a combinatorial problem — we know that greed does not always pay off in the long run — but in the case of spanning trees the idea works perfectly (see Fig. 8).

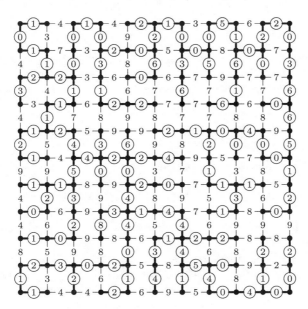

FIGURE 8. A minimum spanning tree.

Maximum Matching

Another problem on this network for which a good algorithm is available is to choose 60 nonoverlapping lines with the maximum possible sum. We may think now of the points as people, instead of as cities, and the numbers now measure the amount of happiness generated between one person and his or her neighbor. The idea is to pair off the people so as to get the maximum total happiness. If men and women alternate in the diagram, with men at the corners, there will be 61 men and 60 women in all, so one man will have no partner; he makes a personal sacrifice for the greater good of the group as a whole. There are exactly 1,801,272,981,919,008 ways to do such a pairing, according to a mathematical theory worked out to solve a physical problem about crystals [19]; Fig. 9 exhibits the best one.

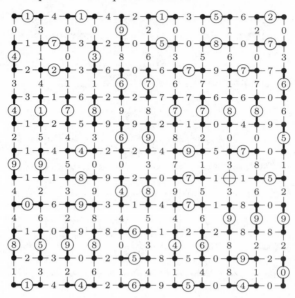

FIGURE 9. The best choice of 60 nonoverlapping lines in the diagram.

It turns out that the circled man (row 7, column 9) is the best to omit, and the others should pair up as shown. Once again we are able to find the optimum solution in 1 or 2 seconds on a computer if we use a suitable algorithm, even though the number of possible arrangements is far too large to examine exhaustively. In this case the algorithm is somewhat more subtle than the ones I have discussed earlier, but it is based on simple ideas. First we add a "dummy" woman who will be paired with the man who gets no real woman. The happiness rating is 0 between the dummy woman and every man. Then if we add or subtract some number from all the happiness ratings touching any particular person, the solution to the problem does not change. A clever way of adjusting these scores can be used so that all 61 of the ratings for the couples matched here are 9, and all the other ratings are 9 or less [20].

An Apparently Harder Problem

From these examples, one might get the idea that a good algorithm can be found for virtually any combinatorial problem. Unfortunately this does not appear to be true, although I did want to demonstrate that considerable progress has been made toward finding good methods. The next problem seems to be much harder: What is the shortest path from the lower left corner to the upper right corner that passes through all 121 points of the grid exactly once?

This is called the traveling salesman problem, because we might think of a salesman who wants to visit each city with minimum travel time. The problem arises frequently in industry — for example, when the goal is to find the best order in which to do n jobs, based on the costs of changing from one job to another. But it has resisted all attacks. We know how to solve medium-sized problems, but the algorithms are not good in the technical sense since the running time goes up rapidly on large cases.

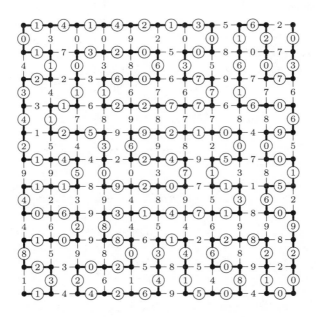

FIGURE 10. A shortest path from lower left to upper right, touching each point just once.

The traveling salesman's path shown in Fig. 10 is as short as possible, and it required several minutes of computer time to verify the fact. To my knowledge, this is the largest network for which the traveling salesman problem had ever been solved exactly, at the time this paper was prepared. I used a method suggested in 1971 by Held and Karp [21], based on a combination of ideas that work well in the spanning tree and matching problems: It is possible to add or subtract numbers from all the lines that touch a particular point, without changing the shape of the minimum tour, and we can use a greedy algorithm to construct a minimum spanning tree for the changed distances. The minimum spanning tree is no longer than the shortest tour, since every tour is a spanning tree; but by properly modifying the distances we can make the minimum spanning tree very nearly a tour, hence comparatively few possibilities need to be tried. I extended the Held and Karp method to take advantage of the fact that each point has at most four neighbors. In this way it was possible to verify at reasonable cost that this tour is optimum; but if I were faced with a larger problem, having say twice as many points to visit, there would be no known method to get the answer in a reasonable amount of time.

In fact, it may well be possible in a few years to prove that no good algorithm exists for the traveling salesman problem. Since so many people have tried for so many years to find a good algorithm, without success, the trend is now to look for a proof that success in this endeavor is impossible. It is analogous to the question of solving polynomial equations: Quadratic equations were resolved in ancient Mesopotamia, and the solution of cubic and quartic equations was found at the beginning of the Renaissance, but nobody was able to solve arbitrary equations of the fifth degree. Finally, during the first part of the 19th century, Abel and Galois proved conclusively that there is no way to solve fifth degree equations in general, using ordinary arithmetic [22]. It is now believed that there is no good algorithm for the general traveling salesman problem, and we are awaiting another Abel or Galois to prove it.

In support of this belief, several important things have already been proved, notably that the traveling salesman problem is computationally equivalent to hundreds of other problems of general interest [23]. If there is a good algorithm for any one of these problems, which for technical reasons are called NP-complete problems, then there will be good algorithms for all the NP-complete problems. Thus, for example, a good algorithm for the traveling salesman problem would lead immediately to a good algorithm for many other difficult problems, such as the optimum scheduling of high school classes, the most efficient way to pack things into boxes, or the best Steiner trees connecting a large number of points. A good solution to any one of these problems will solve them all, so if any one of them is hard they all must be.

A Provably Harder Problem

In recent years, certain problems have, in fact, been shown to be intrinsically hard, in the sense that there never will be a fast way to solve them. Probably the most interesting example of this type was developed in 1974 by L. J. Stockmeyer and A. R. Meyer [24]. The problem is to decide whether or not certain logical statements about whole numbers 0, 1, 2, ... are true or false, even when the form of these statements is severely restricted.

Here are some examples of the sorts of statements we must deal with.

$$048 \leq 1063$$

This statement is clearly true.

$$\forall n \, \exists m \, (m < n + 1)$$

This expression is logical shorthand that can be translated as follows, for people who are not familiar with the new math: "For all numbers n there exists a number m such that m is less than $n + 1$." It is clearly a true statement, since we may take m equal to n.

$$\forall n \, \exists m \, (m + 1 < n)$$

"For all numbers n there exists a number m such that $m + 1$ is less than n." This statement is false, for if $n = 0$ there is no number less than zero; we are considering only statements about nonnegative numbers.

The next example is a little more complicated.

$$\forall a \, \forall b \, (b \geq a + 2 \Rightarrow \exists c \, (a < c \land c < b))$$

"For all numbers a and all numbers b, if b is greater than or equal to $a + 2$ then there exists a number c such that a is less than c and c is less than b." In other words, if b is at least 2 more than a, there is a number c between a and b, and this is obviously true.

Finally we can also make statements about finite sets of numbers; for example

$$\forall F \, (\exists a \, (a \in F) \Rightarrow \exists m \, (m \in F \land \forall a \, (a \in F \Rightarrow m \leq a)))$$

"For all finite sets F of numbers, if there exists a number a such that a is in F then there exists a number m such that m is in F and for all numbers a in F we have $m \leq a$." Informally, the statement says that every finite nonempty set of numbers has a smallest element, and this is true. The similar statement in which "$m \leq a$" is replaced by "$m \geq a$" would also be true, since we're dealing only with finite sets.

The logical statements we shall be concerned with cannot be essentially any harder than these examples. They may not involve subtraction, multiplication, or division; they cannot even involve addition, except addition of a constant. (They cannot involve the formula $x + y$.) Thus the statements must be very simple — much, much simpler than those used every day by mathematicians constructing proofs of theorems.

According to a well-known theorem of Büchi [25], it is possible to decide in a finite number of steps whether or not any statement of the simple kind we have described is true or false, even though these logical statements may concern infinitely many cases.

But the new theorem says that it is impossible actually to do this in the real world, even if we limit ourselves to statements that can be written in no more than 617 symbols: "No realistic algorithm will ever be able to decide truth or falsity for arbitrary given statements of length 617 or less."

In order to understand exactly what this theorem means, we have to know what it means to speak of a "realistic" algorithm. The theorem of Stockmeyer and Meyer is based on the fact that anything that can be done by computer can be done by constructing an electrical circuit, and so they envisage a setup like that shown in Fig. 11. At the top of such a device, one can insert any statement whose truth is to be tested. The logical language involved here makes use of 63 different symbols and a blank character, so we can place the statement (followed if necessary by blanks) into a sequence of 617 positions. Each position is converted into six electrical pulses, whose configuration of "on" and "off" identifies the corresponding character; thus, the letter a might be represented by the six pulses "off, on, on, off, off, on." The resulting 6×617 pulses now enter an electrical circuit or "black box" consisting of AND, OR, and NOT circuits; AND produces a signal that is "on" only when both inputs to AND are "on," OR produces a signal that is "on" when either or both of its inputs are "on," and NOT changes "on" to "off" and vice versa. At the bottom of the circuit, a pulse comes out that is "on" or "off" according to whether the given logical statement of length 617 was true or false.

According to Büchi's theorem, it is possible to construct such an electrical circuit with finitely many components, in a finite amount of time. But Stockmeyer and Meyer [24] have proved that every such circuit must use at least 10^{125} components, and we have seen that this is much larger than the number of protons and neutrons in the entire known universe.

Thus it is hopeless to find an efficient algorithm for this finite problem. We have to face the fact that it can never be done — no matter

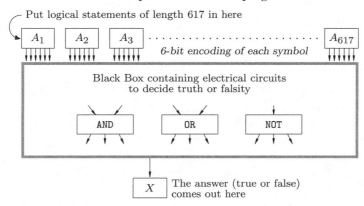

FIGURE 11. Electrical circuit to decide the correctness
of logical statements containing up to 617 characters.

how clever we may become, or how much money and energy is invested
in the project.

What should we do in the face of such limitations? Whenever something has been proved impossible, there is an aspect of the human spirit
that encourages us to find some way to do it anyway. In this particular case, we might try the following sneaky approach: We could build
an electric circuit that gives the correct answer in all simple cases and
that gives a random answer, true or false, in the other cases. Since the
problem is so hard, nobody will be able to know the difference.

But this is obviously unsatisfactory. A better approach would be
to distinguish between levels of truth; for example, the answer might
be "true," "false," or "maybe." And we could give various shades of
"maybe," saying perhaps that the statement is true in lots of cases.

Let's consider the traveling salesman problem again. It is reasonably
likely that, some day, somebody will prove that no good algorithm exists
for this problem. If so, that will be a truly great theorem; but what
should we do when we actually need to solve such a problem?

The answer, of course, is to settle for a tour that is not known to
be the shortest possible one, but is pretty close. It has recently been
observed that we can quickly find a traveling salesman's tour that is
guaranteed to be no worse than 50 percent longer than the shortest possible tour, if the distances satisfy the triangle inequality. And algorithms
have recently been developed for other problems that give "probably correct" answers, where the degree of probability can be specified but the
answer is not absolutely certain.

In this way, computer scientists and mathematicians have been learning how to cope with our finite limitations.

Summary

By presenting these examples, I have tried to illustrate four main points.

1) Finite numbers can be really enormous, and the known universe is very small. Therefore the distinction between finite and infinite is not as relevant as the distinction between realistic and unrealistic.

2) In many cases there are subtle ways to solve very large problems quickly, in spite of the fact that they appear at first to require examination of too many possibilities.

3) There also are cases where we can prove that a fairly natural problem is intrinsically hard, far beyond our conceivable capabilities.

4) It takes a good deal of skill to decide whether a given problem is in the easy or hard class. But even if a problem does turn out to be hard, there are useful and interesting ways to change it into one that can be done satisfactorily.

References and Notes

[1] G. Gamow, *One, Two, Three ... Infinity: Facts & Speculations of Science* (New York: Viking, 1947).

[2] M. A. Morrison and J. Brillhart, "A method of factoring and the factorization of F_7," *Mathematics of Computation* **29** (1975), 183–205.

[3] L. Euler, "Recherches sur une nouvelle espèce de quarrés magiques," *Verhandelingen uitgegeven door het zeeuwsch Genootschap der Wetenschappen te Vlissingen* **9** (1782), 85–239. Reprinted in *Leonhardi Euleri Opera Omnia* (1) **7** (1923), 291–392.

[4] G. Tarry, "Les permutations carrées de base 6," *Mathésis* **20** (1900) Supplement, 23–30.

[5] J. Petersen, "Les 36 officiers," *Annuaire des mathématiciens 1901–1902* (Paris: Laisant & Buhl, 1902), 413–427; P. Wernicke, "Das Problem der 36 Offiziere," *Jahresbericht der Deutschen Mathematiker-Vereinigung* **19** (1910), 264–267; H. F. MacNeish, "Euler squares," *Annals of Mathematics* (2) **23** (1922), 221–227.

[6] M. Hall and D. E. Knuth, "Combinatorial analysis and computers," *American Mathematical Monthly* **72**, part 2, *Computers and Computing*, Slaught Memorial Papers No. 10 (February 1965), 21–28.

[7] C. B. Tompkins, "Machine attacks on problems whose variables are permutations," *Proceedings of Symposia in Applied Mathematics*

6 (American Mathematical Society, 1956), 195–212; L. J. Paige and C. B. Tompkins, "The size of the 10×10 orthogonal latin square problem," *Proceedings of Symposia in Applied Mathematics* **10** (American Mathematical Society, 1960), 71–83.

[8] E. T. Parker, "Computer investigation of orthogonal latin squares of order ten," *Proceedings of Symposia in Applied Mathematics* **15** (American Mathematical Society, 1963), 73–81.

[9] For a complete survey see J. Dénes and A. D. Keedwell, *Latin Squares and Their Applications* (New York: Academic Press, 1974).

[10] See, for example, M. N. Barber and B. W. Ninham, *Random and Restricted Walks* (New York: Gordon & Breach, 1970), Chapter 7.

[11] W. A. Mozart, *Anleitung zum Componiren von Walzern, so viele man will vermittelst zweier Würfel, ohne etwas von der Musik oder Composition zu verstehen* (Berlin: Simrock, 1796); first published by J. J. Hummel of Amsterdam and Berlin, 1793. Reprinted as Mozart's *Musikalisches Würfelspiel*, K. 516f Anh. C 30.01 (Mainz: Schott, 1956). See Martin Gardner, "Melody-making machines," in *Time Travel* (New York: Freeman, 1988), Chapter 7.

[12] The 11 possibilities for bar 8 are all identical, and Mozart gave only two distinct possibilities for bar 16, so the total number of waltzes is 2×11^{14} rather than 11^{16}.

[13] T. H. O'Beirne, *Dice-Composition Music* (Glasgow: Barr & Stroud, 1967).

[14] E. W. Dijkstra, "A note on two problems in connexion with graphs," *Numerische Mathematik* **1** (1959), 269–271.

[15] See, for example, N. Christofides, *Graph Theory, An Algorithmic Approach* (London: Academic Press, 1975), Section 7.4.

[16] First construct the matrix of distances between all pairs of points, then try all possible intermediate junction points.

[17] A determinant formula that specifies the number of spanning trees in a particular graph was discovered by J. J. Sylvester [*Quarterly Journal of Pure and Applied Mathematics* **1** (1857), 42–56] and by C. W. Borchardt [*Journal für die reine und angewandte Mathematik* **57** (1860), 111–121]. When the graph is a square grid, with m rows and m columns, the number of spanning trees seems to be always of the form mx^2 or $2mx^2$, where all the prime factors $> m$ of x are rather small numbers of the form $km \pm 1$; at least this is true when $m \leq 12$. For example, the large number cited in the text corresponds to the case $m = 11$, and in factored form it equals

$2^{15} \cdot 11^2 \cdot 23^2 \cdot 89 \cdot 109 \cdot 199 \cdot 241 \cdot 373 \cdot 397 \cdot 419$. This curious circumstance, which I noticed while preparing the present article, can be explained by factoring the characteristic polynomial of the matrix, as pointed out by Noam Elkies in personal correspondence (1989).

[18] J. B. Kruskal, Jr., "On the shortest spanning subtree of a graph and the traveling salesman problem," *Proceedings of the American Mathematical Society* **7** (1956), 48–50.

[19] E. W. Montroll, "Lattice statistics," in *Applied Combinatorial Mathematics*, edited by E. F. Beckenbach (New York: Wiley, 1964), 105–113.

[20] This is the well-known "Hungarian method" for the assignment problem; for example, see Christofides [15], Section 12.4.

[21] M. Held and R. M. Karp, "The traveling-salesman problem and minimum spanning trees," *Operations Research* **18** (1970), 1138–1162; *Mathematical Programming* **1** (1971), 6–25.

[22] See, for example, C. B. Boyer, *A History of Mathematics* (New York: Wiley, 1968), pp. 555 and 641.

[23] R. M. Karp, "Reducibility among combinatorial problems," in *Complexity of Computer Computations*, edited by R. E. Miller and J. W. Thatcher, (New York: Plenum, 1972), 85–103. See also A. V. Aho, J. E. Hopcroft, J. D. Ullman, *The Design and Analysis of Computer Algorithms* (Reading, Massachusetts: Addison–Wesley, 1974), Chapter 10. For a popular account of related work, see G. B. Kolata, "Analysis of algorithms: Coping with hard problems," *Science* **186** (1974), 520–521.

[24] L. J. Stockmeyer, *The Complexity of Decision Problems in Automata Theory and Logic*, report MAC TR-133 (Ph.D. thesis, Massachusetts Institute of Technology, 1974), Chapter 6. See also Larry Stockmeyer and Albert R. Meyer, "Cosmological lower bound on the circuit complexity of a small problem in logic," *Journal of the ACM* **49** (2002), 753–784.

[25] J. R. Büchi, "Weak second-order arithmetic and finite automata," *Zeitschrift für Mathematische Logik und Grundlagen der Mathematik* **6** (1960), 66–92.

[26] The preparation and publication of this article were supported in part by the National Science Foundation, the Office of Naval Research, and IBM Corporation. Some of the computations were done with the MACSYMA system, supported by the Defense Advanced

Research Projects Agency; others were done on the SUMEX-AIM computer, supported by the National Institutes of Health; still others were done at the Université de Montréal, Centre des Recherches Mathématiques, where a preliminary version of this article was prepared under the auspices of the Chaire Aisenstadt. A lecture based on this material was presented at the AAAS annual meeting in Boston on 22 February 1976, in the session entitled "The Frontiers of the Natural Sciences" organized by R. M. Sinclair.

Addendum

When I prepared this paper I did not realize that it is possible to count the number of paths in grid graphs by a technique known to computer scientists as "discrete dynamic programming" and to combinatorial mathematicians as the "transfer matrix method." This fact was first pointed out to me in 1977 by Richard Schroeppel. The number of paths from corner to corner on an 11×11 grid was computed by John Van Rosendale in 1981 while testing a Cray 1 computer at Boeing Computer Services Company; the exact value turns out to be 1,568,758,030,464,750,013,214,100. By the end of 1995, personal computers were fast enough to calculate this quantity in less than one minute, while in 1976 I had not believed I would ever know the answer in my lifetime! I recently used a similar method to enumerate the paths that go through the center point; this number is exactly 1,243,982,213,040,307,428,318,660 — about 79.3% of the overall total. Moreover, the average length of path is ≈ 91.9009, because the sum of all path lengths is 144,170,284,249,598,867,501,946,128. All three of my Monte Carlo estimates were correct! (Perhaps I was just lucky.)

Exactly 685,736,844,148,461,678,310,714 of the paths (about 43.7%) touch the upper left corner; and 299,749,325,823,584,122,861,402 (about 19.1%) touch all four corners. The latter is very nearly 43.7% of 43.7%.

The total number of paths from corner to corner that touch all 121 points is 1,445,778,936,756,068. During recent years many authors have independently discovered techniques by which such numbers can be computed efficiently as long as the grid is not too large.

The number of 10×10 latin squares with 0 1 2 3 4 5 6 7 8 9 in the first row and column has recently been computed by Eric Rogoyski and Brendan McKay [*Electronic Journal of Combinatorics* **2** (1995), #N3]; it is 7,580,721,483,160,132,811,489,280, slightly less than my estimate of "10^{26} at least."

Functions equivalent to $x \uparrow\uparrow \ldots \uparrow n$ were apparently first considered by Edward Bromhead in *Encyclopædia Britannica, Supplement to the Fourth, Fifth, and Sixth Editions* **3** (Edinburgh: 1824), 569–570.

Chapter 3

Algorithms

An algorithm is a set of rules for getting a specific output from a specific input. Each step must be so precisely defined that it can be translated into computer language and executed by machine.

[Originally published in Scientific American **236**, 4 (April 1977), 63–80.]

Ten years ago the word "algorithm" was unknown to most educated people. Indeed, it was scarcely necessary. But the rapid rise of computer science, which has the study of algorithms as its focal point, has changed all that; the word is now essential. The English language has several other words that almost, but not quite, capture the concept that is needed: procedure, recipe, process, routine, method, rigmarole. Like these things an algorithm is a set of rules or directions for getting a specific output from a specific input. The distinguishing feature of an algorithm is that all vagueness must be eliminated; the rules must describe operations that are so simple and so well defined that they can be executed by a machine. Furthermore, an algorithm must always terminate after a finite number of steps.

A program is the statement of an algorithm in some well-defined language. Thus a computer program represents an algorithm, although the algorithm itself is a mental concept that exists independently of any representation. In a similar way the concept of the number 2 exists in our minds without being written down. Anyone who has prepared a computer program will appreciate the fact that an algorithm must be very precisely defined, with an attention to detail that is unusual in comparison with the other things people do.

Programs for numerical problems were written as early as 1800 B.C., when Babylonian mathematicians at the time of Hammurabi gave rules for solving many types of equations. The rules were stated as step-by-step procedures applied systematically to particular numerical examples.

59

The word algorithm itself originated in the Middle East, although at a much later time. It comes from the last name of the Persian scholar Abu ʻAbd Allāh Muḥammad ibn Mūsā al-Khwārizmī, whose textbook on arithmetic (about A.D. 825) had a significant influence for more than 500 years.

Traditional algorithms were concerned solely with numerical calculation. Experience with computers has shown, however, that the data manipulated by programs can represent virtually anything. Accordingly the emphasis in computer science has now shifted to the study of various structures by which information can be represented, and to the branching or decision-making aspects of algorithms, which allow them to follow one or another sequence of operations depending on the state of affairs at the time. It is precisely these features of algorithms that often make algorithmic models more suitable than traditional mathematical models

Input: $x = $ GRANT

1	2	3	4	5	6	7	8	9	10	11	12	13	14	15	16	17	18	19	20	21	22	23	24	25
WASHINGTON	ADAMS	JEFFERSON	MADISON	MONROE	JACKSON	VAN BUREN	HARRISON	TYLER	POLK	TAYLOR	FILLMORE	PIERCE	BUCHANAN	LINCOLN	JOHNSON	GRANT	HAYES	GARFIELD	ARTHUR	CLEVELAND	McKINLEY	ROOSEVELT	TAFT	WILSON

$\neq$

1	2	3	4	5	6	7	8	9	10	11	12	13	14	15	16	17	18	19	20	21	22	23	24	25
WASHINGTON	ADAMS	JEFFERSON	MADISON	MONROE	JACKSON	VAN BUREN	HARRISON	TYLER	POLK	TAYLOR	FILLMORE	PIERCE	BUCHANAN	LINCOLN	JOHNSON	GRANT	HAYES	GARFIELD	ARTHUR	CLEVELAND	McKINLEY	ROOSEVELT	TAFT	WILSON

$\neq$

$\vdots$ 7 steps later

1	2	3	4	5	6	7	8	9	10	11	12	13	14	15	16	17	18	19	20	21	22	23	24	25
WASHINGTON	ADAMS	JEFFERSON	MADISON	MONROE	JACKSON	VAN BUREN	HARRISON	TYLER	POLK	TAYLOR	FILLMORE	PIERCE	BUCHANAN	LINCOLN	JOHNSON	GRANT	HAYES	GARFIELD	ARTHUR	CLEVELAND	McKINLEY	ROOSEVELT	TAFT	WILSON

=

Output: 17

SEQUENTIAL-SEARCH ALGORITHM (Algorithm A in the text of this chapter) looks for an input word in a table where the entries have not been arranged in any particular order. The table in this example has 25 entries, or keys: KEY[1], KEY[2], and so on up to KEY[25]. Each key is a person's name. Suppose the input word is the name GRANT. Algorithm A searches for GRANT by for the representation and organization of knowledge. Although numerical algorithms certainly have many interesting features, I shall confine the following discussion to nonnumerical ones in order to emphasize the fact that algorithms deal primarily with the manipulation of symbols that need not represent numbers.

Searching a Computer's Memory

In order to illustrate how algorithms can fruitfully be studied, I shall consider in some depth a simple problem of retrieving information. The problem is to discover whether or not a certain word, x, appears in a table of words stored in a computer's memory. The word x might be the name of a person, the number of a mechanical part, a word in some foreign language, a chemical compound, a credit-card number, or almost anything. The problem is interesting only when the set of all possible x's

Input: $x = $ GIBBS

1	2	3	4	5	6	7	8	9	10	11	12	13	14	15	16	17	18	19	20	21	22	23	24	25
WASHINGTON	ADAMS	JEFFERSON	MADISON	MONROE	JACKSON	VAN BUREN	HARRISON	TYLER	POLK	TAYLOR	FILLMORE	PIERCE	BUCHANAN	LINCOLN	JOHNSON	GRANT	HAYES	GARFIELD	ARTHUR	CLEVELAND	McKINLEY	ROOSEVELT	TAFT	WILSON

$\ne$

1	2	3	4	5	6	7	8	9	10	11	12	13	14	15	16	17	18	19	20	21	22	23	24	25
WASHINGTON	ADAMS	JEFFERSON	MADISON	MONROE	JACKSON	VAN BUREN	HARRISON	TYLER	POLK	TAYLOR	FILLMORE	PIERCE	BUCHANAN	LINCOLN	JOHNSON	GRANT	HAYES	GARFIELD	ARTHUR	CLEVELAND	McKINLEY	ROOSEVELT	TAFT	WILSON

$\ne$

⋮ 23 steps later

1	2	3	4	5	6	7	8	9	10	11	12	13	14	15	16	17	18	19	20	21	22	23	24	25
WASHINGTON	ADAMS	JEFFERSON	MADISON	MONROE	JACKSON	VAN BUREN	HARRISON	TYLER	POLK	TAYLOR	FILLMORE	PIERCE	BUCHANAN	LINCOLN	JOHNSON	GRANT	HAYES	GARFIELD	ARTHUR	CLEVELAND	McKINLEY	ROOSEVELT	TAFT	WILSON

$\ne$

Output: 0

comparing it first with KEY[25], which is WILSON, then with KEY[24], which is TAFT, then with ROOSEVELT, and so on. Here GRANT is found to be KEY[17], and the algorithm outputs the corresponding location number, 17 (*left*). If the input had been GIBBS, which is not in the table, Algorithm A would have compared GIBBS with all keys, and the output would have been 0 (*right*).

is too large for the computer to handle all at once; otherwise we could simply set aside one location in the memory for each potential word.

Suppose n different words have been stored in the computer's memory. The problem is to design an algorithm that will accept as its input the word x and will yield as its output the location j where x appears. Thus the output will be a number between 1 and n, if x is present; on the other hand, if x is not in the memory, the output should be 0, indicating that the search was unsuccessful.

It is, of course, easy to solve this problem. The simplest algorithm is to store the words in locations 1 through n and to look at each word in turn. If x is found in location j, the computer should output j and stop, but if the computer exhausts all n possibilities with no success, it should output 0 and stop. Such a description of the search strategy is not precise enough for a computer, however, so the procedure must be stated more carefully. It might be written as a sequence of steps in the following way:

Algorithm A; sequential search.

A1. [Initialize.] Set $j \leftarrow n$. (The arrow here means that the value of variable j is set equal to n, which is the number of words in the table to be searched. This is the initial value of j. Subsequent steps of the algorithm will cause j to run through the sequences of values n, $n-1$, $n-2$, and so on until j reaches either 0 or the number of a location containing the input word x.)

A2. [Unsuccessful?] If $j = 0$, output j and terminate the algorithm. (Otherwise go on to step A3.)

A3. [Successful?] If $x = \mathtt{KEY}[j]$, output j and terminate the algorithm. (The term $\mathtt{KEY}[j]$ refers to the word stored at location j.)

A4. [Repeat.] Set $j \leftarrow j - 1$ (decrease the value of j by 1) and go back to step A2.

This algorithm can be depicted by a flow chart that may help a person visualize the steps [*see illustration*]. One reason it is important to specify the steps carefully is that the algorithm must work in every case. For example, the informal description given first might have suggested an erroneous algorithm that would go directly from step A1 to step A3; such an algorithm would have failed when $n = 0$ (that is, when no words at all were present), since step A1 would set j to 0 and step A3 would refer to the nonexistent $\mathtt{KEY}[0]$.

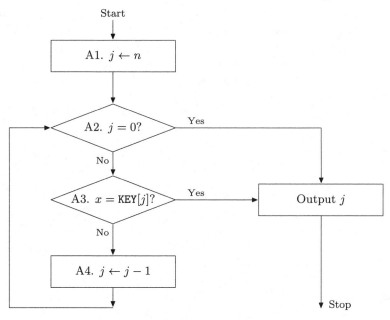

FLOW CHART FOR ALGORITHM A illustrates the logical path by which a brute-force sequential search looks for an input word x in a table of n keys. The algorithm searches for x by comparing it first with KEY$[n]$, then with KEY$[n-1]$, then KEY$[n-2]$, and so on. If x matches some KEY$[j]$, the algorithm outputs j, the location at which x was found. If x is not in the table, the output of the algorithm is 0. The arrow in box A1 ("$j \leftarrow n$") means that the computer is supposed to set j equal to n in that step. The operations in each box are explained in detail in the fuller form of Algorithm A in the text. On the average, Algorithm A must search half of the table to find x. In the worst case, if x equals KEY$[1]$ or if x is not present, Algorithm A must search the entire table.

It is interesting to note that Algorithm A can be improved by giving meaning to the notation KEY$[0]$, allowing a word to be stored in "location 0" as well as in locations 1 through n. Then if step A1 sets KEY$[0] \leftarrow x$ as well as $j \leftarrow n$, step A2 can be eliminated and the search will go about 20 percent faster on many machines. Unfortunately for programmers, the most commonly used computer languages (standard FORTRAN and COBOL) do not allow 0 to be employed as an index for a memory location; thus Algorithm A cannot be so easily improved when it is expressed as a program in those languages.

Algorithm A certainly solves the problem of searching through a table of words, but the solution is not very good unless the number of words to be searched is quite small, say 25 or fewer. If n were as large as a million, a simple sequential search would usually be an unbearably slow way to look through the table. We would hardly go to the expense of building such a large table unless we expected to search it frequently, and we would not want to waste any time during the search. Algorithm A is the equivalent of looking for someone's telephone number by going through a telephone directory page by page, column by column, one line at a time. We can do better than that.

The Advantage of Order

It is, in fact, instructive to consider a telephone directory as an example of such a large table of information. If we want to look up the telephone number of the person who lives at 918 West 35th Street, there is really no better way than to do a sequential search equivalent to Algorithm A, since a standard telephone directory is not organized for searches according to address. But when we look people up by their name, we can

BINARY-SEARCH ALGORITHM (Algorithm B in the text) is a substantial improvement over the sequential search algorithm when the table to be searched is large. The entries in the table must first be arranged in order; here the 25 names are listed alphabetically as in a dictionary. Again the input word sought is GRANT. The algorithm compares GRANT first to the key in the middle location, j, of the table. It calculates the initial value of j by setting the left boundary l of the search to 0 and the right boundary r to $n+1$; in this case r is 26. Then l and r are added together and divided by 2, rounding down to the nearest integer if the answer is not already an integer. The midpoint j of the table is 26/2, or 13, which is the location of LINCOLN (*top*). Since the name GRANT is alphabetically less than LINCOLN, the algorithm discards the entire right half of the table, containing all names alphabetically greater than or equal to LINCOLN. In the remaining half of the table the algorithm calculates a new midpoint, first setting r equal to the location j just examined, which is 13 (*second from top*). The new midpoint j is $(0 + 13)/2$, which must be rounded down to 6, the location of GARFIELD. Since GRANT is alphabetically greater than GARFIELD, the left quarter of the table can be discarded, and the left boundary l is set equal to 6 (*second from bottom*). When the procedure is repeated once more, GRANT is found in position 7 (*bottom*). If the input word x had been GIBBS, Algorithm B would have executed one more step, with l still equal to 6 and r set at 7. The midpoint j would have been 6, which is the current left boundary of the search, meaning that GIBBS is not in the table.

take advantage of alphabetical order. Alphabetical order is a substantial advantage indeed, since a single glance at almost any point in the directory suffices to eliminate many names from further consideration.

If the words of a table appear consistently in some order, there are several ways to design an efficient search procedure. The simplest procedure starts by looking first at the entry in the middle of the table. If the desired word x is numerically or alphabetically less than this middle entry, the entire second half of the table can be eliminated; similarly, if x is greater than the middle entry, one can eliminate the entire first half. Thus a single comparison yields a search problem that is only half as

Input: $x = \mathtt{GRANT}$

$l=0$, $j=13$, $r=26$

1	2	3	4	5	6	7	8	9	10	11	12	13	14	15	16	17	18	19	20	21	22	23	24	25
ADAMS	ARTHUR	BUCHANAN	CLEVELAND	FILLMORE	GARFIELD	GRANT	HARRISON	HAYES	JACKSON	JEFFERSON	JOHNSON	**LINCOLN**	MADISON	McKINLEY	MONROE	PIERCE	POLK	ROOSEVELT	TAFT	TAYLOR	TYLER	VAN BUREN	WASHINGTON	WILSON

$<$

$l=0$, $j=6$, $r=13$

1	2	3	4	5	6	7	8	9	10	11	12	13	14	15	16	17	18	19	20	21	22	23	24	25
ADAMS	ARTHUR	BUCHANAN	CLEVELAND	FILLMORE	**GARFIELD**	GRANT	HARRISON	HAYES	JACKSON	JEFFERSON	JOHNSON	LINCOLN	MADISON	McKINLEY	MONROE	PIERCE	POLK	ROOSEVELT	TAFT	TAYLOR	TYLER	VAN BUREN	WASHINGTON	WILSON

$>$

$l=6$, $j=9$, $r=13$

1	2	3	4	5	6	7	8	9	10	11	12	13	14	15	16	17	18	19	20	21	22	23	24	25
ADAMS	ARTHUR	BUCHANAN	CLEVELAND	FILLMORE	GARFIELD	GRANT	HARRISON	**HAYES**	JACKSON	JEFFERSON	JOHNSON	LINCOLN	MADISON	McKINLEY	MONROE	PIERCE	POLK	ROOSEVELT	TAFT	TAYLOR	TYLER	VAN BUREN	WASHINGTON	WILSON

$<$

$l=6$, $j=7$, $r=9$

1	2	3	4	5	6	7	8	9	10	11	12	13	14	15	16	17	18	19	20	21	22	23	24	25
ADAMS	ARTHUR	BUCHANAN	CLEVELAND	FILLMORE	GARFIELD	**GRANT**	HARRISON	HAYES	JACKSON	JEFFERSON	JOHNSON	LINCOLN	MADISON	McKINLEY	MONROE	PIERCE	POLK	ROOSEVELT	TAFT	TAYLOR	TYLER	VAN BUREN	WASHINGTON	WILSON

$=$

Output: 7

large as the original one. The same technique can now be applied to the remaining half of the table, and so on until the desired word x is either located or proved to be absent. This procedure is commonly known as a binary search.

Although the ideas underlying binary search are simple, some care is necessary in writing the algorithm. First, in a table that has an even number of elements there is no unique "middle" entry. Second, it is not immediately clear when to stop in the case of an unsuccessful search. Teachers of computer science have noticed, in fact, that when students are asked to write a binary-search procedure for the first time, about 80 percent of them get the program wrong, even when they have had more than a year of programming experience! Readers who feel that they understand algorithms fairly well but have never before written a binary-search algorithm might enjoy trying to construct one before reading the following solution.

Algorithm B; binary search. This algorithm employs the same notation as Algorithm A. Moreover, it is assumed that the first word, KEY[1], is less than the second word, KEY[2], which is less than the third word, KEY[3], and so on all the way up to the last word, KEY[n]. This condition can be written KEY[1] < KEY[2] < KEY[3] < $\cdots$ < KEY[n].

B1. [Initialize.] Set $l \leftarrow 0$, $r \leftarrow n + 1$. (The letter l stands for the left boundary of the search and r stands for the right boundary. More precisely, KEY[j] cannot match the given word x unless the location j is both greater than l and less than r.)

B2. [Find midpoint.] Set $j \leftarrow \lfloor (l + r)/2 \rfloor$. (The brackets $\lfloor\ \rfloor$ mean "Round down to the nearest integer." Thus if $(l + r)$ is even, j is set to $(l + r)/2$; if $(l + r)$ is odd, j is set to $(l + r - 1)/2$.)

B3. [Unsuccessful?] If $j = l$, output 0 and terminate the algorithm. (If j equals l, then r must be equal to $l + 1$, since r is always greater than l; therefore x cannot match any key in the table.)

B4. [Compare.] (At this point $j > l$ and $j < r$.) If $x = $ KEY[j], output j and terminate the algorithm. If $x < $ KEY[j], set $r \leftarrow j$ and return to step B2. If $x > $ KEY[j], set $l \leftarrow j$ and return to step B2.

A play-by-play account of Algorithm B as it searches through a table of 25 names is shown in the illustration on the preceding page.

It seems clear that binary search (Algorithm B) is much better than sequential search (Algorithm A), but how much better is it? And when is it better? A quantitative analysis will answer these questions.

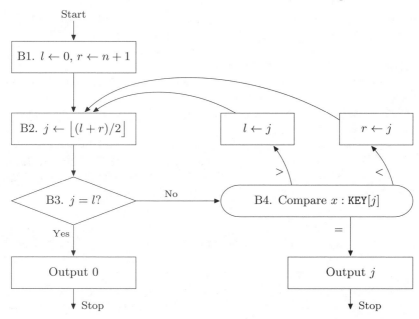

FLOW CHART FOR ALGORITHM B illustrates the rules governing binary search. The algorithm searches for an input word x, in a table of n keys that have previously been arranged in order. First x is compared to the middle entry of the table. If x is greater than ($>$) the middle entry, the left boundary marker l is increased so that x will next be compared to the midpoint of the right half of the table. If x is less than ($<$) the middle entry, the right boundary marker r is decreased so that x will next be compared to the midpoint of the left half of the table. The process continues, with half of the remaining table being discarded each time, until either x is found or the search reveals that x is not present. The half brackets in box B2 ("$\lfloor\ \rfloor$") mean "Round down to the nearest integer." The text explains all operations of Algorithm B in detail and sketches a proof of its correctness.

Quantitative Analysis

First let us analyze the worst cases of algorithms A and B. How long can it possibly take each algorithm to find word x in a table of size n? The answer is easy for Algorithm A. If x equals KEY[1], or if x is not in the table at all, step A3 will be executed n times; that is, the desired word x will be compared with all n entries in the table before the search stops. Furthermore, the algorithm will never execute step A3 more than

n times. When sequential search is applied to a table with a million entries, a million comparisons will be made in the worst case.

The answer is only slightly more difficult for binary search. Since Algorithm B discards half of the table remaining after each execution of step B4, it deals first with the entire table, then with half of the table, then a quarter of the table, then an eighth, and so on. The maximum number of executions of step B4 will be k, where k is the smallest integer such that 2^k is greater than n. For example, when binary search is applied to a table with a million (10^6) entries, k will be equal to 20, since 2^{20} is greater than 10^6 but 10^6 is greater than 2^{19}. Thus if a table with 10^6 entries is searched using Algorithm B, at most only 20 of those entries will ever be examined in any particular search.

From the standpoint of worst-case behavior, one can go further and say that Algorithm B is not only a good way to search; it is actually the *best possible* search algorithm that proceeds solely by comparing x to keys in the table. The reason is that a comparison-based algorithm cannot possibly examine more than $2^k - 1$ different keys during the time it makes its first k comparisons. No matter what strategy is adopted, the first comparison always selects a particular key of the table and the second comparison will be with at most two other keys (depending on whether x was less than or greater than the first key); the third comparison will be with at most four other keys; the fourth comparison will be with at most eight other keys, and so on. Therefore if a comparison-based search algorithm makes no more than k comparisons, the table can contain no more than $1 + 2 + 4 + 8 + \cdots + 2^{k-1}$ distinct keys, and this sum equals $2^k - 1$.

The familiar game of Twenty Questions can be analyzed by reasoning in a similar way. In this game one player thinks of a secret object, and conceals its name on a folded piece of paper. The other players try to guess what the object is by asking up to 20 questions that must be answered only by "Yes" or "No." The other players are also told initially whether the secret object is animal, vegetable, or mineral, or if it is a combination of those supposedly well-defined attributes. By arguing as I have in the preceding paragraph, one can prove that the other players cannot possibly identify more than 2^{23} different objects correctly, no matter how clever their questions are. There are only 2^3 (or eight) possible subsets of the set of attributes {Animal, Vegetable, Mineral}, and there are only 2^{20} possible outcomes of the 20 yes-no questions. Thus the total number of objects one can possibly identify is $2^3 \times 2^{20} = 2^{23}$. The argument holds even when each question asked depends on the answers to the preceding questions.

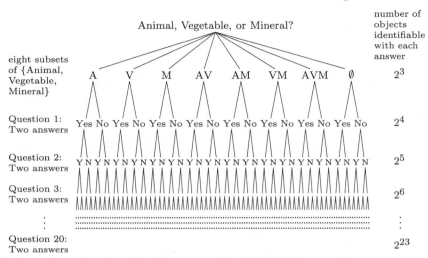

number of
objects
identifiable
with each
answer

Animal, Vegetable, or Mineral?

eight subsets
of {Animal,
Vegetable,
Mineral}

A   V   M   AV   AM   VM   AVM   ∅ 2^3

Question 1:
Two answers   Yes No Yes No Yes No Yes No Yes No Yes No Yes No Yes No 2^4

Question 2:
Two answers   Y N Y N Y N Y N Y N Y N Y N Y N Y N Y N Y N Y N Y N Y N Y N Y N 2^5

Question 3:
Two answers 2^6

⋮   ⋮

Question 20:
Two answers 2^{23}

THE GAME OF TWENTY QUESTIONS demonstrates a fundamental limitation on the power of any branching-search method. One player thinks of an object and describes it as being animal, vegetable, or mineral, or some combination of those characteristics. The opposing players try to guess what the object is by asking as many as 20 questions, which must be answered "Yes" or "No." It can be proved that the players cannot identify more than 2^{23} (or 8,388,608) objects correctly. The reason is that the set of characteristics {Animal, Vegetable, Mineral} has only eight, or 2^3, possible subsets (including the null set ∅ for an object with none of the characteristics), and these eight possibilities combine with only 2^{20} possible outcomes to the 20 yes-no questions. A similar argument can be used to show that a search algorithm cannot find more than $2^{20} - 1$ different key values if it asks at most 20 "less-equal-greater" questions, since $1 + 2 + 4 + 8 + \cdots + 2^{19} = 2^{20} - 1$. Binary search is able to attain this maximum limit, thus it is the most efficient search algorithm of its kind.

Stating this conclusion another way, if more than 2^{23} different objects must be identified, 20 questions will not always be enough. The search problem is similar but not quite the same, since an algorithm for searching does not simply ask yes-no questions. The questions asked by algorithms of the type we are considering have three possible outcomes, namely $x < \texttt{KEY}[j]$ or $x = \texttt{KEY}[j]$ or $x > \texttt{KEY}[j]$. When a table contains 2^k or more entries, the above reasoning proves that k comparisons of x with keys in the table will not always be enough. Therefore every algorithm that searches a table of a million words by making comparisons must in some instances examine 20 or more of those words. In short, binary search has the best possible worst case.

The worst-case behavior of an algorithm is not the whole story, since it is overly pessimistic to base decisions entirely on one's knowledge of the worst that can happen. A more meaningful understanding of the relative merits of algorithms A and B can be gained by analyzing their average-case behavior. If each of the n keys in a table is equally likely to be looked up, what is the average number of comparisons that will be needed? For sequential search (Algorithm A) the answer is the simple average $(1 + 2 + 3 + \cdots + n)/n$, which is equal to $(n + 1)/2$. In other words, to find x with Algorithm A one will on the average have to search through about half of the table.

To determine the average number of comparisons needed to find x using binary search (Algorithm B), the mathematics is only a little more complicated. In this case the answer is $k - \left((2^k - k - 1)/n\right)$, where k is the number of comparisons required in the worst case as discussed earlier. For large values of n this answer is approximately equal to $k - 1$; therefore the average performance of Algorithm B is only about one comparison less than its worst performance. By carefully extending the argument made earlier it is possible to show that binary search is also the best possible algorithm from the standpoint of the average case: Every comparison-based search algorithm must make at least $k - \left((2^k - k - 1)/n\right)$ comparisons on the average, and many such algorithms do much worse.

Better than the Best

As soon as something has been proved impossible, a lot of people immediately try to do it anyway. This seems to be an inherent aspect of human behavior. I have just proved that binary search is the best possible way to search a computer's memory, and so naturally I shall now look for a better way.

In the first place, when the number of words in a table is small, Algorithm A actually turns out to be faster than Algorithm B. Why does this not contradict the proof that binary search is best? The reason is that when comparing Algorithm A and Algorithm B, my arguments so far have considered only the number of comparisons that each algorithm makes. Actually Algorithm A requires less bookkeeping activity; therefore a machine can perform each comparison more quickly. On a typical computer Algorithm A can be made to take about $2n + 6$ units of time, on the average, for a table of size n; Algorithm B, on the other hand, will require an average of about $12 \log_2 n - 11 + 12(k+1)/n$ units of time under the same assumptions. Thus unless there are 20 or more keys to be searched, Algorithm A will be better than Algorithm B. These numbers will vary slightly from computer to computer, but they show that the efficiency of an algorithm cannot be determined by counting only the comparisons made.

There is another reason why Algorithm B can be beaten. When we look up someone's name in a telephone directory and compare the desired name x with the names on a page, our subsequent action is not influenced solely by whether the comparison shows that the desired name is alphabetically less than or greater than the names on the page; we also observe how much less or how much greater, and we turn over a larger chunk of pages if we think we are farther from the goal. The proof given earlier that binary search is best does not apply to algorithms that make use of such things as the degree of difference between x and a particular key. The proof for Twenty Questions can be attacked on similar grounds. For example, the players might notice the length of the secret object's name as it is being written down, or they might be able to gain information from the length of time the player being questioned hesitates before answering "Yes" or "No."

Therefore a human being concerned about efficiency need not begin searching a telephone directory by bisecting it as a computer would; the time-honored method of interpolation with the aid of alphabetical order probably works better in spite of the proof that the binary search is best. In fact, Andrew C. Yao of the Massachusetts Institute of Technology and F. Frances Yao of Brown University have recently shown that the average number of times an interpolation-search algorithm needs to access the table is only $\log_2 \log_2 n$ plus at most a small constant, provided that the table entries are independent and uniformly distributed random numbers. When n is very large, $\log_2 \log_2 n$ is much smaller than $\log_2 n$, so that interpolation search will be significantly faster than binary search. The idea underlying the Yaos' proof is that each iteration of an interpolation search tends to reduce the uncertainty of the position of x from n to the square root of n. (Binary search reduces the uncertainty only from n to $n/2$; sequential search reduces it even less, from n to $n - 1$.) Furthermore, they have proved that interpolation search is nearly the best possible, in a very broad sense: Any algorithm that searches such a random table by making appropriate comparisons must examine approximately $\log_2 \log_2 n$ or more entries, on the average.

These results are of great theoretical importance, although computational experience has shown that an interpolation search is usually not an improvement over binary search in practice. The reason is that the data stored in a table are typically not random enough to conform to the assumption of a uniform distribution; furthermore n is typically small enough that the extra calculation per comparison required by each interpolation outweighs the amount of time saved by reducing the number of comparisons. The simplicity of binary search is one of its virtues, and it is important to maintain a proper balance between theory and practice.

Binary Tree Search

The binary search can be improved, however, in another way, by dropping the assumption that every key in the table is equally likely to be sought. When some keys are known to be far more likely candidates than others, an efficient algorithm will examine the more likely ones first.

Before we explore this notion it will be helpful to look first at the binary search procedure in a different way. Consider the 31 words that are used most frequently in the English language (according to Helen Fouché Gaines in her book *Cryptanalysis*). When these words are arranged alphabetically in the locations KEY[1], KEY[2], KEY[3], ..., KEY[31] of a table, Algorithm B first compares the desired word x to the midpoint KEY[16], which is the word I. If x is alphabetically less than I, the next comparison will be with KEY[8], which is the word BY; if x is greater than I, the next comparison will be with KEY[24], which is THAT. In other words, Algorithm B acts on the table of words by following a structure that looks like an upside-down tree, starting at the top and going down to the left when x is less and down to the right when x is greater [*see illustration*]. It is not hard to see that any algorithm designed to search an ordered table purely by making comparisons can be described by a similar tree with binary (2-way) branching.

The tree for binary search is defined implicitly in Algorithm B by arithmetic operations on l, r, and j. It can also be defined explicitly by storing the tree information in the table of words itself. For this purpose let LEFT[j] be the position in the table at which we are to look if word x is less than KEY[j], and let RIGHT[j] be the position at which we are to look if x is greater than KEY[j]. For example, binary search in a table of 31 words would have LEFT[16] equal to 8 and RIGHT[16] equal to 24, since the search starts at KEY[16] and then proceeds to either KEY[8] or KEY[24]. If the search is to terminate unsuccessfully after determining that the desired word x is less than KEY[j] or greater than KEY[j], we respectively let LEFT[j] equal 0 or RIGHT[j] equal 0. Such 0's are represented by little circles at the bottom of the tree in the accompanying illustration.

Input: $x = \text{FROM}$

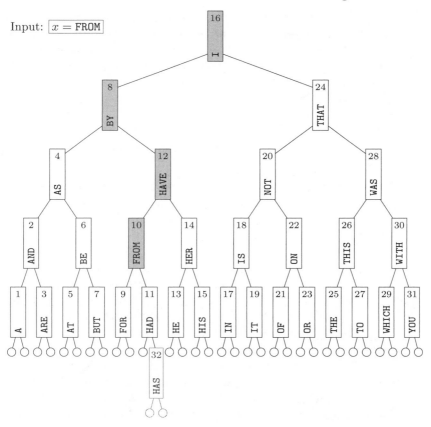

BINARY SEARCH TREE is implicit in Algorithm B. Here a tree graphically illustrates the order in which Algorithm B would probe an alphabetical table of the 31 most common words in English. Starting at the "root," or top, of the tree, the input word x is first compared with the midpoint of the table, the word I. If x is alphabetically smaller than I, the search proceeds down the left branch of the tree; if x is greater, the search proceeds down the right branch. For example, if x is the word FROM, the search first finds that x is less than I, then that x is greater than BY, then that x is less than HAVE, finally that x is equal to FROM. If x were not in the table, the search would stop at one of the 32 zeros (*small circular nodes*) at the bottom of the tree. When branches of the tree are represented explicitly in a computer's memory, rather than implicitly as in Algorithm B (which requires calculation of midpoints), the search goes slightly faster. Explicit branch locations also facilitate the insertion of new information. For example, to add HAS (*word in gray*) to the tree, one simply inserts it in alphabetical order, in place of one of the zeros.

The location of the first key to be examined in a binary tree is traditionally known as the root; in our 31-word example the root is 16. Search algorithms need not start by looking at KEY[16], and other choices of the root may well be more efficient than Algorithm B if some words are looked up much more often than others. A generalized tree-search procedure follows:

Algorithm C; tree search.

C1. [Initialize.] Set j equal to the location of the root of the binary search tree.

C2. [Unsuccessful?] If $j = 0$, output j and terminate the algorithm.

C3. [Compare.] If $x = $ KEY[j], output j and terminate the algorithm. If $x < $ KEY[j], set $j \leftarrow$ LEFT[j] and go back to step C2. If $x > $ KEY[j], set $j \leftarrow$ RIGHT[j] and go back to step C2.

Algorithm C is analogous to a programmed textbook in which, depending on the answers to certain questions, each page tells the reader what page to read next. The algorithm works on any binary tree where all keys accessible from LEFT[j] are less than KEY[j] and all keys accessible from RIGHT[j] are greater than KEY[j], for all locations j in the tree. Such a tree is called a binary search tree.

One of the advantages of Algorithm C over Algorithm B is that no arithmetic calculation is necessary; the search therefore goes slightly faster on a computer. The main advantage of Algorithm C, however, is that the tree structure provides extra flexibility, because the entries in the table can now be rearranged into any order. It is no longer necessary that KEY[1] be less than KEY[2] and so on up to KEY[n]. As long as the pointers LEFT and RIGHT define a valid binary search tree, the actual locations of the keys in the table are irrelevant. This means that we can add new entries to the table without moving all the other entries. For example, the word HAS could be added to the 31-word binary search tree simply by setting KEY[32] $\leftarrow$ HAS and changing RIGHT[j] from 0 to 32, where j is the location of the key HAD. One might think that such additions at the bottom of the tree would upset the balanced structure, but it can be shown mathematically that if new entries are added in random order, the result will almost surely be a reasonably well-balanced tree.

Optimum Binary Search Trees

Since Algorithm C applies to any binary search tree, one can hand-tailor the tree so that the most frequently examined keys are examined

Input: $x = $ FROM

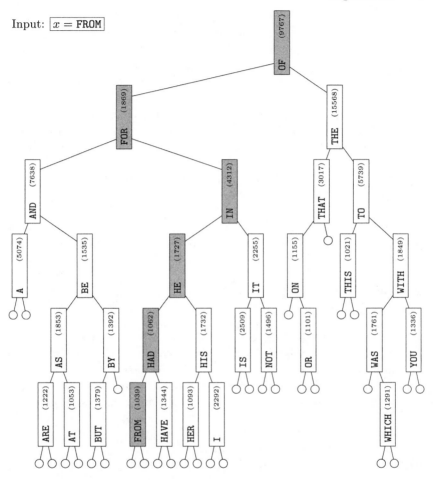

OPTIMUM BINARY SEARCH TREE shows the best order of the 31 words in the tree, based on the relative frequency of each word as estimated by Helen Fouché Gaines. The frequency of each word is represented by the number in parentheses above it. This tree is not as well balanced as the tree implicitly defined by the standard binary-search algorithm and illustrated earlier, so the search will take longer in some cases. For example, to find the word FROM in this tree takes six steps instead of four (*path in gray*). On the average, however, the optimum tree is faster for computer searching, because the more common words are tested sooner. Notice that although the word THE is by far the most frequently used word in English, it is not placed at the root of the tree because it is too far from the center of the alphabet. More than 10^{16} binary search trees are possible for 31 words, yet we can prove that this tree is best.

first. Such tailoring reduces the average time required for a computer to carry out the search, although it cannot reduce the worst-case time. The illustration on the preceding page shows the best possible binary search tree for the 31 most common English words, based on Gaines's estimates of their frequency. The average number of comparisons needed to search for x in this optimum binary search tree is only 3.437, whereas the average number of comparisons needed in the balanced binary search tree is 4.393. It is worth noting that the optimum tree, which is based on the frequencies of the words, does not start by comparing x with the word THE. Even though THE is by far the most common word of English, it comes so late in alphabetical order that it is too far from the middle of the list to serve as the best possible root.

From the standpoint of conventional mathematics it is trivial to find the optimum binary tree for any particular set of n words and frequencies because there are only finitely many search trees. In principle one merely has to list all the trees and choose the one that works best. In practice, however, this observation is useless because the number of possible binary trees with n elements is equal to $(2n)!/n!\,(n+1)!$, where $n!$ stands for the product $1 \times 2 \times 3 \times \cdots \times n$. This formula shows that there are very many binary trees indeed, approximately $4^n/\sqrt{\pi n^3}$ of them, where π is the familiar 3.14159. For example, when n is 31, the total number of possible binary trees is 14,544,636,039,226,909, and each of these 14 quadrillion trees will be optimum for some set of assumed frequencies for the 31 words. How, then, is it possible to show that the particular tree I have chosen is the best one for Gaines's frequencies? The fastest modern computer is far from fast enough to examine 14 quadrillion individual possibilities; even if one tree could be considered per microsecond, the task would take 460 years.

There is, however, an important principle that makes the computation feasible: Every subtree of an optimum tree must also be optimum. In the optimum binary search tree for the 31 most common English words, for example, the subtree to the left of the word OF must represent the best possible way to search for the 20 words A, AND, and so on up to NOT. If there were a better way, it would lead to a better overall tree, and the given tree would therefore not be optimum. Similarly, in that subtree the even smaller subtree to the right of FOR must represent the best possible way to search for the 11 words FROM, HAD, and so on up to NOT. Each subtree corresponds to a set of consecutive words KEY[i], KEY[$i+1$], ..., KEY[j], where $1 \leq i < j \leq n$. It is possible to determine all the optimum subtrees by finding the small ones first and doing the computation in order of increasing values of $j - i$. For each choice of

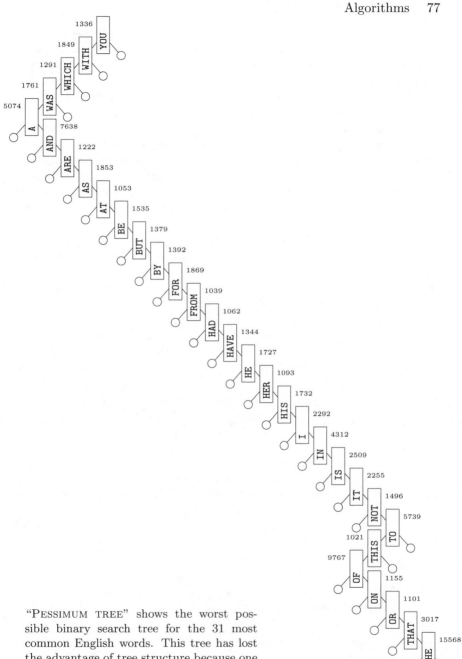

"PESSIMUM TREE" shows the worst possible binary search tree for the 31 most common English words. This tree has lost the advantage of tree structure because one branch of each comparison is always "dead."

indices i and j there are $j - i + 1$ possible roots of the subtree. As one proceeds up the tree with the computation and examines each possible subtree root, the optimum subtrees to the left and right will already have been calculated.

By this procedure the best possible binary search tree for n keys and frequencies can actually be found by doing about n^3 operations. Closer analysis makes it possible to improve the method even further, so that the number of operations is proportional to n^2. In the case of the 31 most common words this means that the optimum binary search tree can be discovered after only about 1000 steps instead of 14 quadrillion.

I should point out that the preceding paragraphs discuss several algorithms whose sole purpose is to determine the best binary search tree. In other words, the output of those algorithms is itself an algorithm for solving another problem! This example helps to explain why computer science has been developing so rapidly as an independent discipline. When we study how to use computers properly, we encounter new problems that are interesting in their own right, and many of these problems require a new and interrelated set of concepts and techniques.

It is amusing and instructive to consider the *worst* possible binary search tree for the 31 most common English words, in order to see how bad things could possibly become with Algorithm C. As in the case of the optimum trees, there is a way to determine such "pessimum" trees after performing about n^2 operations. For the 31 words with Gaines's frequencies the pessimum binary search tree causes Algorithm C to make an average of 19.158 comparisons per search [*see illustration on preceding page*].

How does Algorithm C compare to Algorithm A in this application? The best arrangement for Algorithm A makes KEY[n] the most common word, KEY[$n - 1$] the next most common, and so on; it leads to 9.093 comparisons, on the average, in the 31-word example. The worst arrangement for Algorithm A, in which KEY[n] is least likely, leads to an average of 22.907 comparisons per successful search. Hence the worst case for Algorithm C can never be quite as bad as the worst case for Algorithm A.

Hashing

The algorithms for searching that we have considered so far are closely related to the way people look for words in a dictionary. But there is actually a much better way to search through a large collection of words by computer. It is called *hashing*, and it is a completely different approach that is quite unsuitable for human use because it is based on a

Input: $x = $ HAVE

1	2	3	4	5	6	7	8	9	10	11	12	13	14	15	16	17	18	19	20	21	22	23	24	25	26	27	28	29	30	31	32
THE	HAVE	TO	HIS		BE	FOR	THIS	I	BUT	WAS	HAD	HE	FROM	AT	NOT	THAT	WHICH	AND	AS	OF	ON	IN	ARE	YOU	BY	WITH	IS	IT	HER	OR	A
1	4	3	4		7	7	24	9	11	11	13	13	20	21	17	17	19	19	20	21	29	23	24	29	27	28	28	29	31	1	1

$= \neq \neq$

"HASH" TABLE provides a better way for computers to search through large files of data. For each word x, the computer's ability to do high-speed arithmetic is exploited by computing a hash address $h(x)$ where the search for x is to start. The hash address for each of the 31 most common words is shown below each word; in this example each hash address was obtained by adding the numerical value of each letter (A = 1, B = 2, and so on up to Z = 26) and discarding excess multiples of 32. Sometimes two different words x and y have the same hash address $h(x)$, so that they "collide." If x is not found in position $h(x)$, the search continues leftward through positions $h(x) - 1$, $h(x) - 2$, and so on. For example, the hash address of HIS is H + I + S, or $8 + 9 + 19 - 32 = 4$. The hash address of HAVE is also 4. To search for HAVE the algorithm looks first in position 4 (*light gray*), then in position 3, and finally in position 2 (*dark gray*), where HAVE is located. If the word x is not in the table, the search for x will stop at empty position 5.

machine's ability to do arithmetic reliably at high speeds. The idea is to treat the letters of words as if they were numbers (A = 1, B = 2, C = 3, and so on through Z = 26) and then to hash, or scramble, the numbers in some way in order to get a single number for each word. That number is the so-called hash address of the word; it tells the computer where to look for the word in the table.

In the case of the 31 most common English words we could convert each key into a number between 1 and 32 by adding up the numerical values of its letters and throwing away excess multiples of 32. For example, the hash address of THE would be $20 + 8 + 5 - 32 = 1$; the hash address of OF would be $15 + 6 = 21$; and so on for the rest of the list. In fortunate circumstances each word will lead to a different hash address, and every search will be very fast.

In general, suppose there are m locations in the computer's memory, and suppose that we want to store n keys, where m is greater than n. Since n is equal to 31, we might take m equal to 32. Assume also the existence of a hash function $h(x)$ that converts each possible word x into a number between 1 and m. A good hash function will have the property that $h(x)$ is unlikely to be equal to $h(y)$ if x and y are different words to be put into the table.

Unless m is much larger than n, nearly every hash function will lead to at least a few "collisions" between the values $h(x)$ and $h(y)$, since the probability that n independent random numbers between 1 and m will all be different is extremely small. For example, it is well known that when 23 or more people are present in the same room there is a better than even chance that two of them will have the same birthday. Moreover, in a group of 88 people it is likely that there will be three individuals born on the same day. Although this phenomenon seems paradoxical to many people, the mathematics can be easily checked, and many seemingly impossible coincidences can be explained in the same way.

Another way to state the birthday paradox is to say that a hash function with m equal to 365 and n equal to 23 will have at least one collision, more often than not. Thus any search procedure based on a hash function must be able to deal with the problem of collisions.

Suppose we want to search a table for x and we find that the hash address $h(x)$ already contains another word y. The simplest way to handle the collision is to search through locations $h(x)$, $h(x)-1$, $h(x)-2$, and so on, until we either find x or come to an empty position. If the search runs off one end of the table before it is completed, it resumes at the other end. This procedure, which is known as linear probing, can be spelled out as an algorithm:

Algorithm D; hashing with linear probing.

D1. [Initialize.] Set $j \leftarrow h(x)$.

D2. [Unsuccessful?] If table entry j is empty, output 0 and terminate the algorithm.

D3. [Successful?] If $x = \text{KEY}[j]$, output j and terminate the algorithm.

D4. [Move to next location.] Set $j \leftarrow j-1$; then if $j = 0$, set $j \leftarrow m$. (Location m is considered to be next to location 1.) Return to step D2.

If x is not in the table, and if the algorithm terminates unsuccessfully in step D2 because table entry j is empty, we could set $\text{KEY}[j] \leftarrow x$ using the current value of j. This would insert x into the table so that the algorithm could retrieve it later, because a subsequent search for x will follow the same path as it did the first time, starting at position $h(x)$, moving to $h(x) - 1$ and so on, finding x in position j. Thus the search will proceed properly even when collisions occur.

Returning to the example of the 31 most common English words, suppose that the words have been inserted one by one into an initially empty table in decreasing order of their frequency (THE is inserted first, OF is inserted second, and so on). The result is the hash table shown in the illustration on page 79. Most of the words appear at or near their hash addresses except for the ones that were inserted into the table last; the least frequent word, THIS, has been placed in position 8 although its hash address is 24, because positions 9 through 24 were already filled by the time THIS came along. In spite of such anomalies the average number of times the table must be probed by Algorithm D in order to find a word turns out to be only 1.666 — less than half the average number of comparisons required to find the word with the optimum binary search tree. Of course, the time needed to compute $h(x)$ in step D1 must be added to the time for probing the table. For large collections of data, however, the hashing method will significantly outperform any binary-comparison algorithm.

In practice one would almost never let a hash table get as full as it does in the example. The number m of table positions available is usually chosen to be so large that the table will never become more than 80 or 90 percent full. It can be shown that the average number of probes needed to find one word out of n equally likely words that have been randomly inserted into a table of size m is

$$1 + \frac{n-1}{2m} + \frac{(n-1)(n-2)}{2m^2} + \frac{(n-1)(n-2)(n-3)}{2m^3} + \cdots .$$

Let the symbol α stand for n/m, the fullness ratio or "load factor" of the table. As n approaches infinity it can be shown that the average number of probes required to find any word x in a table approaches the value $1 + (\alpha + \alpha^2 + \alpha^3 + \cdots)/2$, which is equal to $\left(1 + 1/(1 - \alpha)\right)/2$. Furthermore, the true average number of probes will always be less than this limiting value. Therefore when the table being searched is 80 percent full, Algorithm D makes fewer than three probes per successful search on the average.

It is important to note that the stated upper limit on the average number of probes per successful search holds for all tables that have a given load factor $\alpha = n/m$, no matter how large the table is. The same cannot be said about binary-comparison algorithms, because their average running time per successful search will grow arbitrarily large as the number n of words to be searched increases.

Improving Unsuccessful Searches

My statements in the preceding paragraphs about the small number of probes required with Algorithm D apply only to cases where x is actually found in the table. If x is not present, the average number of probes needed to ascertain that fact will be larger, namely

$$1 + \frac{n}{m} + \frac{3n(n-1)}{2m^2} + \frac{2n(n-1)(n-2)}{m^3} + \cdots ;$$

when n is large, this number is approximately equal to $\big(1+1/(1-\alpha)^2\big)/2$. In other words, an average unsuccessful search in a large hash table that is 80 percent full requires nearly 13 probes. Moreover, in our example of the 31 words in 32 spaces, all unsuccessful searches must terminate at the single empty position 5, regardless of the location of the starting address $h(x)$. A precisely analogous situation occurred with the sequential search Algorithm A, where all unsuccessful searches ended at position 0.

In 1973, Ole Amble of the University of Oslo noted that the problem of unsuccessful search could be alleviated by combining the concept of hashing with the concept of alphabetical order. Suppose that the 31 most common English words have been inserted into the table in decreasing alphabetical order instead of in decreasing order of frequency. Since the table is probed by starting at the address $h(x)$ and moving to $h(x) - 1$ and so on, all words lying between the address $h(x)$ and the actual location of x must be alphabetically greater than x, lest there be a collision. A search for x can therefore be terminated unsuccessfully whenever a word alphabetically less than x is encountered. In other words, the following algorithm can be used:

Algorithm E; linear probing in an ordered hash table. This algorithm assumes that KEY[j] is 0 when entry j is empty, and that all input words x have a numerical value that is greater than 0.

E1. [Initialize.] Set $j \leftarrow h(x)$.

E2. [Unsuccessful?] If $x > $ KEY[j], output 0 and terminate the algorithm.

E3. [Successful?] If $x = $ KEY[j], output j and terminate the algorithm.

E4. [Move to next.] Set $j \leftarrow j - 1$; then if $j = 0$, set $j \leftarrow m$. Return to step E2.

The advantage of Algorithm E is illustrated in the ordered hash table on the following page. Suppose we want to determine if HAS is one of

Input: $x = \text{HAS}$

1	2	3	4	5	6	7	8	9	10	11	12	13	14	15	16	17	18	19	20	21	22	23	24	25	26	27	28	29	30	31	32
THE	HAVE	TO	HIS		BE	FOR	AND	I	BUT	WAS	HAD	HE	ARE	AS	NOT	THAT	AT	WHICH	FROM	OF	BY	IN	THIS	IS	IT	ON	WITH	YOU	A	HER	OR
1	4	3	4		7	7	19	9	11	11	13	13	24	20	17	17	21	19	20	21	27	23	24	28	29	29	28	29	1	31	1

(comparisons under positions 22–28): $>\ <\ <\ <\ <\ <\ <$

ORDERED HASH TABLE, which combines the concept of hashing with the advantage of alphabetical order, reveals more quickly when word x is not present. Here all the words between position $h(x)$ and the actual location of x are alphabetically greater than x. Thus an unsuccessful search need not stop only at the empty position 5; it stops as soon as a key value alphabetically less than x is encountered. If the desired word x is HAS, with hash address 28 (*light gray*), the search will stop when it reaches BY in position 22 (*dark gray*).

the 31 most common English words. Its hash address is $8 + 1 + 19 = 28$. With Algorithm E the search terminates in six steps when it reaches $j = 22$ (BY) instead of continuing through the table until it encounters the empty table entry at $j = 5$.

In an ordered hash table the average number of probes per unsuccessful search is reduced to

$$1 + \frac{n}{2m} + \frac{n(n-1)}{2m^2} + \frac{n(n-1)(n-2)}{2m^3} + \cdots,$$

and this number is always less than $\big(1 + 1/(1-\alpha)\big)/2$. Thus the limit for a successful search and the limit for an unsuccessful one are identical. On the average, when an ordered hash table is 80 percent full, Algorithm E will make fewer than three probes regardless of the size of n.

This is all very well if the ordered hash table has been set up by inserting the keys in decreasing alphabetical order as I have described it. In practice, however, one cannot always assume that the words of a table have been entered in such a manner. Tables often grow dynamically with use, and new words enter in random order. The structure of a binary tree (Algorithm C) and of an unordered hash table (Algorithm D) will handle dynamic growth with ease, but the structure of an ordered hash table (Algorithm E) is not so obviously adaptable. Fortunately there is a very simple algorithm for inserting a new word into an ordered hash table:

Algorithm F; insertion into an ordered hash table. This algorithm puts a new word x into an ordered hash table and rearranges the other entries appropriately so that searching with Algorithm E remains valid.

F1. [Initialize.] Set $j \leftarrow h(x)$.

F2. [Compare.] If $x > $ KEY$[j]$, interchange the values of KEY$[j]$ and x. (That is, set x to the former value of KEY$[j]$ and set KEY$[j]$ to the former value of x.)

F3. [Done?] If $x = 0$, terminate the algorithm.

F4. [Move to next.] Set $j \leftarrow j - 1$; then if $j = 0$, set $j \leftarrow m$. Go back to step F2.

If we choose to insert the word HAS into the ordered hash table of the 31 most common English words by means of Algorithm F, the procedure would place HAS in position 22, making room for it by moving BY from position 22 to position 18, moving AT from position 18 to position 15, moving AS from position 15 to position 14, moving ARE from position 14 to position 8 and finally moving AND from position 8 to the empty position 5. That may seem like a lot of work, but it takes only slightly longer than the task of inserting HAS into an unordered hash table using Algorithm D. In general the insertion of a word into an ordered hash table takes the same average number of iterations as the insertion of the same word into an unordered hash table. Furthermore, the average number of words in the table that must be interchanged by way of step F2 to accommodate the new word is

$$\frac{n-1}{2m} + \frac{2(n-1)(n-2)}{3m^2} + \frac{3(n-1)(n-2)(n-3)}{4m^3} + \cdots ;$$

this quantity is approximately equal to $1/(1-\alpha) + \big(\log_e(1-\alpha)\big)/\alpha$, where e is the familiar 2.71828. When α is 80% the average number of interchanges is approximately 2.988. Thus inserting words by Algorithm F is quite a reasonable task.

In this specific case we actually should not have inserted HAS into the table because hash tables ought to have at least one empty position. By coincidence, however, the smallest possible word in alphabetical order (the word A) is present in this completely full table. Hence linear probing with Algorithm E will still work correctly in all cases. If A were not in the table, an empty position would be needed in order to avoid endless searching when the input word x was equal to A.

One of the most useful properties of ordered hash tables is the fact that each one is uniquely determined by its keys. If we use Algorithm F to build an ordered hash table from any set of words, the same table will be obtained regardless of the order in which the words are inserted. Readers may find it entertaining to prove this fact for themselves.

Conclusion

My discussion of ways to search for information stored in a computer's memory is intended to illustrate several important points about algorithms in general:

1) An algorithm must be stated precisely, and the task of doing that is not as easy as one might think.

2) When one tries to solve a problem by computer, the first algorithm that comes to mind can usually be greatly improved.

3) Data structures such as binary trees are important tools for the construction of efficient algorithms.

4) When we start to investigate how fast an algorithm is, or when we try to find the best possible algorithm for a specific application, interesting issues arise and we often find that the questions have subtle answers.

5) Even the "best possible" algorithm can sometimes be improved if we change the ground rules.

6) Since computers "think" differently from people, methods that work well for the human mind are not necessarily the most efficient when they are transferred to a machine.

References

[1] O. Amble and D. E. Knuth, "Ordered hash tables," *The Computer Journal* **17** (1974), 135–142.

[2] D. E. Knuth, "Ancient Babylonian algorithms," *Communications of the ACM* **15** (1972), 671–677. [Reprinted as Chapter 11 of the present volume.]

[3] D. E. Knuth, *The Art of Computer Programming*, Vols. 1–3 (Reading, Massachusetts: Addison–Wesley, 1973).

[4] D. E. Knuth, "Computer Science and its relation to Mathematics," *American Mathematical Monthly* **81** (1974), 323–343. [Reprinted as Chapter 1 of the present volume.]

[5] J. Nievergelt, "Binary search trees and file organization," *Computing Surveys* **6** (1974), 195–207.

[6] A. C. Yao and F. F. Yao, "The complexity of searching an ordered table," *Proceedings of the 17th Annual IEEE Symposium on Foundations of Computer Science* (1976), 173–177.

[An earlier version of the present article was published while the author was a guest professor at the University of Oslo: D. E. Knuth, "Søking etter noe i en EDB-maskin," *Forskningsnytt* **18**, 4 (Norges Almenviten- skapelige Forskningsråd, 1973), 39–42.]

Chapter 4

Algorithms in Modern Mathematics and Computer Science

[Keynote address presented to an international symposium on Algorithms in Modern Mathematics and Computer Science, held in the Khwârizm region of Uzbekistan in September 1979 under the sponsorship of the Soviet and Uzbek Academies of Science. Originally published in Lecture Notes in Computer Science 122 (1981), 82–99. An abridged version entitled "Algorithmic thinking and mathematical thinking" appeared in the American Mathematical Monthly 92 (1985), 170–181.]

My purpose in this paper is to stimulate discussion about a philosophical question that has been on my mind for a long time: What rôle does the notion of an *algorithm* actually play in mathematical sciences?

For many years I have been convinced that computer science is primarily the study of algorithms. My colleagues don't all agree with me, but it turns out that the source of our disagreement is simply that my definition of algorithms is much broader than theirs: I tend to think of algorithms as encompassing the whole range of concepts dealing with well-defined processes, including the structure of data that is being acted upon as well as the structure of the sequence of operations being performed; some other people think of algorithms merely as miscellaneous methods for the solution of particular problems, analogous to individual theorems in mathematics.

In the U.S.A., the sorts of things my colleagues and I do is called Computer Science, emphasizing the fact that algorithms are performed by machines. But if I lived in Germany or France, the field I work in would be called *Informatik* or *Informatique*, emphasizing the stuff that algorithms work on more than the processes themselves. In the Soviet Union, the same field is now known as either *Kibernetika* (Cybernetics), emphasizing the control of a process, or *Prikladnaîa Matematika* (Applied Mathematics), emphasizing the utility of the subject and its

87

ties to mathematics in general. I suppose the name of our discipline isn't of vital importance, since we will go on doing what we are doing no matter what it is called; after all, other disciplines like Mathematics and Chemistry are no longer related very strongly to the etymology of their names. However, if I had a chance to vote for the name of my own discipline, I would choose to call it Algorithmics, a word coined about 16 years ago by J. F. Traub [27, p. 1].

The site of our symposium is especially well suited to philosophical discussions such as I wish to incite, both because of its rich history and because of the grand scale of its scenery. This is an ideal time for us to consider the long range aspects of our work, the issues that we usually have no time to perceive in our hectic everyday lives at home. During the coming week we will have a perfect opportunity to look backward in time to the roots of our subject, as well as to look ahead and to contemplate what our work is all about.

I have wanted to make a pilgrimage to this place for many years, ever since learning that the word "algorithm" was derived from the name of al-Khwârizmî, the great ninth-century scientist whose name means "the Khwârizmian." The Spanish word *guarismo* ("decimal number") also stems from this root. Khwârizm was not simply a notable city (Khiva) as many Western authors have thought, it was and still is a rather large district. In fact, the Aral Sea was at one time known as Lake Khwârizm (see, for example, [17, Plates 9–21]). By the time of the conversion of this region to Islam in the seventh century, a high culture had developed, having for example its own script as well as its own calendar (cf. al-Bîrûnî [21]).

Catalog cards prepared by the U.S. Library of Congress say that al-Khwârizmî flourished between 813 and 846 A.D. It is amusing to take the average of these two numbers, obtaining 829.5, almost exactly 1150 years ago. Therefore we are here at an auspicious time, to celebrate an undesesquicentennial.

Comparatively little is known for sure about al-Khwârizmî's life. His full Arabic name is essentially a capsule biography: Abû 'Abd Allâh Muḥammad ibn Mûsâ al-Khwârizmî, meaning "Mohammed, father of Abdullah, son of Moses, the Khwârizmian." However, the name does not prove that he was born here; it might refer to his ancestors instead of himself. We do know that his scientific work was done in Baghdad, as part of an academy of scientists called the "House of Wisdom," under Caliph al-Ma'mûn. Al-Ma'mûn was a great patron of science who invited many learned men to his court in order to collect and extend the wisdom of the world. In this respect he was building on foundations laid by his predecessor, the Caliph Harûn al-Rashîd, who is familiar to us because of the *Arabian Nights*. The historian al-Ṭabarî added "al-Quṭrubbullî" to al-Khwârizmî's name, referring to the Quṭrubbull district near Baghdad. Perhaps al-Khwârizmî was born in Khwârizm and lived most of his life in Quṭrubbull after being summoned to Baghdad by the Caliph; but the truth will probably never be known.

The Charisma of al-Khwârizmî

It is clear in any event that al-Khwârizmî's work had an enormous influence throughout the succeeding generations. According to the *Fihrist*, a sort of Who's Who and bibliography of 987 A.D., "during his lifetime and afterwards, people were accustomed to rely upon his tables." Several of the books he wrote have apparently vanished, including a historical Book of Chronology and works on the sundial and the astrolabe. But he wrote a short treatise on the Jewish calendar (still extant), and compiled extensive astronomical tables that were in wide use for several hundred years. Of course, nobody is perfect: Some modern scholars feel that those tables were not as accurate as they could have been.

The most significant works of al-Khwârizmî were almost certainly his textbooks on algebra and arithmetic, which apparently were the first Arabic writings to deal with such topics. His algebra book was especially famous; in fact, at least three manuscripts of this work in the original Arabic are known to have survived to the present day, while more than 99% of the books by other authors mentioned in the *Fihrist* have been lost. Al-Khwârizmî's *Algebra* was translated into Latin at least twice during the twelfth century, and this is how Europeans learned about the subject. In fact, our word "algebra" stems from part of the Arabic title of this book, *Kitâb al-jabr wa'l-muqâbala*, "The Book of Aljabr and Almuqâbala." (Historians disagree on the proper translation of this title. My personal opinion, based on a reading of the work and on the early Latin translation *restaurationis et oppositionis* [3, p. 2], together with the fact that *muqâbala* signifies some sort of standing face-to-face, is that it would be best to call al-Khwârizmî's algebra "The Book of Restoring and Equating.")

We can get some idea of the reasons for al-Khwârizmî's success by looking at his *Algebra* in more detail. The purpose of the book was not to summarize all knowledge of the subject, but rather to give the "easiest and most useful" elements, the kinds of mathematics most often needed. He discovered that the complicated geometric tricks previously used in Babylonian and Greek mathematics could be replaced by simpler and more systematic methods that rely on algebraic manipulations alone. Thus the subject became accessible to a much wider audience. He explained how to reduce all nontrivial quadratic equations to one of three forms that we would express as $x^2 + bx = c$, $x^2 = bx + c$, $x^2 + c = bx$ in modern notation, where b and c are positive numbers; note that he has gotten rid of the coefficient of x^2 by dividing it out. If he had known about negative numbers, he would have been delighted to go further and reduce these three possibilities to a single case.

I mentioned that the Caliph wanted his scientists to put all of the existing scientific knowledge of other lands into Arabic texts. Although no prior work is known to have incorporated al-Khwârizmî's elegant approach to quadratic equations, the second part of his *Algebra* (which deals with questions of geometric measurements) was almost entirely based on an interesting treatise called the *Mishnat ha-Middot*, which Solomon Gandz has given good reason to believe was composed by a Jewish rabbi named Nehemiah about 150 A.D. [4]. The differences between the *Mishnat* and the *Algebra* help us to understand al-Khwârizmî's methods. For example, when the Hebrew text said that the circumference of a circle is $3\frac{1}{7}$ times the diameter, al-Khwârizmî added that this is only a conventional approximation, not a proved fact; he also mentioned $\sqrt{10}$ and $\frac{62832}{20000}$ as alternatives, the latter "used by astronomers." The Hebrew text merely stated the Pythagorean theorem, but al-Khwârizmî appended a proof. Probably the most significant change occurred in his treatment of the area of a general triangle: The *Mishnat* simply states Heron's formula $\sqrt{s(s-a)(s-b)(s-c)}$ where $s = \frac{1}{2}(a + b + c)$ is the semiperimeter, but the *Algebra* takes an entirely different tack. Al-Khwârizmî wanted to reduce the number of basic concepts, so he showed how to compute the area in general from the simpler formula $\frac{1}{2}$(base × height), where the height could be computed by simple algebra. Let the perpendicular to the largest side of the triangle from the opposite corner strike the longest side at a distance x from its end; then $b^2 - x^2 = c^2 - (a-x)^2$, hence $b^2 = c^2 - a^2 + 2ax$ and $x = (a^2 + b^2 - c^2)/(2a)$. The height of the triangle can now be computed as $\sqrt{b^2 - x^2}$; thus it isn't necessary to learn Heron's trick.

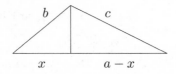

Unless an earlier work turns up showing that al-Khwârizmî learned his approach to algebra from somebody else, these considerations show that we are justified in calling him "the father of algebra." In other words, we can add the phrase "abû al-jabr" to his name! The overall history of the subject can be diagrammed roughly thus:

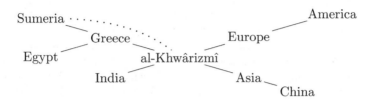

(I have shown a dotted line from Sumeria to represent a plausible connection between ancient traditions that might have reached Baghdad directly instead of via Greece. Conservative scholars doubt this connection, but I think they are too much influenced by obsolete attitudes to history in which Greek philosophers have been regarded as the source of all scientific knowledge.) Of course, al-Khwârizmî never took the subject beyond quadratic equations in one variable, but he did make an important leap away from geometry to abstract reckoning, and he made the subject systematic and reasonably simple for practical use. He was unaware of Diophantus's prior work on number theory, which was even more abstract and further removed from reality, therefore closer to modern algebra. It is difficult to rank either al-Khwârizmî or Diophantus higher than the other, since they had such different aims. The unique contribution of Greek scientists was their pursuit of knowledge solely for its own sake.

The original Arabic version of al-Khwârizmî's small book on what he called the Hindu art of reckoning seems to have vanished. Essentially all we have is an incomplete 13th-century copy of what is probably a 12th-century translation from Arabic into Latin; the original Arabic may well have been considerably different. It is amusing to look at this Latin translation with modern eyes, because it is primarily a document about how to calculate in Hindu numerals (the decimal system) but it uses Roman numerals to express numbers! Perhaps al-Khwârizmî's original treatise was similar in this respect, except that he would have used an alphabetic notation for numbers that was adapted from earlier Greek and Hebrew sources to Arabic; it is natural to expect that the first work on the subject would state problems and their solutions in an old familiar notation. I suppose the new notation became well known shortly after al-Khwârizmî's book appeared, and that might be why no copies of his original are left.

The Latin translation of al-Khwârizmî's arithmetic has blank spaces where most of the Hindu numerals were to be inserted; the scribe never got around to this, but it is possible to make good guesses about how to fill in those gaps. The portion of the manuscript that survives has never yet been translated from Latin to English or any other Western language, although a Russian translation appeared in 1964 [16]. Unfortunately both of the published transcriptions of the Latin handwriting ([3], [29]) are highly inaccurate; see [18]. It would surely be desirable to have a proper edition of this work in English, so that more readers can appreciate its contents. The algorithms given for decimal addition, subtraction, multiplication, and division — if we may call them algorithms, since they omit many details, even though they were written by al-Khwârizmî himself! — have been studied in detail by Îushkevich [9] and Rozenfel'd [16]. They are interesting because they are comparatively unsuitable for pencil-and-paper calculation, requiring lots of crossing-out or erasing; it seems clear that they are merely straightforward adaptations of procedures that were used on an abacus of some sort, in India if not in Persia. The development of methods more suitable for non-abacus calculations seems to be due to al-Uqlîdisî in Damascus about two centuries later [22].

Further details of al-Khwârizmî's works appear in an excellent article by G. J. Toomer in the *Dictionary of Scientific Biography* [26]. This was surely the most comprehensive summary of what was known about Muḥammad ibn Mûsâ in 1973, although I was surprised to see no mention of the plausible hypothesis that local traditions continued from Babylonian times to the Islamic era. Heinz Zemanek has now compiled a great deal of further biographical information in his delightful and insightful contribution to our symposium [32].

Before closing this historical introduction, I want to mention another remarkable man from Khwârizm, Abû Rayḥân Muḥammad ibn Aḥmad al-Bîrûnî (973–1048 A.D.): philosopher, historian, traveler, geographer, linguist, mathematician, encyclopedist, astronomer, poet, physicist, and computer scientist, author of an estimated 150 books [12]. The term "computer scientist" belongs in this list because of his interest in efficient calculation. For example, al-Bîrûnî showed how to evaluate the sum $1 + 2 + \cdots + 2^{63}$ of the number of grains of wheat on a chessboard if a single grain is placed on the first square, two on the second, twice as many on the third, etc.: Using a technique of divide and conquer, he proved that the total is $(((16^2)^2)^2)^2 - 1$, and he gave the answer 18,446,744,073,709,551,615 in three systems of notation (decimal, sexagesimal, and a peculiar alphabetic-Arabic). He also pointed out that this number amounts to approximately 2305 "mountains," if one mountain equals 10000 wâdîs, one wâdî is 1000 herds, one herd is 10000 loads, one load is 8 bidar, and one bidar is 10000 units of wheat ([20]; [21, pp. 132–136]; [23]).

Some Questions

Will Durant has remarked that "scholars were as numerous as the pillars, in thousands of mosques" during that golden age of medieval science. Now here we are, a group of scholars with a chance to be inspired by the same surroundings; and I would like to raise several questions that I believe are important today. *What is the relation of algorithms to modern mathematics?* Is there an essential difference between an algorithmic viewpoint and the traditional mathematical world-view? *Do most mathematicians have an essentially different thinking process from that of most computer scientists?* Among members of university mathematics departments, why do the logicians (and to a lesser extent the combinatorial mathematicians) tend to be much more interested in computer science than their colleagues are?

I raise these questions partly because of my own experiences as a student. I began to study higher mathematics in 1957, the same year that I began to work with digital computers, but I never mixed my mathematical thinking with my computer-science thinking in nontrivial ways until 1961. In one building I was a mathematician, in another I was a computer programmer, and it was as if I had a split personality. During 1961 I was excited by the idea that mathematics and computer science might have some common ground, because BNF notation looked mathematical, so I bought a copy of Chomsky's *Syntactic Structures* and set out to find an algorithm to decide the ambiguity problem of context-free grammars. (I was unaware that a special case of this task had already been proved impossible by Bar-Hillel, Perles, and Shamir.) Naturally I failed to solve that problem, but I did find some useful necessary and sufficient conditions for ambiguity, and I also derived a few other results, like the fact that context-free languages on one letter are regular. Here, I thought, was a nice mathematical theory that I was able to develop with my computer-science intuition; how curious! During the summer of 1962, I spent a day or two analyzing the performance of hashing with linear probing, but this did not really feel like a marriage between my computer science personality and my mathematical personality since it was merely an application of combinatorial mathematics to a problem that has relevance to programming.

I think it is generally agreed that mathematicians have somewhat different thought processes from physicists, who have somewhat different thought processes from chemists, who have somewhat different thought processes from biologists. Similarly, the respective mentalities of lawyers, poets, playwrights, historians, linguists, farmers, and so on, seem to be unique. Each of these groups can probably recognize that other types of people have a different approach to knowledge; and it seems likely that a person gravitates to a particular kind of occupation corresponding to the mode of thought that he or she grew up with, whenever a choice is possible. C. P. Snow wrote a famous book about "two cultures," scientific versus humanistic, but in fact there seem to be many more than two.

Educators of computer science have repeatedly observed that only about 2 out of every 100 students enrolling in introductory programming courses really resonate with the subject and seem to be natural-born computer scientists. (For example, see Gruenberger [8].) I just had some independent confirmation of this, when I learned that 220 out of 11000 graduate students at the University of Illinois are majoring in Computer Science. Since I believe that Computer Science is the study of algorithms, I conclude that roughly 2% of all people "think algorithmically," in the sense that they can reason rapidly about algorithmic processes.

While writing this paper, I learned about some recent statistical data gathered by Gerrit DeYoung, a psychologist-interested-in-computer-science whom I met at the University of Illinois. He had recently made an interesting experiment on two groups of undergraduate students taking different introductory courses in computer science. Group I consisted of 135 students intending to major in computer science, while Group II consisted of 35 social science majors. Both courses emphasized nonnumeric programming and various data and control structures, although numerical problems were treated too. DeYoung handed out a questionnaire that tested each student's so-called quantitative aptitude, a standard test that seems to correlate with mathematical ability; he also asked them to estimate their own performance in class. Afterwards he learned the grades that the students actually did receive, so he had three pieces of data on each student:

A = quantitative aptitude;

B = student's own perception of programming ability;

C = teacher's perception of programming ability.

In both cases B correlated well with C (the coefficient was about .6), so we can conclude that the teachers' grading wasn't random and that there is some validity in these scores. The interesting thing was that there was *no* correlation between A and B or between A and C among the computer science majors (Group I), while there was a pronounced correlation of about .4 between the corresponding numbers for the students of Group II. The reason isn't clear, since many different hypotheses could account for such results; perhaps psychologists know only how to measure the quantitative ability of people who think like psychologists do! At any rate the lack of correlation between quantitative ability and programming performance in the first group reminds me strongly of the feelings I often have about differences between mathematical thinking and computer-science thinking, so further study is indicated.

I believe that the real reason underlying the fact that Computer Science has become a thriving discipline at essentially all of the world's universities, although it was totally unknown twenty years ago, is *not* that computers exist in quantity; the real reason is that the algorithmic thinkers among the scientists of the world never before had a home. We are brought together in Computer Science departments *because we find people who think like we do.* At least, that seems a viable hypothesis, which hasn't been contradicted by my observations during the last half dozen or so years since the possibility occurred to me.

My goal, therefore, is to get a deeper understanding of these phenomena; the "different modes of thought" hypothesis merely scratches the surface and gives little insight. Can we come up with a fairly clear idea of just what algorithmic thinking is, and contrast it with classical mathematical thinking?

At times when I try to come to grips with this question, I find myself almost convinced that algorithmic thinking is really like mathematical thinking, only it concentrates on more "difficult" things. But at other times I have just the opposite impression, that somehow algorithms hit only the "simpler" kinds of mathematics. Clearly such an approach leads only to confusion and gets me nowhere.

While pondering these things recently, I suddenly remembered the collection of expository works called *Mathematics: Its Content, Methods, and Meaning* [1], so I reread what A. D. Aleksandrov had to say in his excellent introductory essay. Interestingly enough, I found that he made prominent mention of al-Khwârizmî. Aleksandrov listed the following characteristic features of mathematics:

- Abstractness, with many levels of abstraction.
- Precision and logical rigor.
- Quantitative relations.
- Broad range of applications.

Unfortunately, however, all four of these features seem to be characteristic also of computer science. Is there really no difference between computer science and mathematics?

A Plan

I decided that I could make no further progress unless I took a stab at analyzing the question "What is mathematics?" — analyzing it in some depth. Many other people have already explored this question, and the answer is obviously that "Mathematics is what mathematicians do." More precisely, the appropriate question should be, "What is good mathematics?" and the answer is that "Good mathematics is what good mathematicians do."

Therefore I took nine books off of my shelf, mostly books that I had used as texts during my student days but also a few more for variety's sake. I decided to take a careful look at page 100 (i.e., a "random" page) in each book and to study the first result on that page. This way I could get a sample of what good mathematicians do, and I could attempt to understand the types of thinking that seem to be involved.

From the standpoint of computer science, the notion of "types of thinking" is not so vague as it once was, since we can now imagine trying to make a computer program discover the mathematics. What sorts of capabilities would we have to put into such an artificially intelligent program, if it were to be able to come up with the results on page 100 of the books I selected?

In order to make this experiment fair, I was careful to abide by the following ground rules: (1) The books were all to be chosen first, before I studied any particular one of them. (2) Page 100 was to be the page examined in each case, since I had no *a priori* knowledge of what was on that page in any book. If somehow page 100 turned out to be a bad choice, I wouldn't try anything sneaky like searching for another page number that would give results more in accord with my prejudices. (3) I would not suppress any of the data; every book I had chosen would appear in the final sample, so that I wouldn't introduce any bias by selecting a subset.

The results of this experiment opened up my eyes somewhat, so I would like to share them with you. Here is a book-by-book summary of what I found.

Book 1: Thomas's Calculus

I looked first at the book that had introduced me to higher mathematics, the calculus text by George B. Thomas [25] that I had used as a college freshman. On page 100 he treats the following problem: *What value of x minimizes the travel time from $(0, a)$ to $(x, 0)$ to $(d, -b)$, if you must go at speed s_1 from $(0, a)$ to $(x, 0)$ and at some other speed s_2 from $(x, 0)$ to $(d, -b)$?*

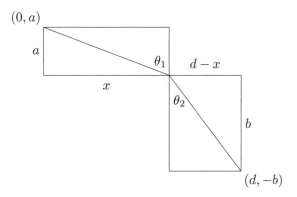

In other words, we want to minimize the function

$$f(x) = \frac{\sqrt{a^2 + x^2}}{s_1} + \frac{\sqrt{b^2 + (d - x)^2}}{s_2}.$$

The solution is to differentiate $f(x)$, obtaining

$$f'(x) = \frac{x}{s_1 \sqrt{a^2 + x^2}} - \frac{d - x}{s_2 \sqrt{b^2 + (d - x)^2}} = \frac{\sin \theta_1}{s_1} - \frac{\sin \theta_2}{s_2}.$$

As x runs from 0 to d, the value of $(\sin \theta_1)/s_1$ starts at zero and increases, while the value of $(\sin \theta_2)/s_2$ decreases to zero. Therefore the derivative starts negative and ends positive; there must be a point where it is zero, i.e., $(\sin \theta_1)/s_1 = (\sin \theta_2)/s_2$, and that's where the minimum occurs. Thomas remarks that this is "Snell's Law" in optics; somehow light rays know how to minimize their travel time.

The mathematics involved here seems to be mostly a systematic procedure for minimization, based on formula manipulation and the correspondence between formulas and geometric figures, together with some reasoning about changes in function values. Let us keep this in mind as we look at the other examples, to see how much the examples have in common.

Book 2: Survey of Mathematics

Returning to the survey volumes edited by Aleksandrov et al. [1], we find page 100 in the chapter on Analysis by Lavrent'ev and Nikol'skiĭ. It shows how to deduce the derivative of the function $\log_a x$ in a clever way:

$$\frac{\log_a(x+h) - \log_a x}{h} = \frac{1}{h}\log_a\frac{x+h}{x} = \frac{1}{x}\log_a\left(1 + \frac{h}{x}\right)^{x/h}.$$

The logarithm function is continuous, so we have

$$\lim_{h\to 0}\frac{1}{x}\log_a\left(1 + \frac{h}{x}\right)^{x/h} = \frac{1}{x}\log_a\lim_{h\to 0}\left(1 + \frac{h}{x}\right)^{x/h} = \frac{1}{x}\log_a e,$$

since it has already been proved that the quantity $(1 + \frac{1}{n})^n$ approaches a constant called e, when n approaches infinity through integer or non-integer values. Here the reasoning involves formula manipulation and an understanding of limiting processes.

Book 3: Kelley's General Topology

The third book I chose was a standard topology text [11], where page 100 contains the following exercise: "*Problem A. The image under a continuous map of a connected space is connected.*" No solution is given, but I imagine something like the following was intended. First we recall the relevant definitions, that a function f from topological space X to topological space Y is continuous when the inverse image $f^{-1}(V)$ is open in X, for all open sets V in Y; a topological space X is connected when it cannot be written as a disjoint union of two nonempty open sets. Thus let us try to prove that Y is connected, under the assumption that f is continuous and X is connected, where $f(X) = Y$. If $Y = V_1 \cup V_2$, where V_1 and V_2 are disjoint and open, then $X = f^{-1}(V_1) \cup f^{-1}(V_2)$, where $f^{-1}(V_1)$ and $f^{-1}(V_2)$ are disjoint and open. It follows that either $f^{-1}(V_1)$ or $f^{-1}(V_2)$ is empty, say $f^{-1}(V_1)$ is empty. Finally, therefore, V_1 is empty, since $V_1 \subseteq f(f^{-1}(V_1))$. Q.E.D.

(Note that no properties of "open sets" were needed in this proof.)

The mathematical thinking involved here is somewhat different from what we have seen before; it consists primarily of constructing chains of implications from the hypotheses to the desired conclusions, using a repertoire of facts like "$f^{-1}(A \cap B) = f^{-1}(A) \cap f^{-1}(B)$". This is analogous to constructing chains of computer instructions that transform some input into some desired output, using a repertoire of subroutines, although the topological facts have a more abstract character.

Another type of mathematical thinking is involved here, too, and we should be careful not to forget it: Somebody had to define the concepts of continuity and connectedness in a way that would lead to a rich theory having lots of applications, thereby generalizing many special cases that had been proved before the abstract pattern was perceived.

Book 4: From the 18th Century

Another book on my list was Struik's *Source Book in Mathematics*, which quotes authors of famous papers written during the period 1200–1800 A.D. Page 100 is concerned with Euler's attempt to prove the fundamental theorem of algebra, in the course of which he derived the following auxiliary result: "*Theorem 4. Every quartic polynomial* $x^4 + Ax^3 + Bx^2 + Cx + D$ *with real coefficients can be factored into two quadratics.*"

Here's how he did it. First he reduced the problem to the case $A = 0$ by setting $x = y - \frac{1}{4}A$. Then he was left with the problem of solving $(x^2 + ux + \alpha)(x^2 - ux + \beta) = x^4 + Bx^2 + Cx + D$ for u, α, and β, so he wanted to solve the equations $B = \alpha + \beta - u^2$, $C = (\beta - \alpha)u$, $D = \alpha\beta$. These equations lead to the relations $2\beta = B + u^2 + C/u$, $2\alpha = B + u^2 - C/u$, and $(B + u^2)^2 - C^2/u^2 = 4D$. But the cubic polynomial $(u^2)^3 + 2B(u^2)^2 + (B^2 - 4D)u^2 - C^2$ goes from $-C^2$ to $+\infty$ as u^2 runs from 0 to ∞, so it has a positive root, and the factorization is complete.

(Euler went on to generalize, arguing that every equation of degree 2^n can be factored into two of degree 2^{n-1}, via an equation of odd degree $\frac{1}{2}\binom{2^n}{2^{n-1}}$ in u^2 having a negative constant term. But this part of his derivation was not rigorous; Lagrange and Gauss later pointed out a serious flaw.)

When I first looked at this example, it seemed to be more "algorithmic" than the preceding ones, probably because Euler was essentially explaining how to take a quartic polynomial as input and to produce two quadratic polynomials as output. Input/output characteristics are significant aspects of algorithms, although Euler's actual construction is comparatively simple and direct so it doesn't exhibit the complex control structure that algorithms usually have. The types of thinking involved here seem to be (a) to reduce a general problem to a simpler special case (by showing that A can be assumed zero, and by realizing that the resulting sixth-degree equation in u was really a third-degree equation in u^2); (b) formula manipulation to solve simultaneous equations for α,

β, and u; (c) generalization by recognizing a pattern for the case of 4th degree equations that apparently would extend to degrees 8, 16, etc.

Book 5: Abstract Algebra

My next choice was another standard textbook, *Commutative Algebra* by Zariski and Samuel [31]. Their page 100 is concerned with the general structure of arbitrary fields. Suppose k and K are fields with $k \subseteq K$; the *transcendence degree* of K over k is defined to be the cardinal number of any "transcendence basis" L of K over k, namely a set L such that all of its finite subsets are algebraically independent over k and such that all elements of K are algebraic over $k(L)$; i.e., the elements of K are roots of polynomial equations whose coefficients lie in the smallest field containing $k \cup L$. The exposition in the book has just found that this cardinal number is a well-defined invariant of k and K, i.e., that all transcendence bases of K over k have the same cardinality.

Now comes Theorem 26: *If $k \subseteq K \subseteq \mathcal{K}$, the transcendence degree of $\mathcal{K}$ over k is the sum of the transcendence degrees of K over k and of $\mathcal{K}$ over K.* To prove the theorem, Zariski and Samuel let L be a transcendence basis of K over k and $\mathcal{L}$ a transcendence basis of $\mathcal{K}$ over K; the idea is to prove that $L \cup \mathcal{L}$ is a transcendence basis of $\mathcal{K}$ over k, after which the result will follow since L and $\mathcal{L}$ are disjoint.

The required proof is not difficult and it is worth studying in detail. Let $\{x_1, \ldots, x_m, X_1, \ldots, X_M\}$ be a finite subset of $L \cup \mathcal{L}$, where the x's are in L and the X's in $\mathcal{L}$, and assume that they satisfy some polynomial equation over k, namely

$$\sum_{\substack{e_1, \ldots, e_m \geq 0 \\ E_1, \ldots, E_M \geq 0}} \alpha(e_1, \ldots, e_m, E_1, \ldots, E_M) \, x_1^{e_1} \ldots x_m^{e_m} X_1^{E_1} \ldots X_M^{E_M} = 0 \, , \quad (*)$$

where all the $\alpha(e_1, \ldots, e_m, E_1, \ldots, E_M)$ are in k and only finitely many α's are nonzero. This equation can be rewritten as

$$\sum_{E_1, \ldots, E_M \geq 0} \beta(E_1, \ldots, E_M) \, X_1^{E_1} \ldots X_M^{E_M} = 0 \, , \qquad (**)$$

where

$$\beta(E_1, \ldots, E_M) = \sum_{e_1, \ldots, e_m \geq 0} \alpha(e_1, \ldots, e_m, E_1, \ldots, E_M) \, x_1^{e_1} \ldots x_m^{e_m}$$

is a polynomial in the X's with coefficients in K. Hence all of the coefficients are zero by the algebraic independence of $\mathcal{L}$ over K. These coefficients $\beta(E_1, \ldots, E_M)$ in turn are polynomials in the x's with coefficients in k, so all the β's must be zero; this makes all the α's zero. In other words, any finite subset of $L \cup \mathcal{L}$ is algebraically independent.

Finally, all elements of K are algebraic over $k(L)$ and all elements of $\mathcal{K}$ are algebraic over $K(\mathcal{L})$. It follows from the previously developed theory of algebraic extensions that all elements of $\mathcal{K}$ are algebraic over $k(L)(\mathcal{L})$, the smallest field containing $k \cup L \cup \mathcal{L}$. Hence $L \cup \mathcal{L}$ satisfies all the criteria of a transcendence basis.

Note that the proof involves somewhat sophisticated "data structures," i.e., representations of complex objects, in this case polynomials in many variables. The key idea is to make a mathematical pun, based on the equivalence between the polynomial over k in $(*)$ and the polynomial over $k(L)$ in $(**)$. In fact, the structure theory of fields being developed in this part of Zariski and Samuel's book is essentially a theory about data structures by which all elements of the field can be represented and manipulated. Theorem 26 is not as important as the construction of transcendence bases that appears in its proof.

Another noteworthy aspect of this example is the way infinite sets are treated. Finite concepts have been generalized to infinite ones by saying that all finite subsets must have the property; this allows algorithmic constructions to be applied to the subsets.

Book 6: Metamathematics

I chose Kleene's *Introduction to Metamathematics* [13] as a representative book on logic. Page 100 talks about "disjunction elimination": Suppose we are given (1) $\vdash A \vee B$ and (2) $A \vdash C$ and (3) $B \vdash C$. Then by a rule that has just been proved, (2) and (3) yield

$$(4) \quad A \vee B \vdash C.$$

From (1) and (4) we may now conclude "(5) $\vdash C$". Kleene points out that this is the familiar idea of reasoning by cases. If either A or B is true, we can consider case 1 that A is true (then C holds), or case 2 that B is true (and again C holds). It follows that statement C holds in any case.

The reasoning in this example is simple formula manipulation, together with an understanding that familiar thought patterns are being generalized and made formal.

I was hoping to hit a more inherently metamathematical argument here, something like "anything that can be proved in system X can also be proved in system Y," since such arguments are often essentially algorithms that convert arbitrary X-proofs into Y-proofs. But page 100 was more elementary, this being an introductory book.

Book 7: Knuth

Is my own work [14] algorithmic? Well, page 100 isn't especially so, since it is part of an introduction to mathematical techniques that I presented before getting into the real computer science content. The problem discussed on that page is to get the mean and standard deviation of the number of "heads" in n coin flips, when each independent flip comes up "heads" with probability p and "tails" with probability $q = 1 - p$. I introduce the notation p_{nk} for the probability that k heads occur, and observe that

$$p_{nk} = p \cdot p_{(n-1)(k-1)} + q \cdot p_{(n-1)k}.$$

To solve this recurrence, I introduce the generating function

$$G_n(z) = \sum_{k \geq 0} p_{nk} z^k$$

and obtain $G_n(z) = (q + pz)G_{n-1}(z)$, $G_1(z) = q + pz$. Hence $G_n(z) = (q + pz)^n$, and

$$\text{mean}(G_n) = n \,\text{mean}(G_1) = pn; \quad \text{var}(G_n) = n \,\text{var}(G_1) = pqn.$$

Thus, the recurrence relation is set up by reasoning about probabilities; it is solved by formula manipulation according to patterns that are discussed earlier in the book. I like to think that I was being like al-Khwârizmî here—not using a special trick for this particular problem, rather illustrating a general method.

Book 8: Pólya and Szegő

The good old days of mathematics are represented by Pólya and Szegő's famous *Aufgaben und Lehrsätze*, recently available in an English translation with many new Aufgaben [19]. Page 100 contains a real challenge:

$$\textbf{217.} \quad \lim_{n \to \infty} \int_{-\pi}^{\pi} \frac{n!\, 2^{2n \cos \theta}}{\left| (2ne^{i\theta} - 1) \ldots (2ne^{i\theta} - n) \right|} \, d\theta = 2\pi.$$

Fortunately the answer pages provide enough of a clue to reveal the proof that the authors had in mind. We have $|2ne^{i\theta} - k|^2 = 4n^2 + k^2 - 4nk \cos \theta = (2n - k)^2 + 4nk(1 - \cos \theta) = (2n - k)^2 + 8nk \sin^2 \theta/2$. Replacing θ by $x/\sqrt{n}$ allows us to rewrite the integral as

$$\frac{n!\, 2^{2n}}{\sqrt{n}\,(2n - 1) \ldots (n + 1)n} \int_{-\infty}^{\infty} f_n(x)\, dx,$$

where $f_n(x) = 0$ for $|x| > \pi\sqrt{n}$, and otherwise

$$f_n(x) = 2^{2n(\cos(x/\sqrt{n})-1)} \prod_{1 \le k \le n} \left(1 + \frac{8nk}{(2n-k)^2} \sin^2 \frac{x}{2\sqrt{n}}\right)^{-1/2}$$

$$= \exp\left((2\ln 2)n \left(\cos \frac{x}{\sqrt{n}} - 1\right)\right.$$

$$\left. - \sum_{k=1}^{n} \frac{1}{2} \ln\left(1 + \frac{8nk}{(2n-k)^2} \sin^2 \frac{x}{2\sqrt{n}}\right)\right)$$

$$= \exp\left(-x^2 \ln 2 + O\left(\frac{x^4}{n}\right)\right.$$

$$\left. + \frac{1}{2} \sum_{k=1}^{n} \left(\frac{-2nk}{(2n-k)^2} \frac{x^2}{n} + O\left(\frac{x^4}{n^2}\right)\right)\right)$$

$$= \exp\left(-x^2 \ln 2 - (1 - \ln 2)x^2 + O\left(\frac{1+x^4}{n}\right)\right).$$

Thus, $f_n(x)$ converges uniformly to e^{-x^2} in any bounded interval. Furthermore we have $|f_n(x)| \le 2^{2n(\cos x/\sqrt{n}-1)}$ and

$$\cos \frac{x}{\sqrt{n}} - 1 \le -\frac{x^2}{2n} + \frac{x^4}{24n^2}$$

$$\le -\left(\frac{1}{2} - \frac{\pi^2}{24}\right)\frac{x^2}{n} \qquad \text{for } |x| \le \pi/\sqrt{n},$$

since the cosine function is "enveloped" by its Maclaurin series; therefore $|f_n(x)|$ is less than the integrable function e^{-cx^2} for all n, where $c = 1 - \pi^2/12$. From this uniformly bounded convergence we are justified in taking limits past the integral sign,

$$\lim_{n \to \infty} \int_{-\infty}^{\infty} f_n(x)\,dx = \int_{-\infty}^{\infty} e^{-x^2}\,dx = \sqrt{\pi}.$$

Finally, the coefficient in front of $\int_{-\infty}^{\infty} f_n(x)\,dx$ is $2^{2n+1}n!^2/\sqrt{n}(2n)!$, which is equal to $2\sqrt{\pi}\left(1 + O(1/n)\right)$ by Stirling's approximation, and the result follows.

This derivation gives some idea of how far mathematics had developed between the time of al-Khwârizmî and 1920. It involves formula manipulation and an understanding of the asymptotic limiting behavior of functions, together with the idea of inventing a suitable function f_n that will rigorously permit us to make the interchange $\lim_{n\to\infty} \int_{-\infty}^{\infty} f_n(x)\,dx = \int_{-\infty}^{\infty} \lim_{n\to\infty} f_n(x)\,dx$. The definition of $f_n(x)$ requires a clear understanding of how functions like $\exp x$ and $\cos x$ behave.

Book 9: Bishop's Constructive Analysis

The last book I chose to sample turned out to be most interesting of all from the standpoint of my quest; it was Errett Bishop's *Foundations of Constructive Analysis* [2], a book that I had heard about but never before read. The interesting thing about this book is that it reads essentially like ordinary mathematics, yet it is entirely algorithmic in nature if you look between the lines.

Page 100 of Bishop's book completes his discussion of the Stone-Weierstrass theorem, which began on page 97. The first result on page 100 is Corollary 3, which reads as follows in the case $n = 1$: *Every uniformly continuous function on a compact set $X \subseteq \mathbf{R}$ can be arbitrarily closely approximated on X by polynomial functions over* $\mathbf{R}$. And here is his proof: "By Lemma 5, the function $x \mapsto |x - x_0|$ can be arbitrarily closely approximated on X by polynomials. The theorem then follows from Corollary 2."

We might call this a compact proof! Before unwrapping it to explain what Lemma 5 and Corollary 2 are, I want to stress that Bishop's proof, which he called a "person program" as opposed to a computer program [2, p. 355] is essentially an algorithm. The algorithm takes any constructively given compact set X and continuous function f and tolerance ϵ as input, and it outputs a polynomial that approximates f to within ϵ on all points of X. Furthermore the algorithm operates on algorithms, since f is given by an algorithm of a certain type, and since real numbers are essentially algorithms themselves.

I will try to put Bishop's implicit algorithms into an explicit form, using a language analogous to Pascal [30], even though the capabilities of today's programming languages have to be stretched considerably to reflect his constructions. First let's consider Lemma 5, which states that for each $\epsilon > 0$ there exists a polynomial $p : \mathbf{R} \to \mathbf{R}$ such that $p(0) = 0$ and $\big||x| - p(x)\big| \le \epsilon$ for all $|x| \le 1$. Bishop's proof, which makes the lemma an algorithm, is essentially the following.

> **function** *Lemma5* (ϵ: *positive_real*): **polynomial of** *real*;
> **var** N: *integer*;
> g, p: **polynomial of** *real*;

begin $N :=$ an integer that is $\geq 4/\epsilon^2$;
$g(t) := \sum_{n=0}^{N} \binom{1/2}{n}(-t)^n$; { an approximation to $\sqrt{1-t}$ }
$p(t) := g(1 - t^2) - g(1)$; { an approximation to $|t|$ }
$Lemma5 := p$;
end.

Here N has been chosen sufficiently large that we have

$$\left| g(t) - \sqrt{1-t} \right| \leq \sum_{n=N+1}^{\infty} \left| \binom{1/2}{n} \right|$$

$$= \sum_{n=N+1}^{\infty} \frac{1 \cdot 3 \cdot \ldots \cdot (2n-3)}{2 \cdot 4 \cdot 6 \cdot \ldots \cdot 2n}$$

$$< \sum_{n=N+1}^{\infty} \frac{1}{2n^{3/2}}$$

$$< \int_{N}^{\infty} \frac{dx}{2x^{3/2}}$$

$$= \frac{1}{N^{1/2}}$$

$$\leq \frac{\epsilon}{2}$$

for $0 \leq t \leq 1$.

In this algorithm I did not spell out the precise definition of N, but any easily computed integer $\geq 4/\epsilon^2$ could be used. A positive real number ϵ in Bishop's system is not simply an element of data that is stored in computer memory; it is an algorithm that defines a sequence $\epsilon_1, \epsilon_2, \ldots$ of rational numbers with the property that

$$|\epsilon_m - \epsilon_n| \leq 1/m + 1/n \qquad \text{for all } m, n \geq 1,$$

together with an index j such that $\epsilon_j > 1/j$. The value of ϵ is then defined to be $\lim_{n \to \infty} \epsilon_n$. If we set $M = \lceil 2/(\epsilon_j - 1/j) \rceil$, it is not difficult to prove that $\epsilon \geq 1/M$; hence we may set $N := 4M^2$ in $Lemma5$. Notice that I would *not* be allowed to set $N := \lceil 4/\epsilon^2 \rceil$ directly, because the ceiling function $\lceil x \rceil$ is not computable for arbitrary real numbers x. (We cannot tell in finitely many steps whether or not a given real number is an integer.)

The other missing component of the proof on page 100 of Bishop's book is Corollary 2, which states that if X is any compact metric space and if G is the set of all functions $x \mapsto \rho(x, x_0)$, where $x_0 \in X$ and where $\rho(x, y)$ denotes the metric distance from x to y, then "$\mathfrak{A}(G)$ is dense in $C(X)$." That is, all uniformly continuous real-valued functions on X can be approximated to arbitrarily high accuracy by functions obtained from the functions of G by a finite number of operations of addition and multiplication, together with multiplication by real numbers. Bishop's Corollary 2 turns out to be false as it stands, in the case that X contains only one point, since G and $\mathfrak{A}(G)$ then consist only of the zero function. I noticed this oversight while trying to formulate his proof in an explicitly algorithmic way. But the defect is easily remedied.

For our purposes it is best to reformulate Corollary 2 as follows: "*Let X be a compact metric space containing at least two points, and let G be the set of all functions of the form* $x \mapsto c\rho(x, x_0)$, *where* $c > 0$ *and* $x_0 \in X$. *Then G is a separating family over X.*" I'll repeat his definition of separating family in a minute; first I want to mention his Theorem 7, the Stone-Weierstrass theorem whose proof I shall not discuss in detail, namely the fact that $\mathfrak{A}(G)$ is dense in $C(X)$ whenever G is a separating family of uniformly continuous functions over a compact metric space X. In view of this theorem, my reformulation of Corollary 2 leads to the corollary as he stated it.

A *separating family* is a collection of real-valued functions G over X, together with a function δ from the positive reals $\mathbf{R}^+$ into $\mathbf{R}^+$, and also together with two selection algorithms σ and τ. Algorithm σ takes elements x, y of X and a positive real number ϵ as input, where $\rho(x, y) \geq \epsilon$, and selects an element g of G such that for all z in X we have

(i) $\rho(x, z) \leq \delta(\epsilon)$ implies $|g(z)| \leq \epsilon$,

(ii) $\rho(y, z) \leq \delta(\epsilon)$ implies $|g(z) - 1| \leq \epsilon$.

Algorithm τ takes an element y of X and a positive real number ϵ as input, and selects an element g of G such that (ii) holds for all z in X.

Thus the reformulated Corollary 2 is an algorithm that takes a nontrivial compact metric space X as input and yields a separating family (δ, σ, τ), where σ and τ select functions of the form $c\rho(x, x_0)$. Here is the construction, amended to correct the error noted above:

function *Corollary2* (X: *compact_metric_space*;
$\qquad\qquad y_0, y_1$: X*-element*): X*-separating_family*;
$\quad$ { y_0 and y_1 are assumed to be distinct elements of X }

var δ: **function** (ϵ: *positive_real*): *positive_real*;
  d: **function** (x, y: *X-element*): *positive_real*;
  σ: **function** (x, y: *X-element*; ϵ: *positive_real*): $C(X)$;
  τ: **function** (y: *X-element*; ϵ: *positive_real*): $C(X)$;
begin $d(x, y) := X.\rho(x, y)$; { this is the distance function in X }
$\delta(\epsilon) := \min\left(\epsilon^2, \frac{1}{4}\epsilon d(y_0, y_1)\right)$;

$\sigma(x, y, \epsilon) := \big($**function** $g(z$: *X-element*): *real*;
          begin $g := d(x, z)/d(x, y)$ **end**$\big)$;
$\tau(y, \epsilon) := \big($**function** $g(z$: *X-element*): *real*; **var** r: *rational*;
          begin $r :=$ rational number such that
$$\left|d(y, y_1)/d(y_0, y_1) - r\right| \le 1/4;$$
$$g := \big(\textbf{if } r \le 1/2 \textbf{ then } d(y_0, z)/d(y_0, y)$$
$$\textbf{else } d(y_1, z)/d(y_1, y)\big) \textbf{ end}\big);$$
Corollary2 $:= (\delta, \sigma, \tau)$;
end.

My notation for the complicated types involved in these algorithms is not the best possible, but I hope it is reasonably comprehensible without further explanation. The selection rule σ determined by this algorithm has the desired property since, for example, $\rho(x, y) \ge \epsilon$ and $\rho(y, z) \le \delta(\epsilon) \le \epsilon^2$ implies that $|g(z) - 1| = |\rho(x, z) - \rho(x, y)|/\rho(x, y) \le \rho(y, z)/\rho(x, y) \le \epsilon$. The selection rule τ has the desired property by a similar proof; if $r \le \frac{1}{2}$ we have $d(y, y_1) \le \frac{3}{4}d(y_0, y_1)$ and $d(y, y_0) \ge \frac{1}{4}d(y_0, y_1)$, otherwise $d(y, y_1) \ge \frac{1}{4}d(y_0, y_1)$. It is necessary to work indirectly via a rational number r because a test like "**if** $d(y, y_1) \le \frac{1}{2}d(y_0, y_1)$" would not be finitely computable.

Bishop's proof of Corollary 3 can now be displayed explicitly as an algorithm in the following way. If X is a compact subset of the real numbers $\mathbf{R}$, under Bishop's definition, we can compute $M = \text{bound}(X)$ such that $-M \le x \le M$ for all x in X. Let us assume that his Theorem 7 is a procedure whose input parameters consist of a compact metric space X, a separating family (δ, σ, τ) over X that selects functions from some set $G \subseteq C(X)$, a uniformly continuous function $f : X \to \mathbf{R}$, and a positive real number ϵ. The output of this procedure is an element A of $\mathfrak{A}(G)$, namely a finite sum of terms of the form $Cg_1(x)\ldots g_m(x)$ where $m \ge 1$ and each $g_i \in G$; this output satisfies $|A(x) - f(x)| \le \epsilon$ for all x in X.

Here is the fleshed-out form of Corollary 3. We assume* that there is a way to determine when a compact metric space contains at least

---

*Oops: Patrick Cégielski pointed out in 2009 that this assumption fails; there's no algorithm to decide if, say, $\{y_0, y_1\}$ contains two distinct points,

two points, and to compute two of its points in such a case.

> **function** *Corollary3* (*X*: *compact_real_set*;
>   *f*: *X-continuous_function*;
> ϵ: *positive_real*): **polynomial of** *real*;
> **var** *p*, *q*, *r*: **polynomial of** *real*;
>   *M*, *B*: *rational*;
> y_0, y_1: *X-element*;
>   *A*: $\mathfrak{A}(G)$-*element*, where *G* is the set of functions $x \mapsto c|x - x_0|$;
> **begin** $M := bound(X)$; $y_0 := element(X)$;
> **if** *trivial*(*X*) **then** $r(x) := f(y_0)$ { a constant function }
> **else begin** $y_1 := element(X \setminus \{y_0\})$;
> $A := Theorem7\big(X, Corollary2(X, y_0, y_1), f, \epsilon/2\big)$;
> $B :=$ suitable function of *A*, see the text below;
> $p(t) := Lemma5\big(\epsilon/(2MB)\big)(t)$;
> $q(t) := 2Mp\big(t/(2M)\big)$;
>   { now $\big|q(x - y) - |x - y|\big| \le \epsilon/B$ for all *x*, *y* in *X* }
> $r(x) :=$ substitute $cq(x - x_0)$ for each factor $g_i(x) = c|x - x_0|$
>   of each term of *A*;
>   **end**;
>   *Corollary3* := *r*;
>   **end**.

The number *B* should be chosen so that $\big|q(x - x_0) - |x - x_0|\big| \le \epsilon/B$ implies that $\big|r(x) - A(x)\big| \le \frac{1}{2}\epsilon$. This bound depends on *M* and on the structure of the terms of *A* in a straightforward way.

Clearly it would be extremely interesting from the standpoint of high-level programming language design to find an elegant notation in which Bishop's constructions are simultaneously readable and explicit.

Tentative Conclusions

What insights do we get from these nine randomly selected examples of mathematics? In the first place, they point out something that should have been obvious to me from the start, that there is no such thing as "mathematical thinking" as a single isolated concept. Mathematicians use a variety of modes of thought, not just one. My question about computer-science thinking as distinct from math thinking therefore needs to be reformulated. Indeed, when I reflect further about my

---

when y_0 and y_1 are Bishop-style reals. Further correction is necessary.

student days, I realize that I would not only wear my CS hat when programming computers and my math hat when taking courses. I also had other hats representing various modes of thought that I used when I was editing a student magazine or when I was acting as officer of a fraternity or dating my future wife or playing the sousaphone, etc. Al-Bîrûnî's biography shows that he had more hats than anybody else.

Thus, it seems better to think of a model in which people have a certain number of different modes of thought, something like genes in DNA. It is probable that computer scientists and mathematicians overlap in the sense that they share several modes of thought, yet there are other modes peculiar to one or the other. Under this model, different areas of science would be characterized by different "personality profiles."

I tried to distill out different kinds of reasoning in the nine examples, and I came up with nine categories that I tentatively would diagram as follows. (Two ⋆'s means a strong use of some reasoning mode, while one ⋆ indicates a mild connection.)

	Formula manipulation	Representation of reality	Behavior of function values	Reduction to simpler problems	Dealing with infinity	Generalization	Abstract reasoning	Information structures	Algorithms
1 (Thomas)	★★	★★	★★						
2 (Lavrent'ev/Nikol'skiĭ)	★★		★		★★				
3 (Kelley)	★					★★	★★		
4 (Euler)	★★		★★	★		★★			★
5 (Zariski/Samuel)	★			★	★★	★	★★	★★	
6 (Kleene)	★					★★	★★		★
7 (Knuth)	★★	★		★					
8 (Pólya/Szegő)	★★		★★	★★	★★				
9 (Bishop)	★★		★★	★★	★	★★	★★		★
"Algorithmic thinking"	★	★★		★★			★★	★★	★★

These nine categories aren't precisely defined, and they may represent combinations of more fundamental things. For example, both formula manipulation and generalization involve the general idea of pattern recognition, spotting certain kinds of order. Another fundamental distinction might be in the type of "visualization" needed, whether it be geometric or abstract or recursive, etc. Thus, I am not at all certain of the categories; they are simply put forward as a basis for discussion.

I have added a tenth row to the table labeled algorithmic thinking, trying to make it represent my perception of the most typical thought processes used by a computer scientist. Since computer science is such a young discipline, I don't know what books would be appropriate candidates from which to examine page 100; perhaps some of you can help me round out this study. It seems to me that most of the modes of thought listed in the table are common in computer science as well as in mathematics, with the notable exception of "reasoning about infinity." Infinite-dimensional spaces seem to be of little relevance for computer scientists, although most other branches of mathematics have been extensively applied in many ways.

One of the most striking differences that I have observed between the habits of computer scientists and traditional mathematicians is that a computer scientist tends to be much more willing to deal with a multitude of quite different cases. Data structures in computer science needn't be homogeneous, and algorithms can involve many different kinds of steps. (See [28] for a stimulating account of related issues.) Sometimes this tolerance for diversity is a weakness of computer scientists, because we don't try as hard as we should to find uniform laws. But sometimes it is a strength, because we can deal fluently with concepts that are inherently nonuniform.

Computer scientists will also notice, I think, that two types of thinking are absent from the examples we have studied. In the first place, there is almost no notion of "complexity" or economy of operation in what we have discussed. Bishop's mathematics is constructive, but it does not have all the ingredients of an algorithm because it ignores the "cost" of the constructions. If we carry out the details of his Stone-Weierstrass theorem with respect to simple functions, we are likely to wind up with a polynomial approximation of degree 10^6, say, although a suitable polynomial of degree 6 could have been found by a more efficient scheme. Bishop did remark [2, p. 3] that he regarded his work as only a first step, after which efficient constructions should come to the fore; but the entire content of his book has a completely different flavor.

The other missing concept that seems to separate mathematicians from computer scientists is related to the "assignment operation" :=, which changes values of quantities. More precisely, I would say that the missing concept is the dynamic notion of the *state* of a process: "How did I get here? What is true now? What should happen next if I'm going to get to the end?" Changing states of affairs, or snapshots of a computation, seem to be intimately related to algorithms and algorithmic thinking. Many of the concepts of data structures, which are so fundamental in computer science, depend very heavily on an ability to reason about the notion of process states, and we rely on this notion also when studying the interaction of collections of processes that are acting simultaneously.

Our nine examples don't have anything resembling "$n := n + 1$," except for Euler's discussion where he essentially begins by setting $x := x - \frac{1}{4}A$. The assignment operations in Bishop's constructions aren't really assignments; they are simply definitions of quantities, and those definitions won't be changed. This discrepancy between classical mathematics and computer science is well illustrated by the fact that Burks, Goldstine, and von Neumann did not actually have the notion of assignment in their early notes on computer programming; they used a curious in-between concept instead (see [15]).

The closest thing to "$:=$" in classical mathematics is the reduction of a relatively hard problem to a simpler one, since the simpler problem replaces the former one. Al-Khwârizmî did this when he divided both sides of a quadratic equation by the coefficient of x^2; so I shall conclude this lecture by once again paying tribute to al-Khwârizmî, a remarkable pioneer in our discipline.

The preparation of this paper was supported in part by the National Science Foundation and the Office of Naval Research. My wife and I wish to thank our Uzbek hosts for their incomparable hospitality. Many people too numerous to name have contributed their insights during informal discussions about the topics listed here. The algorithmic proof of Corollary 2 in section 9 corrects a serious error in the original versions of this paper; I thank David Gladstein for calling this error to my attention.

References

[1] A. D. Aleksandrov, A. N. Kolmogorov, and M. A. Lavrent'ev, eds., *Mathematics: Its Content, Methods and Meaning* **1** (Cambridge, Massachusetts: MIT Press, 1963). Translated by S. H. Gould and T. Bartha from *Matematika: Eë Soderzhanie, Metody i Znachenie* (Moscow: Akademiiâ Nauk SSSR, 1956).

[2] Errett Bishop, *Foundations of Constructive Analysis* (New York: McGraw–Hill, 1967). Revised version, *Constructive Analysis* by Errett Bishop and Douglas Bridges, *Grundlehren der mathematischen Wissenschaften* **279** (Springer, 1985). [The error in "Corollary 2" of the original book is corrected in the revision, whose corresponding "Corollary (5.16)" requires the compact space to have a positive diameter.]

[3] Baldassarre Boncompagni, ed., "Algoritmi de Numero Indorum," *Trattati d'Aritmetica* **1** (Rome, 1857).

[4] Solomon Gandz, "The Mishnat Ha Middot," *Proceedings of the American Academy for Jewish Research* **4** (1933), 1–104. Reprinted in S. Gandz, *Studies in Hebrew Astronomy and Mathematics* (New York: Ktav, 1970), 295–400.

[5] Solomon Gandz, "Sources of al-Khowârizmî's Algebra," *Osiris* **1** (1936), 263–277.

[6] Solomon Gandz, "The origin and development of the quadratic equations in Babylonian, Greek, and early Arabic algebra," *Osiris* **5** (1938), 405–557.

[7] Solomon Gandz, "The algebra of inheritance," *Osiris* **5** (1938) [sic], 319–391.

[8] Fred Gruenberger, "The role of education in preparing effective computing personnel," in F. Gruenberger, ed., *Effective vs. Efficient Computing* (Englewood Cliffs, New Jersey: Prentice–Hall, 1973), 112–120.

[9] A. P. Ĭushkevich, "Arifmeticheskiĭ traktat Mykhammeda Ben Musa Al-Khorezmi," *Trudy Institut Istorii Estestvoznaniĩâ i tekhniki* **1** (1954), 85–127.

[10] Louis Charles Karpinski, ed., Robert of Chester's Latin Translation of the *Algebra* of Al-Khowarizmi, *University of Michigan Humanistic Series* **11**, part 1 (Ann Arbor, 1915), 164 pp. Reprinted in 1930.

[11] John L. Kelley, *General Topology* (Princeton: D. Van Nostrand, 1955).

[12] E. S. Kennedy, "al-Bīrūnī," *Dictionary of Scientific Biography* **2** (New York: Charles Scribner's Sons, 1970), 147–158.

[13] Stephen Cole Kleene, *Introduction to Metamathematics* (Princeton: D. Van Nostrand, 1952).

[14] Donald E. Knuth, *Fundamental Algorithms* (Reading, Massachusetts: Addison–Wesley, 1968).

[15] Donald E. Knuth and Luis Trabb Pardo, "The early development of programming languages," *Encyclopedia of Computer Science and Technology* **7** (New York: Marcel Dekker, 1977), 419–493. Reprinted in *A History of Computing in the Twentieth Century*, N. Metropolis, J. Howlett, and G.-C. Rota, eds. (New York: Academic Press, 1980), 197–273.

[16] Ĭu. Kh. Kopelevich and B. A. Rozenfel'd, translators, Mukhammad al'-Khorezmi: *Matematicheskie Traktaty* (Tashkent: Akademiĩâ

Nauk Uzbekskoĭ SSR, 1964). [Includes al-Khwârizmî's arithmetic and algebra, with commentaries by B. A. Rozenfel'd.]

[17] Seyyed Hossein Nasr et al., *Historical Atlas of Iran* (Tehran, 1971).

[18] D. Pingree, review of [29], *Mathematical Reviews* **30** (July 1965), 1–2.

[19] G. Pólya and G. Szegő, *Problems and Theorems in Analysis* **1** (Berlin: Springer, 1972). A revised and enlarged translation of their *Aufgaben und Lehrsätze aus der Analysis* **1** (Berlin: Springer, 1925).

[20] Ed. Sachau, "Algebraisches über das Schach bei Bîrûnî," *Zeitschrift der Deutschen Morgenländischen Gesellschaft* **29** (1876), 148–156.

[21] C. Edward Sachau, transl. and ed., al-Bîrûnî's *Chronology of Ancient Nations* (London: William H. Allen, 1879).

[22] A. S. Saidan, *The Arithmetic of al-Uqlīdisī* (Dordrecht: D. Reidel, 1975).

[23] S. Kh. Sirazhdinov and G. P. Matvievskaīā, *Abu Raĭkhan Beruni i Ego Matematicheskie Trudy* (Moscow: Prosveshchenie, 1978).

[24] D. J. Struik, ed., *A Source Book in Mathematics, 1200–1800* (Cambridge, Massachusetts: Harvard University Press, 1969).

[25] George B. Thomas, *Calculus and Analytic Geometry*, 2nd ed. (Cambridge, Massachusetts: Addison–Wesley, 1956).

[26] G. J. Toomer, "al-Khwārizmī," *Dictionary of Scientific Biography* **7** (New York: Charles Scribner's Sons, 1973), 358–365.

[27] J. F. Traub, *Iterative Methods for the Solution of Equations* (Englewood Cliffs, New Jersey: Prentice–Hall, 1964).

[28] G. S. Tseytin, "From logicism to proceduralism (an autobiographical account)," *Lecture Notes in Computer Science* **122** (1981), 390–396.

[29] Kurt Vogel, ed., Mohammed Ibn Musa Alchwarizmi's *Algorismus*, Das früheste Lehrbuch zum Rechnen mit indischen Ziffern (Aalen/Osnabrück: Otto Zeller Verlagsbuchhandlung, 1963). [This edition contains a facsimile of the manuscript, from which a correct transcription can be deduced.]

[30] N. Wirth, "The programming language Pascal," *Acta Informatica* **1** (1971), 35–63.

[31] Oscar Zariski and Pierre Samuel, *Commutative Algebra* **1** (Princeton: D. Van Nostrand, 1958).

[32] Heinz Zemanek, "Al-Khorezmi: His background, his personality, his work and his influence," *Lecture Notes in Computer Science* **122** (1981), 1–81.

This souvenir medal was given to the conference participants.

Note on the spelling of Khwârizm: In the first and second editions of my book [14] I spelled Muḥammad ben Mûsâ's name "al-Khowârizmî," following the convention used in most American books up to about 1930 and perpetuated in many other modern texts. Recently I learned that "al-Khuwârizmî" would be a more proper transliteration of the Arabic letters, since the character in question currently has an 'oo' sound; the U.S. Library of Congress uses this convention. The Moorish scholars who brought Arabic works to Spain in medieval times evidently pronounced the letter as they would say a Latin 'o'; and it is not clear to what extent this particular vowel has changed its pronunciation in the East or the West, or both, since those days. At any rate, from about 1935 until the present time, the leading American scholars of oriental mathematics history have almost unanimously agreed on the form "al-Khwârizmî" (or its equivalent, al-Khwārizmī, which is easier to type on conventional typewriters). They obviously know the subject much better than I do, so I shall happily conform to their practice from now on.

Additional References

Mathematical explanations for lack of correlation between statistical measurements on nonrandom populations are discussed in the following papers, which might be relevant to the data of Gerrit DeYoung:

[33] C. A. Akemann, A. M. Bruckner, J. B. Robertson, S. Simons, and Max L. Weiss, "Conditional correlation phenomena with application to university admission strategies," *Journal of Educational Statistics* **8** (1983), 5–44.

[34] C. A. Akemann, A. M. Bruckner, J. B. Robertson, S. Simons, and Max L. Weiss, "Asymptotic conditional correlation coefficients for truncated data," *Journal of Mathematical Analysis and Applications* **99** (1984), 350–434.

Chapter 5

Algorithmic Themes

[Written for the 100th birthday of the American Mathematical Society. Originally published in A Century of Mathematics in America, *edited by Peter L. Duren, Volume 1 (Providence, Rhode Island: American Mathematical Society, 1988), 439–445.]*

I like to think of mathematics as a vast musical instrument on which one can play a great variety of beautiful melodies. Many generations of mathematicians have provided us with rich tonal resources that offer limitless possibilities for harmonious combination.

A great performance of mathematics can be as exciting to the audience as it is to the person controlling the instrument. Whether we are replaying a classic theme, or improvising a new one, or just fooling around, we experience deep pleasure when we encounter patterns that fit together just right, or when we can pull out all the stops in order to unify independent voices and timbres.

This analogy isn't perfect, because mathematics is the music as well as the organ for its creation. But a view of mathematics as a multivoiced mechanism helps me understand the relationship between mathematics and its infant step-child called computer science. I believe computer science has made and will continue to make important contributions to mathematics primarily because it provides an inspiration for new themes and rhythms by which the delicious modulations of mathematics can be enjoyed and enriched.

Computer science is not the same as mathematics, nor is either field a subset of the other. I believe that there is roughly as much difference between a computer scientist and a mathematician as there is between a mathematician and a physicist (although the distance from computer science to physics is greater than the other two distances). People like

115

myself look at mathematics as a device for articulating computer science, but there is of course a converse relation: Many mathematicians see computer science as an instrument for developing mathematics. Both viewpoints are valid, yet I wish to stress the latter, which I believe is more significant for mathematicians. Computer science is now enriching mathematics — as physics did in previous generations — by asking new sorts of questions, whose answers shed new light on mathematical structures. In this way computer science makes fundamental improvements to the mathematical ensemble. When good music is played, it influences the builders of musical instruments; my claim is that the cadences of computer science are having a profound and beneficial influence on the inner structure of mathematics. (In a similar way, applications of computers to physics, medicine, psychology, mathematics, art — and, yes, music — are improving the core of computer science. But that's another story.)

I must admit that my intuitive impressions about the distinction between mathematics and computer science are not universally shared. Such opinions cannot be demonstrated like theorems. But I know that I experience a conscious "culture shock" when I switch from a mathematician's way of thinking to that of a computer scientist and back again.

For example, I recall that when I was studying the properties of Dedekind sums [10], I began that work with the mentality I had when I was a graduate student of mathematics. Then I got stuck. The next day I looked at the remaining problems with computer science eyes, and I saw how to write an algorithm and to ask new questions; this led me to another plateau. Once again I was stuck, since my computer science ideas had now been exhausted. So I put a mathematical cap on again and was able to move further. Such alternation continued over a period of weeks, and I could distinctly feel the transitions.

Another example, perhaps more convincing to someone besides myself, is based on my experiences with a mathematical novelette called *Surreal Numbers* [8]. When I wrote that little book I was definitely relishing the perspective of a pure mathematician, with no illusions that the book would be of the slightest interest to a computer scientist. Subsequent book reviews bore out this hypothesis: The work was praised in the *Bulletin* as "an exciting and stimulating book which 'turns on' the reader" [2], and Gian-Carlo Rota recently wrote (while reviewing another book) that "Surreal numbers are an invention of the great J. Conway. They may well go down in history as one of the great inventions of the century" [14]. But the consensus in computer-science circles is that "The book is a failed experiment" [16].

I would like to think that those book reviews prove my point about the difference between computer scientists and mathematicians. But the argument is not conclusive, because there are different kinds of mathematicians too. For example, I showed the manuscript of *Surreal Numbers* to George Pólya before it was published; he replied as follows [12]:

> I must confess, I am prejudiced against the case you have chosen for a case study. I simply cannot imagine that mathematically unsophisticated young people can be interested in this kind of "abstract" topic and even develop creativity on it. I cannot get rid of my prejudice — to be honest, I cannot even really wish to get rid of it, it is in my constitution: I can develop interest only in starting from concrete, or "relatively concrete" situations (difficulties, questions, observations, ...).

Perhaps Pólya was constitutionally a computer scientist?

If I had to put my finger on the greatest difference between mathematicians and computer scientists, I would say that mathematicians have a strong preference for uniform rules, coupled with a strong dislike for case-by-case analysis; computer scientists, by contrast, are comfortable and fluent with highly nonuniform structures (like the different operations performed by real computers, or like the various steps in long and complex algorithms). This tolerance of nonuniformity is the computer scientists' strength as well as their weakness; it's a strength because they can bring order into situations where no clean mathematical models exist, but it's a weakness because they don't look hard enough for uniformity when a uniform law is actually present. The gulf that separates uniform laws, which are a mathematician's staple food, from nonuniform algorithms and data structures, which are bread and butter to a computer scientist, has been described beautifully by G. S. Tseytin [15], who tells about an evolution in his own thinking.

There are other differences between our fields and our mentalities. For example, a computer scientist is less concerned with infinite and continuous objects, and more concerned with finite (indeed small) and discrete ones. A computer scientist is concerned about efficient constructions, etc. But such things are more or less corollaries of the main uniform/nonuniform dichotomy.

My purpose in this essay is not to dwell on perceived differences between mathematics and computer science, but rather to say *vive la différence*, and to emphasize mathematics. Indeed, much of my own work tries to have a foot planted firmly in each camp.

What is it that I do? I like to call it "analysis of algorithms" [5, 6]. The general idea is very simple: Given an algorithm, I try to understand its quantitative behavior. I ask how much time the algorithm will take to perform its task, given a probability distribution of its inputs.

I remember vividly how I first became interested in this topic. The year was 1962, and I was a graduate student in mathematics; however, I was spending the summer earning some money by writing a computer program (a FORTRAN compiler). As I worked on that program I came to the part where an interesting algorithm called "hashing" was appropriate, and I had recently heard a rumor that two of Feller's students at Princeton had tried unsuccessfully to analyze the speed of hashing. Programming was hard work, so I took a break one weekend and tried to solve this reportedly unsolvable problem. With a stroke of luck, I found the answer (see [7, pp. 529–530] and [9]); somehow my experience in programming the method had helped in the analysis. The nice thing was that the answer involved an interesting type of mathematical function I hadn't seen before:

$$1 + \frac{n}{m} + \frac{n(n-1)}{m^2} + \frac{n(n-1)(n-2)}{m^3} + \cdots .$$

(Later I would find this and similar functions arising in connection with many other algorithms.)

Well, it was fun to analyze the performance of hashing, and I soon realized that a lot more algorithms were out there waiting to be studied. I had heard about a comparatively new subject called "queuing theory"; gosh, I thought, if an entire subdiscipline can be devoted to the study of one small class of algorithms, surely there is much interesting work to be done in the study of *all* classes of algorithms. There was clearly more than a lifetime's worth of things to be done, and I decided that I wanted to spend a major part of my own life doing some of them. Not only was the mathematics good, the results were appreciated by programmers, so there was a double payoff.

Analysis of algorithms has been the central focus of my work ever since. After more than 25 years, I still find no shortage of interesting problems to work on. And the main point is that these problems almost invariably have a clean mathematical structure, appealing in its own right. Some applications of mathematics are no doubt boring, but the problems suggested by important algorithms have consistently turned out to be exciting. Indeed, overstimulation has been the real drawback; I need to find ways to *stop* thinking about analysis of algorithms, in order to do various other things that human beings ought to do.

Time and again I experience "the incredible effectiveness of mathematics": Looking at a new computer method (such as an algorithm for information retrieval called Patricia), I'll find that its running time depends on quantities that mathematicians have been studying for hundreds of years (such as the gamma function, hyperbolic cosine, and zeta function in the case of Patricia [7, exercise 6.3–34]).

One of the most venerable algorithms of all is Euclid's procedure for calculating greatest common divisors. I tried unsuccessfully to analyze it in 1963, so I asked several of my teachers for help. The problem is this: Let τ_n be the number of steps taken by Euclid's algorithm to determine that m and n are relatively prime, averaged over the $\varphi(n)$ nonnegative integers m that are less than n and prime to n. If we assume that the fraction m/n behaves like a random real number, Lévy's theory of continued fractions suggests that τ_n will be asymptotically $12 \ln 2/\pi^2$ times $\ln n$. My empirical calculations in 1963 confirmed this and showed, in fact, that

$$\tau_n \approx \frac{12 \ln 2}{\pi^2} \ln n + 1.47 \,.$$

In the first (1969) edition of [4] I discussed this conjecture and wrote

> We have only given plausible grounds for believing that the related quantity τ_n is asymptotically $(12 \ln 2/\pi^2) \ln n$, and the theory does not suggest any formula for the empirically determined constant 1.47. The heuristic reasoning, and the overwhelming empirical evidence . . . , mean that for all practical purposes the analysis of Euclid's algorithm is complete. From an æsthetic standpoint, however, there is still a gaping hole left.

Research by Heilbronn [3] and Dixon [1] soon established the constant $12 \ln 2/\pi^2$, and Porter [13] proved that

$$\tau_n = \frac{12 \ln 2}{\pi^2} \ln n + C + O(n^{-1/6+\epsilon}) \,.$$

John Wrench and I subsequently determined that Porter's constant $C = 1.4670780794\ldots$ has the closed form

$$C = \frac{6 \ln 2}{\pi^2} \left(3 \ln 2 + 4\gamma - \frac{24}{\pi^2} \zeta'(2) - 2 \right) - \frac{1}{2} \,.$$

Therefore I could happily say in the second edition of [4] that "conjecture (48) is fully proved."

A more surprising development occurred when A. C. Yao and I decided to analyze the primitive version of Euclid's algorithm that is based on subtraction instead of division. Consider the average σ_n of all partial quotients of the regular continued fractions for m/n, where $1 \leq m \leq n$; this is the average running time of the subtractive algorithm for gcd. If we assume that rational fractions behave like almost all real numbers, a theorem of Khintchine states that the sum of the first k partial quotients will be approximately $k \log_2 k$. And since $k = O(\log n)$, we expect $\sigma_n = O(\log n \log \log n)$. However, Yao and I proved that

$$\sigma_n = \frac{6}{\pi^2}(\ln n)^2 + O\big(\log n (\log \log n)^2\big).$$

Therefore rational numbers tend to have larger partial quotients than their real counterparts — even though Heilbronn showed that the kth quotient of a rational number m/n approaches the corresponding distribution of a real number, for all fixed k as $n \to \infty$. This is the most striking case I know where the analogy between discrete and continuous values leads to an incorrect estimate.

Different kinds of algorithms lead to different corners of mathematics. In fact, I think that by now my colleagues and I have used results from every branch of mathematics (judging by the categories in *Mathematical Reviews*), except one. The lone exception is the topic on which I wrote my Ph.D. dissertation: finite projective planes. But I still have hopes of applying even that to computer science some day.

Here's a curious identity that illustrates some of the diversity that can arise when algorithms are analyzed: Let $\|x\|$ denote the distance from x to the nearest integer. Then

$$\cdots + \tfrac{1}{8}\|8x\|^2 + \tfrac{1}{4}\|4x\|^2 + \tfrac{1}{2}\|2x\|^2 + \|x\|^2$$
$$+ 2\|\tfrac{1}{2}x\|^2 + 4\|\tfrac{1}{4}x\|^2 + 8\|\tfrac{1}{8}x\|^2 + \cdots = |x|.$$

The sum is doubly infinite, converging at the left because $\|x\| \leq \tfrac{1}{2}$, and converging at the right because $\|x/2^k\|$ is ultimately equal to $|x/2^k|$. The identity holds for all real x; I stumbled across it when working on an algorithm based on Brownian motion [11].

Analysis of algorithms is only one small aspect of the interaction between mathematics and computer science. I have chosen to mention a few autobiographical examples only because I understand them better than I can understand some of the deeper things. I could have touched instead on some of the recent advances in algebra and number theory that have occurred as new algorithms for algebraic operations and factorization have been found. Or I could have highlighted the exciting field of discrete and computational geometry that is now opening up. And so on.

My point is rather that a great deal of interesting work remains to be done, even after a person has invented an algorithm to solve some mathematical problem. We can ask, "How good is the algorithm?" and this question will often lead to a host of relevant issues. Indeed, there will be enough good stuff to keep subsequent generations of mathematicians happy for another century at least.

References

[1] John D. Dixon, "The number of steps in the Euclidean algorithm," *Journal of Number Theory* **2** (1970), 414–422.

[2] Aviezri S. Fraenkel, Review of *On Numbers and Games* by J. H. Conway and *Surreal Numbers* by D. E. Knuth, *Bulletin of the American Mathematical Society* **84** (1978), 1328–1336.

[3] Hans A. Heilbronn, "On the average length of a class of finite continued fractions," *Abhandlungen aus Zahlentheorie und Analysis = Number Theory and Analysis*, edited by Paul Turán (New York: Plenum, 1968/1969), 87–96.

[4] Donald E. Knuth, *Seminumerical Algorithms*, Vol. 2 of *The Art of Computer Programming* (Reading, Massachusetts: Addison–Wesley, 1969).

[5] Donald E. Knuth, "The analysis of algorithms," *Actes du Congrès International des Mathématiciens 1970*, **3** (Paris: Gauthier-Villars, 1971), 269–274.

[6] Donald E. Knuth, "Mathematical analysis of algorithms," *Proceedings of IFIP Congress 1971*, **1** (Amsterdam: North-Holland, 1972), 19–27.

[7] Donald E. Knuth, *Sorting and Searching*, Vol. 3 of *The Art of Computer Programming* (Reading, Massachusetts: Addison–Wesley, 1973).

[8] Donald E. Knuth, *Surreal Numbers:* How two ex-students turned on to pure mathematics and found total happiness (Reading, Massachusetts: Addison–Wesley, 1974).

[9] Donald E. Knuth, "Computer Science and its relation to Mathematics," *American Mathematical Monthly* **81** (April 1974), 323–343. [Reprinted as Chapter 1 of the present volume.]

[10] Donald E. Knuth, "Notes on generalized Dedekind sums," *Acta Arithmetica* **33** (1977), 297–325.

[11] Donald E. Knuth, "An algorithm for Brownian zeroes," *Computing* **33** (1984), 89–94.

[12] George Pólya, letter to the author dated July 8, 1973.

[13] J. W. Porter, "On a theorem of Heilbronn," *Mathematika* **22** (1975), 20–28.

[14] Gian-Carlo Rota, review of *An Introduction to the Theory of Surreal Numbers* by H. Gonshor, *Advances in Mathematics* **66** (1987), 318.

[15] G. S. Tseytin, "From logicism to proceduralism (an autobiographical account)," in *Algorithms in Modern Mathematics and Computer Science*, A. P. Ershov and D. E. Knuth, eds., *Lecture Notes in Computer Science* **122** (1981), 390–396.

[16] Eric Weiss, "Mathematics on the beach," *Abacus* **1**, 3 (Spring 1984), 44.

Chapter 6

Theory and Practice, I

[A speech given at the inauguration ceremony for the Fletcher Jones professorship at Stanford University, 2 December 1977.]

I would like to begin by quoting some remarks made by James Sylvester[1] in his inaugural address, when he became Savilian Professor of Mathematics at the University of Oxford about 100 years ago:

> *Qui condis laeva condis collegia dextra,*
> *Nemo tuarum unam vicit utraque manu.*
> [KWEE coan-DIS lai-WAH coan-DIS col-LAYG-i-a DEX-tra,
> NAY-mo too-AR oo-NAM WEE-kit oo-TRAH-kwe mah-NU.]

(pause) I suppose he got a pretty good laugh in those days.

It is customary at occasions like this for the speaker to reflect a bit on his career and his field of activity. Since I'm on sabbatical leave this year I'm supposed to have lots of time for such reflection, and so I prepared this talk by going on an ego trip and taking a look back at my professional life since my college days.

Because of my mathematical orientation the first thing I did was to check over my vita and gather a few quantitative statistics, with the aid of a pocket calculator. I learned from my CV that I have received four patents; that I'm on the editorial boards of twelve technical journals and one encyclopedia. I've been the Ph.D. advisor for fourteen students who have finished their theses, and of two others who I hope will finish soon. (Right, Luis and Lyle?) I have published five books, containing a total of 2261 printed pages, 2488 exercises, and 2231 answers to the exercises[2]. And I've written 90 technical papers, amounting to over 1300 more published pages.

Well, that just about sums me up. For twenty years I've been grinding out page after page, and I think only my secretary Phyllis has read more than half of those papers.

Now today I'm deeply honored to be appointed to the Fletcher Jones chair, the first of what we all hope will become a series of endowed professorships in the Computer Science Department at Stanford. Receiving such an honor makes me very happy, because quite frankly it gives me some tangible evidence that my professional work has been a success.

Recently I was struck by the thought that few people ever really feel successful. The most ambitious among us work and work, but regard every achievement as just a small stepping stone to an ever grander project. Never do they sit back and say, "I've been successful, and worked hard; now let me relax and enjoy the rest of my life."

I don't want to make such a mistake, so today at this time it seems fitting that I announce to all of you *my retirement from active work as a computer scientist.* I've been successful, and worked hard; now I wish to relax and enjoy the rest of my life.

After all, most of the easy research problems in our field have been solved by now, and it's getting harder and harder to push computer science any further. If I continue to work actively, I'll have to compete with a lot of you in the race to discover that rapidly vanishing and ever scarcer resource known as a "computer science research topic." It has also become clear to me that I should abandon the task of writing Volume 4, because it would be impossible to complete it. All these years of toil, writing books one word at a time, have meant countless hours when I was sitting all alone, concentrating hard and unable to be with my wife and children. Furthermore, there's nothing more that I could achieve anyway by continuing to work so hard, since Nobel didn't set up a prize for mathematicians, much less for computer scientists. Next month I'll be 40 years old; that's too old to win the Fields Medal, but a good age at which my life can begin anew.

In summary, now that I have been appointed to this chair, it is my intention to "sit on it."[3]

$$* - * - * - * - *$$

Some of you who know me will realize that I have a peculiar sense of humor. I occasionally say preposterous things under the assumption that nobody will take them seriously. I hope none of you really believed any of this nonsense about my early retirement; I was of course only kidding. It was fun for me to make such an announcement — for once in my life — and I wanted to give a sort of unpredictable speech today. But the point I really wish to make is that such talk of ceasing activity in computer science is quite absurd.

The subject is just too fascinating. Far from being faced with a dearth of research problems, we find that every day brings interesting new questions that cry out for solution. We haven't even begun to scratch the tip of the iceberg, and each question answered leads to a host of new ones. Of course some days turn out to be more inspiring than others, but at the present time I know of no upper bounds on the amount of interesting computer science research awaiting us.

Furthermore it is always exciting to teach Stanford students, and I can't imagine ever getting tired of that.

I must admit being satisfied to know that my work has had some measure of success. I believe that this success is due mainly to two things. In the first place I've been blessed with a wonderful wife, who has stood by me through many complicated years. The only thing I really meant seriously, when I spoke about quitting business a few moments ago, was the part about not spending enough time with my family. This is a perpetual problem for people in service occupations, and I need to keep working at it to find the right balance, precisely because it is all too easy to get wrapped up in computer science. I can't possibly express enough thanks to my wife for all the years of understanding support she has given me. The main reason I cited those statistics before, about the total number of pages and so on, was to make it clear how long-suffering she has been; anybody who has gotten pleasure out of anything I have written ought to thank her as much as me. (Jill, I haven't been the greatest husband, and I certainly don't deserve all you've done for me, but you know that I'm trying to improve. And when Volume 7 is finally done, I promise to spend a full year just with you. ... Before I go to work on that calculus book.)

The second reason that I think my work has been successful is that the main theme of my professional life has been to combine theory and practice. I'm very grateful that my college education was in pure mathematics, at the same time as I had a part-time job writing assemblers and compilers. It seems to me that both theory and practice are essential, and my life's work has been to keep blending them with each other. You can't get very far in practical work without abstract theories that permit you to think at a higher level, and at the same time theoretical work becomes dead if it doesn't receive fresh inspirations from practical problems in the "real world." The real joy of computer science for me has been that it is a rich source of ideas and techniques that not only achieve some useful purposes in the world but that are at the same time associated with theories that are beautiful from a purely mathematical standpoint.

In this regard I want especially to thank Bob Floyd for teaching me that mathematics and computer programming go together. He probably doesn't realize how much his ideas in the early 1960s have influenced my entire career. (On the other hand he probably doesn't want to be held responsible for all of my crazy opinions — just the good ones.) I am especially glad to be part of a Computer Science Department in which all theoretical work is firmly grounded in practical questions.

This is a golden time for computer science. The students and faculty here are teeming with exciting ideas, and I believe this creative ferment is due to the fact that we are maintaining an excellent balance between theory and practice. For such a fortunate climate of opinion we must especially thank the late founder of our department, George Forsythe, who was primarily responsible for shaping its philosophy. All of us who knew George have engraved a permanent endowed chair for him in our hearts. I can certainly vouch for the fact that George was the most influential person in my own decision to come to Stanford, and of course that was one of the best things ever to happen to me.

Furthermore the Computer Science Department has been blessed with the enlightened support of Stanford's central administration — at least most of the time — and our present chairman Ed Feigenbaum is also to be congratulated on his efficient handling of our affairs.

Another reason it is so pleasant for me to be here is the fact that I have the greatest secretary in the world, Phyllis Winkler. She actually does most of my work, sometimes making highly technical corrections to my papers and letters, so I suspect that she really knows more computer science than any of us. But she never admits it, I guess because she enjoys being a secretary. She does all these things for me while serving as secretary to several other people and keeping everyone's spirits up with her contagious laughter.

Above all, my feelings today are of gratitude for the many people who have helped me, too numerous to mention. For me, today is Thanksgiving Day. I had the good fortune to talk with my mother on the telephone this morning and to thank her for all the sacrifices she and my dad had to make while raising me and putting me through college. I am grateful to them especially for the Christian education I received and for the chance to learn piano and organ. Nobody could hope for better parents than I have had.

Finally in closing, I want to thank also two other people who have been sources of inspiration for me in recent years. The first is Norm Pfotenhauer, the pastor of Bethany Lutheran Church in Menlo Park; you might say he has been the curator of my soul during the time I have been at Stanford. The second is George Pólya, whose name I am proud to stand behind in my office in Polya Hall. Many of you know that Professor Pólya will be celebrating his 90th birthday a few days from now; yet he has published several books during the last three years ... tonight he will be at Asilomar to deliver a lecture to the California Mathematics Council ... and next quarter he will be teaching course CS150 in our department! I hope that in future years I may be able to serve computer science and mathematics as George Pólya has.

Notes

1. James Joseph Sylvester, *Collected Works* 4, page 278. This quotation actually has nothing to do with the subject of my talk; it's just my idea of a "different" way to start. Sylvester was speaking of Johns Hopkins University, from which he had just resigned to accept an even better position at Oxford, and this couplet means:

> You who establish colleges with left hand and right,
> Nobody surpassed one of yours using both hands.

(Thanks to Prof. Mike Wigodsky of Stanford's Classics Department and Prof. Hendrik Lenstra of Berkeley's Mathematics Department for hints about translation and pronunciation.)

2.

	exercises	answers	pages
Volume 1	879	803	656
Volume 2	701	653	636
Volume 3	864	767	738
Surreal Numbers	22	0	125
Mariages Stables	22	8	106

3. Henry Fonzarelli Winkler, *Happy Days*, ABC Television series, 1974–1984.

Chapter 7

Theory and Practice, II

[A speech given in the ancient Greek theater of Epidaurus on 16 July 1985, as part of the 12th International Colloquium on Automata, Languages, and Programming. Originally published in Bulletin of the EATCS 27 (October 1985), 15–21.]

It is a great privilege to be able to deliver a lecture in this place. For the past several months I've been practicing with pebbles in my mouth, hoping to be able to give a suitable oration for the occasion.

Can you all hear me? Every American visitor to Greece knows that this amphitheater has perfect acoustics, and when I was preparing my talk I began to wonder whether the theory of acoustics is symmetrical. If A can hear B perfectly, does it follow that B can hear A perfectly? If so, an audience's laughter or applause might be deafening to the speaker's eardrums. In spite of this risk, I decided to prepare a few jokes, so that if you laugh at the right times I will know that somebody is listening.

My subject is 'Theory and Practice'. The talk will be partly autobiographical, because I'm hoping that some of my recent experiences with the blending of theory and practice will prove to be valuable to many of you.

What a thrill it is to be in Greece, where theory was born! Mankind owes a tremendous debt to the people who first went beyond the practical needs of everyday life to the realm of abstract thought. The revolutionary ideas of Hellenic philosophy — that some facts can be proved rigorously, that intuitive assumptions and rules of inference can be made explicit, that ideal mental models can far transcend concrete physical models — all these insights have had incredibly profound effects on all aspects of civilization, especially in science, and particularly in computer science. To properly recognize this debt, we should change the initials of the organization that sponsors our annual conferences: The European Association for Theoretical Computer Science, 'EATCS', should really be called 'EAΘCS'.

Photo by Gregory Mentzas

Have you ever wondered about the origin of the word 'theory'? My first guess was that it might be etymologically related to '$\theta\varepsilon\acute{o}\varsigma$', God — perhaps (I thought) because the early followers of Pythagoras submitted so devoutly to his theories. But if I had known more about the Greek language, I wouldn't have made that conjecture, because the 'o' in 'theology' is an omicron while the 'o' in 'theorem' is an omega. The word 'theory' actually comes from the same root as the word 'theater' — which makes it all the more appropriate that we should be meeting here tonight. According to the dictionaries I consulted, the root word '$\theta\acute{\varepsilon}\bar{a}$' (a sight) led to '$\theta\acute{\varepsilon}\bar{a}\tau\varrho o\nu$' (a place for viewing) and '$\theta\varepsilon\omega\varrho\acute{o}\varsigma$' (a spectator), as well as '$\theta\varepsilon\acute{\omega}\varrho\eta\mu a$' (a seeing, a spectacle, an object of study).

And what about 'practice'? It's another Greek word, indeed another theatrical word: Practice means performance.

You can see how these root words dichotomize the notions of theory and practice: Theoreticians sit in the audience and watch, while practitioners are on stage actually doing something. The lexicon also told me that 'πρακτικός' means 'active' and 'strong'; thus we can say that theory is to practice as rigor is to vigor.

The importance of abstract theory to the ancient Greek people is illustrated by a scene in a play that has certainly been performed many times in the theater where we are now gathered. Aristophanes's comedy *The Birds* includes a cameo appearance of the astronomer Meton, who comes on stage carrying rulers and compasses, claiming that he can square the circle! Where else on earth would a playwright think of including such a scene?

I like to think that one of the people who have witnessed Aristophanes's play, in this very theater, was Plato's student Eudoxus, who is thought to be the inventor of Euclid's algorithm, the oldest nontrivial computational technique — an amazing method that is still of great importance today. Although the historical evidence is fragmentary, I think it highly likely that Eudoxus had a deep understanding of continued fractions, even in the case of irrational numbers. And I believe it is clear that Eudoxus was a significantly better mathematician than any other human being born before his time. I have long been looking forward to making a pilgrimage to Greece so that I could have some experience of the places where he lived. For me, Eudoxus is the great granddaddy of algorithmic analysis.

But what did the great Greek philosophers themselves have to say about theory and practice? Here's an interesting quote from Aristotle's book on politics [2]: "Enough has been said about the *theory* of wealth-getting; we will now proceed to the *practical* part." Aristotle goes on to tell a story about Thales of Miletus, who was the world's first mathematician, in the sense that several theorems have been credited to him [3]. (Theorems such as "base angles of an isosceles triangle are equal" and "the angle inscribed in a semicircle is a right angle" were supposedly his discoveries, while earlier mathematical results were anonymous.) Aristotle tells us that, to Thales, the primary question was not 'What do we know?' but 'How do we know it?'. Yet Thales also reportedly put his knowledge to practical use: Anticipating by scientific observations that the olive crop would be especially good one year, he obtained a monopoly on all the oil presses, later raising a large sum of money because he could name his own price.

There's also more to the story. Aristotle tells us that Thales didn't really want to get rich, he only wanted to prove that a philosopher could easily make money if he chose to do so; critics had been taunting him, saying "If you're so smart, why aren't you rich?" Through most of the later Hellenic period, the intellectual ideal was knowledge for its own sake, apart from its uses or applications.

Plato loved binary trees, and said [10] that "We may divide the sciences at large into two types, which may be called the science of action (πρακτική) and the science of knowing (γνωστική)." It turns out that he included the art of numerical calculation under the science of knowing, but only because a theoretician could in principle check a calculation, not that a theoretician would actually stoop to perform one. Aristotle continued this tradition of organizing knowledge into hierarchies, with one kind of science taking precedence over another; for example, he frequently pointed out that geometry is applied to optics, and optics in turn is applied to the theory of the rainbow.

Such perceptions were no doubt valuable in their day, but Archimedes contributed important new insights about 100 years later when he pointed out that the correct data structure for knowledge is more complicated than a tree. Archimedes found that after applying his theoretical knowledge to practical problems, he obtained new intuitions that led to substantially better theories. For example, while working on the problem of designing ship hulls so that boats would be stable, he came up with the famous "Method" [1] by which he could prove amazing facts about the centers of gravity of solids, anticipating many techniques of modern calculus. Alfréd Rényi once put the following words into Archimedes's mouth, in an imaginary dialog [12] that might have taken place in the third century B.C.: "Odysseus used the wooden horse to smuggle himself and some Greek soldiers into Troy. But I [Archimedes] used my machines to smuggle an idea into the public mind of the Greek world, the idea being that mathematics — not only its elements, but also its most subtle parts — can be applied successfully to practical purposes. ... Conversely, a concern with applications can aid in pure mathematical research."

Archimedes's contemporary Apollonius wrote an essay called *Quick Delivery*, now unfortunately lost, that reportedly dealt with the subject of efficient methods of calculation [3]. Apollonius is said to have obtained an approximation to π whose accuracy was unprecedented, by applying his new computational methods. These examples, and many more that could be given, all serve to illustrate Charles Hutton's maxim that 'To be learned in an art, &c, the Theory is sufficient; to be a master of it, both the Theory and practice are requisite." [6]

(holding up a copy of [11]) A few hours ago I was delighted to find this magazine on the streets of Nafplion. Can you see the title?

Contemporary Greek "practice," from [11, p. 56].

ΠΡΑΚΤΙΚΗ! I'm really glad to see the spirit of *πρακτική* continuing strong in present-day Greece.

While I was preparing this talk I happened to meet Alan Perlis, who is a master at the art of creating epigrams. I told him that I was going to speak at Epidaurus, and he said I should definitely relay the following message to everyone here: "Alas, man can only achieve immortality posthumously." Then I asked him for some wisdom related to my subject of theory and practice. He replied, "Truth is not where you find it, but where you put it."

I would also like to quote John von Neumann's famous words on the subject [14]. After stating his belief that the best inspirations of modern mathematics originated outside of mathematics, in the sciences, he pointed out that the converse is also true: "At a great distance from its empirical source, or after much 'abstract' inbreeding, a mathematical subject is in danger of degeneration. ...Whenever this stage is reached, the only remedy seems to me to be the rejuvenating return to the source."

Well, it's clear that many people much wiser than I have said important things about the relationship between theory and practice. Why therefore should I dare to think that I could give a lecture on a subject that is already so well covered? What could I possibly add to the comments of all the great people who have established the great traditions of which I'm so proud to play a small part? There are two main reasons why I decided that 'Theory and Practice' must be the topic to discuss tonight. First, our discipline of computer science seems to be one in which theory and practice are more intimately related than in any other field, because of the nature of computing machines themselves. And second, my present situation gives me an unusual opportunity to reflect on these relationships, because of the somewhat heterodox research that I am just now in the process of completing.

During the past several years I've been intensively involved with practical software developments. This has brought me to a personal turning point; the software project will soon be finished, and I'm about to return to my main life's work, namely to write about *The Art of Computer Programming*. Therefore it's natural for me to be musing about what I have learned from my odyssey into the real world of software creation.

The most important lesson, for me, was that *software is hard*; and it takes a long time. From now on I shall have significantly greater respect for every successful software tool that I encounter. My original plan was to spend one year working on algorithms for typography; but that was in the spring of 1977, so you can see that it has taken more than eight years to finish the job. Even so, if my health continues to be good, I think it will turn out that those eight years were not wasted, because they will have improved my efficiency enough that I'll be able to recover the time during the next decade or so. Most importantly, those eight years were surely not wasted, because I learned an enormous number of things that will "feed" the theoretical work that I do in the future.

Software creation not only takes time, it's also much more difficult than I thought it would be. Why is this so? I think the main reason is that a longer attention span is needed when working on a large computer program than when doing other intellectual tasks. A great deal of technical information must be kept in one's head, all at once, in high-speed random-access memory somewhere in the brain. I found to my dismay that I could not be writing large programs while teaching my regular classes; I simply couldn't do justice to both activities simultaneously, nor could I be happy if the programs were left unwritten. So I reluctantly took occasional leaves of absence from university teaching. In this sense I believe that program-writing is substantially more demanding than book-writing.

Another reason that programming is harder than the writing of books and research papers is that programming demands a significantly higher standard of accuracy. Programs don't simply have to make sense to another human being, they must make sense to a computer. For example, I wrote the entire TEX compiler and desk-checked it before I did any debugging on a machine. At that point I had in my hands a document of some 500 pages, containing the program and an informal proof of its correctness. It seemed to me that this document was in some ways similar to the first proof by Feit and Thompson [4] of the famous theorem that all simple groups of odd order are cyclic. My program didn't require as much creativity or daring as their theorem did, but the program was about as detailed and as lengthy as their proof, and both works involved about the same number of paradigms. If I had submitted the program to human referees for verification, they would presumably have found a few problems that could readily be fixed, after which I might have published my program as a theoretical demonstration that "there exists a way to compile TEX." But of course the computer was a much sterner taskmaster than any human referees would be; therefore I had to spend another five months of intense activity before my program actually ran well enough for me to believe that it did the right things.

While working on these programs my theoretical brain didn't go dormant. (At least, I don't think it did; other people will have to judge this, not me.) Stimulating new problems kept coming up all the time. For example, more than a dozen interesting subproblems arose while I was working on the new METAFONT interpreter. I learned, for example, the amazing algorithm of Morrison and Moler [9] for Pythagorean addition $(\sqrt{x^2 + y^2})$, and this led me naturally to think of an interesting new way to calculate the geometric mean of two fixed-point numbers $(\sqrt{xy})$ using only single-precision arithmetic. I developed slightly improved digital algorithms for trigonometric functions, and this experience led to a completely new digital method for plotting parametric Bézier spline curves. I worked out a new kind of programming language that attempts to do for macros what SIMULA did for procedures. I also extended the "dynamic online" linear equation solver of the old METAFONT system so that equations can be deleted as well as inserted, while they are in the midst of being solved. My student John Hobby discovered three important new methods of computer graphics: one to choose angles at a designer's knot points, one to choose appropriate cubic splines when adjacent angles are given, and one to draw curves that have nearly uniform thickness on a discrete raster. Hobby's curve-drawing algorithm is especially striking because it involves a beautiful interplay between geometry and number theory; the ancient Greek mathematicians would have really loved it. His work incidentally is based on the convolution theory of Guibas, Ramshaw, and Stolfi [5], a significant contribution to pure mathematics that was inspired by the prototype of METAFONT a few years ago.

METAFONT, as a computer program, includes interesting data structures for recording pixel patterns and displaying them on a screen; it has subtle algorithms for rounding the envelope of a curve to a raster; and so on. I can't give you the details, without drawing equations and pictures, but they will be published elsewhere. I think you will agree with me when you see them that the theoretical ideas inspired by these practical problems are more than interesting enough to compensate for some of the more laborious aspects of real-world programming.

Rather than postpone all the details to a later publication, however, I do want to discuss with you in more detail two of the interesting subproblems that came up while I was working on METAFONT last year. The first is a combinatorial task for which I have a method that works satisfactorily in practice, but I suspect one of you might be able to think of a way to reduce the worst-case solution time. The problem is this: Given n integers $x_1 \ldots x_n$ and a number $m < n$, find m integers $y_1 \ldots y_m$ that minimize the distance from the x's to the y's. More precisely, every x_i should be within distance d of some y_j, and we want to choose the y's so that d is as small as possible. For example, if $x_1 \ldots x_n$ are the odd numbers $1, 3, 5, \ldots, 2n - 1$, and if $m = \frac{1}{2}n$, then the best solution is to choose the y's to be 2, 6, 10, and so on; every x is within one unit of a y. I won't tell you tonight just how I implemented a solution to this problem, but I'd be glad to see your ideas later.

The other subproblem I want to mention has to do with ellipses, and I bring it up for several reasons. First, we all know that conic sections were among the greatest loves of early Greek mathematicians, from Menæchmus of Athens to Apollonius of Perga; so I want to pay homage to this ancient tradition by showing that new applications can lead to pleasant new aspects of old theories, even when the theories have existed for more than 2000 years. Second, I want to try to explain why this small idea of mine pleased me so much when I hit on it, even though I'm sure that it is not really a major contribution either to theory or to practice.

The problem is simply this: A user of METAFONT is allowed to specify an arbitrary affine transformation by specifying the images of the three points $(0,0)$, $(1,0)$, and $(0,1)$. METAFONT is then supposed to compute the image of the unit circle under this affine transformation. The image will, of course, be an ellipse, and we want to compute its center of gravity, its major and minor axes, and its angle of inclination with respect to the coordinate system.

Well, this is hardly a new problem, but there was a new twist when I faced it. Namely, I had already implemented the rest of METAFONT and I wanted to solve this ellipse problem in the simplest way based on subroutines that were already present. METAFONT is a highly portable program, and I had purposely refrained from using machine-dependent things like floating-point numbers. I had implemented everything from scratch, using scaled integers, so that identical results would be obtained on all computers. These already-written subroutines formed a coherent unit, and I didn't want to implement something completely different or out of character just for the special ellipse problem; I wanted to keep the METAFONT code elegant.

Now I'm going to tell you the solution, just in case you're good at visualizing formulas that are heard rather than seen. The problem can obviously be reduced to the case that the origin is fixed, so we can formulate it as follows: Given two pairs of real numbers (p, q) and (r, s), find axes (a, b) and angles (θ, ϕ) such that a certain complicated four-dimensional trigonometric relation holds between the parameters. The essence of the relation in question is that the following two affine transformations should be identical: One transformation takes $(0, 0)$ into $(0, 0)$, $(1, 0)$ into (p, q), and $(0, 1)$ into (r, s); the other affine transformation, which should turn out to be the same, consists of a rotation by ϕ followed by multiplication of the x and y coordinates by a and b, then a rotation by θ. This means in particular that the unit circle is mapped into an ellipse with semi-axes (a, b), rotated by θ. Well, it turns out that the values of $a - b$ and $\theta - \phi$ are respectively the Pythagorean sum and the arctangent of the pair $(p - s, q + r)$; similarly $a + b$ and $\theta + \phi$ are the Pythagorean sum and arctangent of $(p + s, q - r)$. METAFONT already had subroutines for Pythagorean sum and for arctangent, so it was extremely easy to solve the four simultaneous nonlinear equations without needing any more basic tools.

I hope some of you can understand why this little discovery made me so jubilant: I love to have programs that fit together nicely. The poet Edna St. Vincent Millay once wrote that "Euclid alone has looked on Beauty bare" [13]; but I think there can be raw beauty also in mundane practical things such as computer programs. That is why I have called my books *The Art of Computer Programming.*

My experiences of the past few years have been so positive that I now wish to make a strong recommendation to the members of the EAΘCS: I urge you to consider devoting more of your time to questions of actual implementation. I sincerely believe that all of you will benefit from more programming activity, especially now that parallel computations are beginning to be really feasible. It's a great time to put many of our abstract theoretical ideas to the test.

Of course I realize that software development takes a lot of time; perhaps the younger members of the audience had better wait until they get tenure, before they become too involved with programming! What I'm saying, though, is that the best way for a theoretician to spend a sabbatical, or even to spend the time between sabbaticals, is to work intensively on applications.

Mrs. Mercouri has reminded us that there is an important moral dimension to be added to this discussion. Not all applications of computing machines are beneficial, and I certainly do not want to encourage anyone to write code for anything that the programmer does not personally believe is valuable. Nor should you write programs if you really hate practical work; by all means concentrate on what you love to do, because that is what you will do best. But I do want to stress that nobody should ever have to be ashamed if they have a secret love for writing computer programs that actually work; on the contrary, we should greatly appreciate such achievements, and we should encourage the practical endeavors of our colleagues and our students as well as ourselves.

I suppose I actually have a secret motivation for suggesting that you all abandon pure theory for a few years and go into software: I desperately need time to catch up with the literature, and I yearn for a decreased flow of papers to journals, so that I'll have a chance to finish my books.

On the other hand, it isn't true that practical work implies a decreased number of publications. I have in fact been agitating recently for the notion of computer programs as works of literature [7], and I'm hoping to see more publications of complete, runnable algorithms. My own programs for TEX and METAFONT are being published [8] and I certainly rank them among the most significant achievements of my life.

Therefore in conclusion I say: Let us not confuse big-Omicron with big-Omega by making a theology out of theory. Let us rather practice what we preach. This will not only give the world better applications, it will ultimately give the world better theory.

Special thanks are due to Prof. Christos Papadimitriou and to Her Excellency the Minister of Culture of the Hellenic Republic, Mrs. Melina Mercouri, for making this event possible. The text of Mrs. Mercouri's remarks can be found in *Bulletin of the EATCS* **27** (October 1985), 13–14.

References

[1] Archimedes, *Method*, edited by Thomas L. Heath (Cambridge University Press, 1912).

[2] Aristotle, *Politica*, translated by Benjamin Jowett (Oxford, 1885), I.11.

[3] Carl B. Boyer, *A History of Mathematics* (New York: Wiley, 1968), page 158.

[4] Walter Feit and John G. Thompson, "Solvability of groups of odd order," *Pacific Journal of Mathematics* **13** (1963), 775–1029.

[5] Leo Guibas, Lyle Ramshaw, and Jorge Stolfi, "A kinetic framework for computational geometry," *Proceedings of the 24th Annual Symposium on the Theory of Computing* (1983), 100–111.

[6] Charles Hutton, *A Mathematical and Philosophical Dictionary* **2** (London, 1795), 585.

[7] Donald E. Knuth, "Literate programming," *The Computer Journal* **27** (1984), 97–111. [Reprinted as Chapter 4 of *Literate Programming*.]

[8] Donald E. Knuth, *Computers and Typesetting*, 5 vols. (Reading, Massachusetts: Addison–Wesley, 1986).

[9] Donald Morrison and Cleve Moler, "Replacing square roots by Pythagorean sums," *IBM Journal of Research and Development* **27** (1983), 577–581.

[10] Plato, *Politicus*, edited by J. Burnet (Oxford, 1900–1907), 258e.

[11] Πρακτική **49** (July 1985). [This magazine contains several dozen algorithms for knitting and other kinds of needlework, as well as for food preparation.]

[12] Alfréd Rényi, *Dialógusok on matematikáról* (Budapest: Akadémiai Kiādó, 1965); *Dialogues on Mathematics* (San Francisco: Holden-Day, 1967).

[13] Edna St. Vincent Millay, *Collected Sonnets* (New York: Harper, 1941), page 45.

[14] John von Neumann, "The Mathematician," in Robert B. Heywood, ed., *The Works of the Mind* (University of Chicago Press, 1947), 180–196.

Chapter 8

Theory and Practice, III

[An after-dinner talk given at the Franklin Institute on 16 October 1986, in connection with a special convocation marking the fortieth anniversary of the creation of ENIAC.]

It's quite an honor for me to be invited to ENIAC's 40th birthday party, because I was only 8 years old when that machine was born. I certainly hope that the people of *my* generation will be able to pass on to our students the many things that we have learned from the people who are assembled in this room.

Although I grew up long after computers had been invented, I've always been interested in the early machines, and in fact when I was 30 years old I came to the Moore School specifically to look at the archives of the ENIAC and EDVAC projects. I don't know where those papers are now, but at that time they were kept in half a dozen cardboard boxes, squirreled away in a storeroom right under the seats of the football stadium. As I paged through those papers, I got a feeling for the tempo and scale of the work on ENIAC, a glimmer of what went on during those years, so I feel a special appreciation for what was achieved.

One of the first things I found in those archives was a copy of John Mauchly's original memo of 1942, which proposed working on an electronic computing machine. There was a little slip of paper still attached to it with a rusty paper clip, saying something like "This sounds interesting, John, let's talk about it" — initialed by JGB [John Grist Brainerd].

Some of the other things I remember seeing were mimeographed notes from the air-raid warden, Art Burks, telling everybody what should be done during blackouts. There were some letters from IBM, mentioning a machine that IBM was "building for Harvard." And there was an interesting episode about photographers from the New York Times who came to take pictures of ENIAC when it was first announced. If my memory is correct, somebody objected that the women weren't dressed properly in the first set of photographs, so everybody had to come back and take a whole new set of pictures.

Above all, I remember that most of the papers in the archives were carbon copies of letters and purchase orders from Dr. Brainerd, as he tried to buy tubes, tubes, and more tubes.

On the same trip I had the pleasure of visiting John and Kay Mauchly at their home in Ambler. John showed me several letters he had written in the 40s about algorithms and programming languages. I hope his correspondence from those days will find its way to appropriate archives, since it is certainly valuable for the history of many parts of computer science.

Three years later it turned out by coincidence that I was able to attend ENIAC's 25th birthday party, held in Chicago's Museum of Science and Industry. Thus it has been possible for me to feel rather close to the ENIAC, even though I had only seen it in pictures until this morning, when I had a chance to touch it for the first time.

Since tonight's celebration is taking place in the Franklin Institute, I decided to look up Poor Richard's Almanac for 1736. I wanted to see what words of wisdom Benjamin Franklin had to offer us 250 years ago, because almanacs have an amazing way of predicting future events. Here's what he said, for the dates October 16 and 17, 1736: "New Titles of Honour make Men ridiculous!"*

I continued reading and learned that in November of the same year he had something to say about fine dinners such as we have had tonight: "I saw few die of Hunger, [but] of Eating 100,000."

Also in September, 1736, he included a special message for me: "He that speaks much is much mistaken." I will therefore try to keep this after-dinner speech from running on too long.

According to your dinner programs, the general subject of my remarks tonight is supposed to be 'Theory and Practice'. I want to say a few words about this because I'm hoping that some of my recent experiences with the blending of theory and practice will prove to be valuable to many of you as they were for me.

Professor Gorn told me that I was invited to speak here tonight because I've recently been working intensively on computer systems for printing. He thought I might have something to say that ties in with the work of America's master printer of the 18th century, the great man whose statue stands before us.

---

*Several members of the audience and I received honorary doctorates from the University of Pennsylvania as part of the festivities earlier that day.

And indeed, I feel a special kinship with Benjamin Franklin as well as with the ENIAC. Both Ben and I were heavily involved with printing when we were 40 years old, although our rôles were sort of reversed in other respects: Franklin did his main typographical work as a young man, and he essentially retired from printing at age 41 in order to investigate the theory of electricity. In my case I started out by developing mathematical theories, and it wasn't until age 39 that I took up the practice of printing. Yet both of us were strongly drawn to working with type because of our love of books. And both of us seem to have had good experiences in combining theory with practice.

Have you ever wondered about the origin of the word 'theory'? My first guess was that it might be etymologically related to the Greek word '$\theta\varepsilon\delta\varsigma$', God — perhaps (I thought) because the early followers of Pythagoras submitted so devoutly to Pythagorean doctrines. But if I had known more about the Greek language, I wouldn't have made that conjecture, because the 'o' in 'theology' is an omicron while the 'o' in 'theorem' is an omega. The word 'theory' actually comes from the same root as the word 'theater'. According to the dictionaries I consulted, the root word '$\theta\acute{\varepsilon}\bar{\alpha}$' (a sight) led to '$\theta\acute{\varepsilon}\bar{\alpha}\tau\varrho o\nu$' (a place for viewing) and '$\theta\varepsilon\omega\varrho\delta\varsigma$' (a spectator), as well as '$\theta\varepsilon\acute{\omega}\varrho\eta\mu\alpha$' (a seeing, a spectacle, an object of study).

And what about 'practice'? It's another Greek word, indeed another theatrical word: Practice means performance. You can see how these root words dichotomize the notions of theory and practice: Theoreticians sit in the audience and watch, while practitioners are on stage actually doing something. The lexicon also told me that '$\pi\varrho\alpha\kappa\tau\iota\kappa\delta\varsigma$' means 'active' and 'strong'; thus we can say that theory is to practice as rigor is to vigor.

Poor Richard never had much to say about the relation of theory to practice, but I did find one relevant maxim in his almanac for 1753: "Many have quarreled about religion that never practiced it."

Since 'theory' and 'practice' both come from Greek words, I decided to look at what ancient Greek philosophers had to say about the relation between them. Here's an interesting quote from Aristotle's book on politics: "Enough has been said about the *theory* of wealth-getting; we will now proceed to the *practical* part."

Aristotle goes on to tell a story about Thales of Miletus, who was the world's first mathematician, in the sense that several theorems have been credited to him. (Theorems such as "base angles of an isosceles triangle are equal" and "the angle inscribed in a semicircle is a right angle" were supposedly his discoveries, while earlier mathematical results were anonymous.) Aristotle tells us that, to Thales, the primary question was not 'What do we know?' but 'How do we know it?'. Yet Thales also reportedly put his knowledge to practical use: Anticipating by scientific observations that the olive crop would be especially good one year, he went out and got a monopoly on all the oil presses, later raising a large sum of money because he could name his own price.

A talk entitled 'Theory and Practice' after a dinner that celebrates ENIAC might well have the subtitle 'Mauchly and Eckert' in many people's minds, because historians have generally characterized John Mauchly as the visionary on the project and Pres Eckert as the man who got things done. This is, of course, an oversimplification. It may be true that Mauchly tended to be theoretically inclined, and that Eckert tended to lean more toward practice, but actually both of them combined theory and practice very nicely in their work. Each one complemented the other beautifully, so that as a team they were able to accomplish great things that neither of them would have been able to do alone. This was not because one did the theory and the other did the practice; it was rather that they focused on different aspects of the problems. Nowadays we would say that Eckert was more involved with hardware and Mauchly with software.

I chose to talk about theory and practice tonight because I believe that the discipline of computer science is one in which theory and practice are more intimately related than they are in any other field. This is due to the nature of computing machines themselves. And this strong inter-relationship is especially striking to me right now because I have just come to a turning point in my life: During the past nine years I've been working on practical software development, related to printing, but I'm now turning back to my main life's work, which is to write about the theoretical underpinnings of efficient computer programs. At such a time I can't help but reflect on what a theoretician like me has learned from such a long excursion into the practical world.

I should remark that my work has been to develop computer *software*, while many of you have been developing computer *hardware*; people often think that these are quite different, and in some ways they are. Indeed, Poor Richard once said that "The horse thinks one thing, and he that saddles him [thinks] another." But actually there is not much difference nowadays between software design and hardware design, so I think my recent experiences are probably relevant to all aspects of computer science.

The most important lesson I learned during the past nine years is that *software is hard*; and it takes a long time. From now on I shall have significantly greater respect for every successful software tool that I encounter. My original plan was to spend one year working on algorithms for typography; but that was in the spring of 1977, and I soon found that much more work would be needed to finish the job. Even so, if my health continues to be good, I think it will turn out that those nine years were not wasted, because they will have improved my efficiency enough that I'll be able to recover the time during the next decade or so. Most importantly, those nine years were surely not wasted, because I learned an enormous number of things that will "feed" the theoretical work that I do in the future.

Software creation is not only time-consuming, it's also much more difficult than I thought it would be. Why is this so? I think the main reason is that a longer attention span is needed when you're working on a large computer program than when you're doing other intellectual tasks. I read in Time magazine that cots were brought in to the old ENIAC lab so that Eckert and others could work through the night. Those of you who slept in those cots will know what I mean when I speak of the need for an unusually long attention span. A great deal of technical information must be kept in one's head, all at once, in high-speed random-access memory somewhere in the brain. I found to my dismay that I could not be writing large programs while teaching my regular classes; I simply couldn't do justice to both activities simultaneously, nor could I be happy if the programs were left unwritten. So I reluctantly took occasional leaves of absence from university teaching. I'm ashamed to admit this, and I know that it sets a dangerous precedent; but the difficulty of creating innovative software while teaching seems to be so great that universities may well have to adjust their present policies if they are going to be able to provide leadership in software creation.

Two hundred years ago, Benjamin Franklin was governor of Pennsylvania; he was also building a new wing of his house, based on some ideas he had for reducing the danger of fire; he was also helping one of his grandsons get established in the printing business; he was also discussing a radical reform of English spelling with Noah Webster, based on a new phonetic alphabet of his own design; and he was also involved in various other activities. He was a truly amazing man, but I don't believe he could have done any of those other things while developing a large software system!

The amount of technical detail in a large system is one thing that makes programming more demanding than book-writing. Another is that programming demands a significantly higher standard of accuracy.

Programs don't simply have to make sense to another human being, they must make sense to a computer. For example, I wrote the entire TEX compiler and desk-checked it before I did any debugging on a machine. At that point I had in my hands a document of some 500 pages, containing the program and an informal proof of its correctness. If I had submitted the program to human referees for verification, they would presumably have found a few problems that could readily be fixed, after which I might have published my program as a theoretical demonstration that "there exists a way to compile TEX." But of course the computer was a much sterner taskmaster than any human referees would be; therefore I had to spend another five months of intense activity before my program actually ran well enough for me to believe that it did the right things.

While working on these programs my theoretical brain didn't go dormant. (At least, I don't think it did; other people will have to judge that, not me.) Stimulating new problems kept coming up all the time. For example, while I was working on the new METAFONT interpreter, my students and I stumbled onto some really nice new ways to draw images on a TV screen, and these led to new ideas and approaches to basic mathematical concepts. The new ideas are so interesting, they might even change the way geometry is taught in high schools some day.

Thus the practical work has had a significant benefit on my theoretical work. Conversely, the computer systems I worked on would have been significantly poorer without the theory that went into them. I'm really happy about the way the past nine years have turned out, and I think the successes were essentially due to the interplay between theory and practice. The world gets better theoretical tools as it gets better practical tools.

A former director of the Franklin Institute, Dr. Henry Butler Allen, once described Benjamin Franklin as a 'philosophical engineer'. I think that's an excellent characterization of Franklin's personality, so I'm pretty sure Old Ben would have agreed with the sentiments I've expressed tonight. The theories I've been talking about have been quite mathematical, therefore rather different from anything Franklin himself ever did; it's fair, I think, to say that he was a *polymath* who excelled at everything *except* mathematics.* Yet he had an unusually good intuition for numerical relationships as applied to economic growth, and he loved new things; furthermore, he was addicted to chess. Therefore I have little doubt that he would have welcomed the improvements that mathematics and computer science have brought to the practice of printing and vice versa.

There has been only one negative outcome: My work on typography has made me so conscious of the low-level details of printing that I can no longer read any books without being intensely aware of the shapes and spacing of all the individual letters. When I sit down in a restaurant and look at the menu, I subconsciously study the fonts of type so carefully that it sometimes takes me five minutes before I realize that the menu is about food. I hope I'll soon get over this, but I fear that I'll retain the scars all my life, because Benjamin Franklin also had the same problem. For example, when he was 73, he found the typefaces in Boston newspapers so unreadable that he said, "If you should ever have any Secrets that you wish to be well kept, get them printed in those Papers." At the age of 81, Franklin wrote to Bodoni in Italy, criticizing the shape of the letter 'T' on one of Bodoni's title pages. This was 40 years after Franklin had retired as an active printer, so I imagine I too am destined to be superconscious of type for the rest of my life. Practical work does have its risks.

Well, I had better stop now; for, as Poor Richard says, "Early to bed, and Early to Rise, etc."

Note added August, 2001: After seeing an article by Paul C. Pasles in the *American Mathematical Monthly* **108** (2001), 489–511, I now am happily able to retract that statement. Pasles discusses a previously unpublished 16×16 magic square constructed by Franklin in 1765, a nontrivial arrangement that has intimate connections with binary numbers.

Chapter 9

Theory and Practice, IV

*[A keynote address for the 11th World Computer Congress (Information Processing 89), held in San Francisco, 28 August 1989. Originally published in Theoretical Computer Science **90** (1991), 1–15.]*

[SLIDE 0 to be shown during introduction of the speaker]

Slide 0.

Good morning! I want to welcome you all to the San Francisco Bay area and to nearby Silicon Valley, where I live at Stanford University. [SLIDE 1] In recent years the people around here have been taking advantage of an idea that originated, I think, in the international road signs that have spread from Europe to the rest of the world: the idea of *icons*, as graphic representations of information. Icons have now become so pervasive, in fact, that I think people might soon be calling this place Silly Icon Valley.

The title of my talk this morning is "Theory and Practice," and in order to be up-to-date I want to begin by showing you two icons that

149

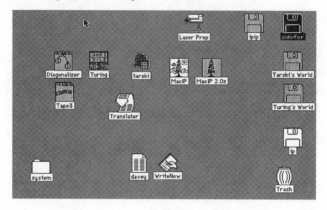

Slide 1.

might make suitable pictographs for the notions of theory and practice. I didn't have any trouble finding such images, because the reference section of our local telephone directory contains lots of icons these days. Looking at those pages, I immediately spotted an image that seems just right to depict theory — a light bulb of inspiration [SLIDE 2]. And what

Slide 2.

about practice? Right next to that light bulb in the phone book was another suitable image — a hand carrying a briefcase [SLIDE 2 + 3].

Slide 2 + 3.

Theory and *Practice.* Both of these English words come from the Greek language, and their root meanings are instructive [SLIDE 4]. The Greek θεωρία means seeing or viewing, while πρακτική means doing, performing. We owe to ancient Hellenic philosophers the revolutionary notion of theory as the construction of ideal mental models that transcend concrete physical models. They taught us systems of logic by which intuitive assumptions and rules of inference can be made explicit; therefore significant statements can be rigorously and conclusively

Θεωρία πρακτική

seeing   doing

Slide 4.

proved. Throughout the ages, practitioners have taken such theories and applied them to virtually every aspect of civilization. [SLIDE 4 + 5] Thus, we can say that theory is to practice as rigor is to vigor.

Θεωρία πρακτική

seeing   doing

rigor   vigor

Slide 4 + 5.

Theory *and* Practice [SLIDE 6 + 7]. The English word 'and' has several meanings, one of which corresponds to the mathematical notion of 'plus'. When many people talk about theory and practice, they are thinking about the sum of two disjoint things. In a similar way, when we refer to 'apples and oranges', we're talking about two separate kinds of fruit.

 +

Slide 6 + 7.

Slide 6 + 8.

[SLIDE 6 + 8] But I wish to use a stronger meaning of the word 'and', namely the logician's notion of 'both and', which corresponds to the *intersection* of sets rather than a sum. The main point I want to emphasize this morning is that both theory and practice can and should be present simultaneously. Theory and practice are not mutually exclusive; they are intimately connected [SLIDE 6 + 8 + 9]. They live together and support each other.

Slide 6 + 8 + 9.

This has always been the main credo of my professional life. I have always tried to develop theories that shed light on the practical things I do, and I've always tried to do a variety of practical things so that I have a better chance of discovering rich and interesting theories. It seems to me that my chosen field, computer science — information processing — is a field where theory and practice come together more than in any other discipline, because of the nature of computing machines.

I came into computer science from mathematics, so you can suspect that I have a soft spot in my heart for abstract theory. I still like to think of myself as a mathematician, at least in part; but during the 1960s I became disenchanted with the way mathematics was going. I'll try to explain why, by saying a few things about the history of mathematical literature [SLIDE 10]. The first international journal of mathematics was founded in 1826 by a man named August Leopold Crelle. I think its title was significant: *Journal für die reine und angewandte Mathematik*, a journal for pure and applied mathematics. In many people's eyes, 'pure mathematics' corresponds to 'theory' and 'applied mathematics' corresponds to 'practice'; so there we have it, theory and practice.

This venerable journal is still being published today, currently in volume number 398. [SLIDE 11] Another journal with the equivalent title in French began publication ten years later. This one too has continued to

TOME 68 FASCICULE 1 1989

NEUVIÈME SÉRIE

Journal für die reine und angewandte Mathematik

gegründet 1826 von

August Leopold Crelle

fortgeführt von
C. W. Borchardt, K. Weierstrass, L. Kronecker, L. Fuchs,
K. Hensel, L. Schlesinger, H. Hasse, H. Rohrbach

gegenwärtig herausgegeben von

Simon Donaldson · Willi Jäger
Martin Kneser · Horst Leptin · Samuel J. Patterson
Peter Roquette · Michael Schneider

unter Mitwirkung von
J. Arthur (Toronto), T. tom Dieck (Göttingen), O. Forster (München),
P. R. Halmos (Santa Clara), F. Hirzebruch (Bonn),
R. Howe (New Haven), Y. Ihara (Tokyo), H. Koch (Berlin), J. Lindenstrauss (Jerusalem)

JRMAA8

Band 398

JOURNAL
DE
MATHÉMATIQUES
PURES ET APPLIQUÉES

W
DE
G

Walter de Gruyter · Berlin · New York 1989

gauthiervillars

Slide 10.   Slide 11.

the present day, and both journals still mention both pure and applied mathematics in their titles. But there was a time when the only applied mathematics you could find in these journals consisted of applications to pure mathematics itself.

[NO SLIDE] When theory becomes inbred — when it has grown several generations away from its roots, until it has completely lost touch with the real world — it degenerates and becomes sterile. I was attracted to computer science because its theory seemed much more exciting and interesting to me than the new mathematical theories I was hearing about in the 60s. I noticed that computer science theory not only had a beautiful abstract structure, it also answered questions that were relevant to things I wanted to do. So I became a computer scientist.

History teaches us that the greatest mathematicians of past centuries combined theory and practice in their own careers. For example, let's consider Carl Friedrich Gauss, who is often called the greatest

Slide 12.

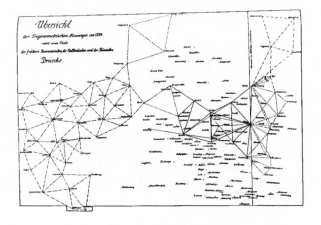

Slide 13.

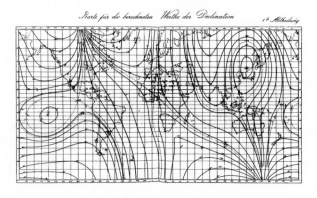

Slide 14.

mathematician of all time because of the deep theories he discovered. [SLIDE 12] Here is an excerpt from one of his diaries; Gauss left behind thousands of pages of detailed computations. His practical work with all these numbers led him to discover the method of least squares and the so-called Gaussian distribution of numerical errors. [SLIDE 13] He also made measurements of the earth and drew this map as a basis for land surveys in parts of Germany, the Netherlands, and Denmark. [SLIDE 14] His study of magnetism led him to publish a series of world maps such as this one. Thus Gauss was by no means purely a theoretician. His practical work went hand in hand with his theoretical discoveries in geometry and physics.

One of the main reasons I've chosen to speak about Theory and Practice this morning is that I've spent the past 12 years working on a project that has given me an unusual opportunity to observe how theory and practice support each other. [NO SLIDE] My project at Stanford University has led to the development of two pieces of software called TeX and METAFONT: TeX, a system for typesetting, and METAFONT, a system for generating alphabets and symbols. [SLIDE 15] Here are the icons for TeX and METAFONT.

Slide 15.

Throughout my experiences with the TeX project, I couldn't help noticing how important it was to have theory and practice present simultaneously in equal degrees. One example of this is the method for hyphenating words that was discovered by my student Frank Liang. [SLIDE 16] Suppose we want to find permissible places to break up the word 'hyphenation'. Liang's idea is to represent hyphenation rules by a set of patterns, where each pattern is a string of letters separated by numerical values. We find all the patterns that appear as substrings of the given word, as shown here; and then we calculate the maximum of all the numbers that occur between each pair of adjacent letters. If the resulting number is odd, it represents a place to break the word; but if it is even, we don't insert a potential hyphen.

$$h\ y\ p\ h\ e\ n\ a\ t\ i\ o\ n$$

$${}_0h_0y_3p_0h_0$$
$${}_0h_0e_2n_0$$
$${}_0h_0e_0n_0a_4$$
$${}_0h_0e_0n_5a_0t_0$$
$${}_1n_0a_0$$
$${}_0n_2a_0t_0$$
$${}_1t_0i_0o_0$$
$${}_2i_0o_0$$
$${}_0o_2n$$

$${}_0h_0y_3p_0h_0e_2n_5a_4t_2i_0o_2n_0$$
$$h\ y\text{-}p\ h\ e\ n\text{-}a\ t\ i\ o\ n$$

Slide 16.

The beauty of Liang's method is that it is highly accurate, it runs fast, and it takes up very little space inside a computer. Moreover, it works with all languages, not just English: Successful sets of patterns have already been found for French, German, Italian, Spanish, Portuguese, Swedish, Icelandic, Russian, and other languages. Thus, it is a uniform method able to support international communication. Liang discovered this unified method only after considerable theoretical study of other techniques, which solved only special cases of the problem. And his practical work also had a theoretical payoff, because it led him to discover a new kind of abstract data structure called a dynamic trie, which has turned out to be of importance in other investigations. I think it's reasonable to compare this with some of Gauss's work; Gauss worked with masses of numerical data while Liang worked with masses of linguistic data, but in both cases there was an enrichment of practice that would have been impossible without the theory and an enrichment of theory that would have been impossible without the practice.

[NO SLIDE] That was an example from TEX; let me give another example, this time from METAFONT. One of the key problems of discrete geometry is to draw a line or curve that has approximately uniform thickness although it consists entirely of square black-or-white pixels. The obvious way to solve this problem is to draw a solid line of the desired thickness, without thinking about the underlying raster, and then to digitize the two edges of that line separately and fill in the region inside. But this obvious approach doesn't work. [SLIDE 17] For example, here are two straight lines of slope 1/2 and thickness 1 that were drawn by the obvious method. When we digitize the two edges and fill the inner region, [SLIDE 17 + 18] the lower line comes out 50% darker than the upper one, because it happens to fall in a different place on the raster.

Slide 17.

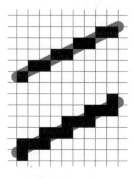
Slide 17+18.

There's a better way, which I'll call the diamond method. Imagine a diamond-shaped pen tip, one pixel tall. [SLIDE 19] Draw a line or curve with this pen, and then digitize the edges. Now you get a line or curve

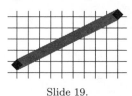
Slide 19.

that has nearly uniform thickness, regardless of where it falls on the raster. The "obvious" method I mentioned before corresponds to lines that you would draw when the tip of the pen is a circle of diameter 1 instead of a diamond. The track of a circular pen nib does not digitize well, but the track of a diamond-shaped pen nib does.

[SLIDE 20] Here's another example, using circular and diamond-shaped pens to draw a circle whose radius is 7.5. In this case the circular pen gives a digital track [SLIDE 20 + 21] that's noticeably heavier when it travels diagonally than when it is traveling horizontally or vertically. The diamond pen gives a much nicer digital circle without such glitches.

My student John Hobby found a beautiful way to extend these ideas to curves of greater thickness. [SLIDE 22] Here, for example, is an octagon-shaped pen nib that turns out to give the best results when

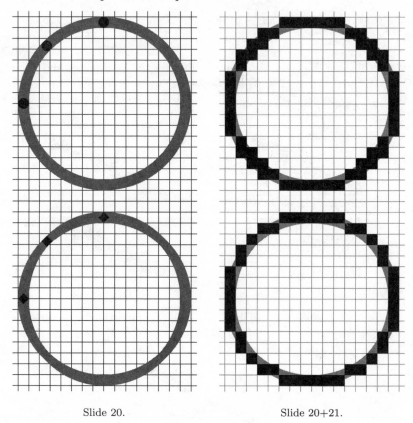

Slide 20.   Slide 20+21.

you want to draw curves that are slightly less than 3 pixels thick. Hobby developed METAFONT's polygonal method of curve drawing by creating a truly elegant combination of number theory and geometry. His work is one of the nicest blends of theory and practice I have ever seen: It's

Slide 22.

a case where deep theoretical results have made an important contribution to a practical problem, and where the theory could only have been discovered by a person who was thoroughly familiar with both the practice of digitization and with mathematical theories that had been developed for quite different problems.

[NO SLIDE] I want to mention also a third example. This one isn't as important as the other two, but I can't resist telling you about it because I just thought of it four days ago. I decided last week to make some extensions to TEX so that the system will be more useful for languages other than English. The new standard version of TEX will support 8-bit character sets instead of only the 7-bit ASCII code. Furthermore it will allow you to hyphenate words from several different languages within the same paragraph, using different sets of patterns for each language. One of the new features will be an extension of the mechanism by which TEX makes ligatures in the text, and that's the method I want to explain now.

Suppose two letters occur next to each other in a word that is to be typeset by the computer; I'll call those letters α and ω. [SLIDE 23] The present version of TEX allows the font designer to say that the letters α and ω should be replaced by a ligature, say λ. This is the way, for example, that an 'f' followed by an 'i' is converted into a symbol for 'fi' that looks better.

$$\alpha\omega \to \lambda$$
$$\text{fi} \to \text{fi}$$

Slide 23.

The new version of TEX will extend this mechanism as follows. A new letter λ will be inserted between α and ω, and the original letters might still remain. [SLIDE 24] There are nine cases, depending on what letters are kept and depending on where TEX is instructed to look next for another possible ligature. (The little caret between letters in this picture shows where TEX is focusing its attention.) The first case here shows the old ligature mechanism; the middle seven cases are new; and the bottom case is the normal situation where no ligature is to be inserted.

$$\alpha_\wedge\omega \to \lambda_\wedge$$
$$\alpha_\wedge\omega \to \alpha_\wedge\lambda$$
$$\alpha_\wedge\omega \to \alpha \ \lambda_\wedge$$
$$\alpha_\wedge\omega \to \lambda_\wedge\omega$$
$$\alpha_\wedge\omega \to \lambda \ \omega_\wedge$$
$$\alpha_\wedge\omega \to \alpha_\wedge\lambda \ \omega$$
$$\alpha_\wedge\omega \to \alpha \ \lambda_\wedge\omega$$
$$\alpha_\wedge\omega \to \alpha \ \lambda \ \omega_\wedge$$
$$\alpha_\wedge\omega \to \alpha \ \omega_\wedge$$

Slide 24.

This new mechanism has a potential danger: A careless user can now construct ligature instructions that will get TeX into an infinite loop. [SLIDE 25] For example, suppose we have the four rules shown at the top of this illustration. Then when 'a' is followed by 'z', the rules set off a chain reaction that never stops.

$$a_\wedge z \to a\ b_\wedge z$$
$$b_\wedge d \to b\ c_\wedge d$$
$$b_\wedge z \to b_\wedge d\ z$$
$$c_\wedge d \to a_\wedge$$

$$a_\wedge z \to a\ b_\wedge z$$
$$\to a\ b_\wedge d\ z$$
$$\to a\ b\ c_\wedge d\ z$$
$$\to a\ b\ a_\wedge z$$
$$\to a\ b\ a\ b_\wedge z$$
$$\to \quad \cdots$$

Slide 25.

To minimize this danger, I need an algorithm that will take a given set of ligature rules and decide if it can spawn an infinite loop. And that's where computer science theory comes to the rescue! [SLIDE 26] We can define a function f on letter pairs according to the nine ligature possibilities, as shown here. This definition is recursive. It's not hard to see that f is well defined if and only if there are no infinite ligature loops; we can understand this from the theory of deterministic pushdown automata. (The value of $f(\alpha, \omega)$ represents the letter just preceding the cursor when the cursor first moves to the right of the original ω.) And we can check whether or not f is well defined by using a small extension of an important algorithm called depth-first search.

$$\alpha_\wedge \omega \to \lambda_\wedge \qquad\qquad f(\alpha, \omega) = \lambda$$
$$\alpha_\wedge \omega \to \alpha_\wedge \lambda \qquad\qquad f(\alpha, \omega) = f(\alpha, \lambda)$$
$$\alpha_\wedge \omega \to \alpha\ \lambda_\wedge \qquad\qquad f(\alpha, \omega) = \lambda$$
$$\alpha_\wedge \omega \to \lambda_\wedge \omega \qquad\qquad f(\alpha, \omega) = f(\lambda, \omega)$$
$$\alpha_\wedge \omega \to \lambda\ \omega_\wedge \qquad\qquad f(\alpha, \omega) = \omega$$
$$\alpha_\wedge \omega \to \alpha_\wedge \lambda\ \omega \qquad\qquad f(\alpha, \omega) = f\big(f(\alpha, \lambda), \omega\big)$$
$$\alpha_\wedge \omega \to \alpha\ \lambda_\wedge \omega \qquad\qquad f(\alpha, \omega) = f(\lambda, \omega)$$
$$\alpha_\wedge \omega \to \alpha\ \lambda\ \omega_\wedge \qquad\qquad f(\alpha, \omega) = \omega$$
$$\alpha_\wedge \omega \to \alpha\ \omega_\wedge \qquad\qquad f(\alpha, \omega) = \omega$$

Slide 26.

I like this example not only because it gives an efficient, linear-time algorithm for testing whether or not a ligature loop exists. This practical problem also showed me how to extend the theory of depth-first search in a way that I hadn't suspected before. And I have a hunch the extended theory will have further ramifications, probably leading to additional applications having nothing to do with ligatures or typesetting.

What were the lessons I learned from so many years of intensive work on the practical problem of setting type by computer? One of the most important lessons, perhaps, is the fact that SOFTWARE IS HARD [SLIDE 27]. From now on I shall have significantly greater respect for every successful software tool that I encounter. During the past decade

Software

is

HARD

Slide 27.

I was surprised to learn that the writing of programs for TEX and for METAFONT proved to be much more difficult than all the other things I had done (like proving theorems or writing books). The creation of good software demands a significantly higher standard of accuracy than those other things do, and it requires a longer attention span than other intellectual tasks.

My experiences also strongly confirmed my previous opinion that the best theory is inspired by practice and the best practice is inspired by theory [SLIDE 28]. The examples I've mentioned, and many others, convinced me that neither theory nor practice is healthy without the other.

The best theory
is
inspired by practice

~

The best practice
is
inspired by theory

Slide 28.

But I don't want to give the impression that theory and practice are just two sides of the same coin. No. They deserve to be mixed and blended, but sometimes they also need to be pure. I've spent many an hour looking at purely theoretical questions that go way beyond any practical application known to me other than sheer intellectual pleasure. And I've spent many an hour on purely practical things like pulling weeds in the garden or correcting typographic errors, not expecting those activities to improve my ability to discover significant theories. [SLIDE 29] Still, I believe that most of the purely practical tasks I undertake do provide important nourishment and direction for my theoretical work; and I believe that the hours I spend contemplating the most abstract questions of pure mathematics do have a payoff in sharpening my ability to solve practical problems.

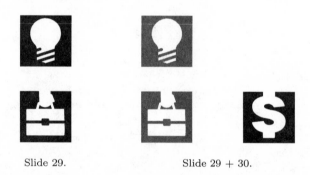

Slide 29.   Slide 29 + 30.

When I looked for an icon that would be appropriate for 'practice', I was tempted to use another one instead of the briefcase — a symbol for money! [SLIDE 29 + 30] It seems that people who do practical things are paid a lot more than the people who contribute the underlying theory. Somehow that isn't right. The past decade has, in fact, witnessed a very unfortunate trend in the patterns of funding for basic, theoretical research. We used to have a pretty well balanced situation in which both theory and practice were given their fair share of financial support by enlightened administrators. But in recent years, greater and greater amounts of research dollars have been switched away from basic research and earmarked for mission-oriented projects. The people who set the budgets have lost consciousness of the fact that the vast majority of the crucial ideas that go into the solution of these mission-oriented problems were originally discovered by pure scientists, who were working alone, independently, on basic research stimulated by intellectual curiosity. At the present time the scientific community faces a crisis in which a substantial number of the world's best scientists in all fields cannot get financial support for their work unless they subscribe to somebody else's agenda telling them what to do. We need to go back to a system where people who have demonstrated an ability to devise significant new theories are given a chance to set their own priorities. We need a lot of small projects devised by many independent scientists, instead of concentrating most of our resources on a few huge projects with predefined goals. [SLIDE 29 + 30 + 31] In other words, we need a balance between theory and practice in the budgets for scientific research, as well as in the lives of individual scientists. Otherwise we'll face a big slump in our future abilities to tackle new problems.

Slide 29 + 30 + 31.

These comments hold true for industry as well as for the university community. Many of the graduates of Stanford's Computer Science Department who have written Ph.D. theses about theoretical subjects have now taken jobs in Silicon Valley and elsewhere; and they have in most cases been able to work with enlightened managers who encourage them to continue doing basic research. I think it's fair to state that these so-called theoreticians are now considered to be among the key employees of the companies for which they work.

Slide 32.

[SLIDE 32] Speaking of key employees reminds me that this is a keynote speech; indeed, this morning is surely the only time in my life when I'll be able to give the keynote address to an IFIP Congress. So I would like to say something memorable, something of value, something that you might not have expected to hear. I thought about David

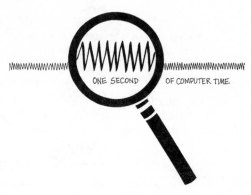

ONE SECOND   OF COMPUTER TIME

Slide 33.

Hilbert's famous address to the International Congress of Mathematicians in 1900, when he presented a series of problems as challenges for mathematicians of the 20th century. My own goals are much more modest than that; but I *would* like to challenge some of you in the audience to combine theory and practice in a way that I think will have a high payoff.

[SLIDE 33] My challenge problem is simply this: *Make a thorough analysis of everything your computer does during one second of computation.* The computer will execute several hundred thousand instructions during that second; I'd like you to study them all. The time when you conduct this experiment should be chosen randomly; for example, you might program the computer itself to use a random number generator to decide just what second should be captured and recorded.

Many people won't be able to do this experiment easily, because they won't have hardware capable of monitoring its own activities. But I think it should be possible to design some tracing software that can emulate what the machine would have done for one second if it had been running freely.

Even when the machine's instructions are known, there will be problems. The sequence of operations will be too difficult to decipher unless you have access to the source code from which the instructions were compiled. University researchers who wish to carry out such an experiment would probably have to sign nondisclosure agreements in order to get a look at the relevant source code. But I want to urge everyone who has the resources to make such a case study to do so, and to compare notes with each other afterwards, because I am sure the results will be extremely interesting; they will tell us a lot about how we can improve our present use of computers.

I discussed this challenge problem with one of the botanists at Stanford, since I know that biologists often make similar studies of plant and animal life in a randomly chosen region. [SLIDE 34] She referred me to a recent project done in the hills overlooking Stanford's campus, in which all plants were identified in several square blocks of soil. The researchers added fertilizer to some of the plots, in an attempt to see what this did to the plant life. Sure enough, the fertilizer had a significant effect on the distribution of species.

Study site

Studies were carried out on Jasper Ridge Biological Preserve in San Mateo County, Northern California. A serpentine outcrop bisects a low-lying ridge (max. elevation 189 m) situated on the eastern side of the Santa Cruz mountains. The climate is a Mediterranean-type with a mean-annual rainfall of 480 mm and a virtually rain-free period from May to September. The serpentine soil is extremely nutrient poor (0.192% N, 0.029% P; C. Chu, unpublished work) and has a Ca/Mg ratio of 0.034 and a high Ni concentration (216 ppm, acetic acid extraction; B. Streit, unpublished work). The vegetation has been described by McNaughton (1968) and studied in detail by Hobbs and Mooney (1985). The main annual species present at the study site are *Lasthenia californica* and *Plantago erecta* (authorities given in Table 1). A diverse collection of other annual species is also present, together with several species of perennial bunch grasses, notably *Sitanion jubatum* and *Stipa pulchra*.

Experimental procedure

In November 1982, we set up grids in the serpentine grassland which formed part of a long-term experiment on herbivore exclusion. Each grid measured 1 × 3 m and was subdivided into 12, 50 × 50 cm quadrats. Three sets of 2 adjacent grids were used for the present study, and each set was fenced using 1 m high chicken wire (2 cm mesh) to exclude rabbits and deer. Within each grid 2 adjacent 50 × 50 cm quadrats were chosen at random and supplied with 56 g Osmocote slow release fertiliser (14.0% N as 7.4% NO3, 6.6% NH4; 14.0% P; 14.0% K) in December 1982 and again in 1983.
At the beginning of April in the years 1983–86 we recorded the species present in each fertilised (50 × 50 cm) quadrat and in an equivalent number of unfertilised quadrats (i.e. 12 quadrats each in fertilised and unfertilised). The unfertilised quadrats analysed were located one quadrat away from the fertilised areas to obviate cross contamination.

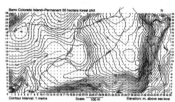

Fig. 3.1. Topographic map of the 50 hectare plot on Barro Colorado Island, Panama (BCI). Contour lines are drawn for each metre of elevational change. Dotted lines mark permanent trails through the plot. Grid marks indicate the corners of 1250, 20×20 metre quadrats. A stream in the lower left corner drains a seasonal swamp (left of centre). Grades on the steeper slopes range between 10 and 20%.

3.4   A neotropical forest case study

In 1980 we began a long-term study of a half-square kilometre plot of tropical forest on Barro Colorado Island (BCI), Panama (Hubbell & Foster, 1983), a 15 km² nature reserve in Gatun Lake. In this plot (Fig. 3.1), we have completely identified, measured, and mapped to the nearest metre all free-standing woody plants with a 1 cm or greater stem diameter at breast height (dbh). There are nearly a quarter of a million trees, saplings, and shrubs in the 50-hectare plot, representing approximately 300 species. The plot is located in 'old-growth' forest (Foster & Brokaw, 1982). Recent palaeoecological surveys of the site reveal that the forest has never been clearcut for agriculture: fossil corn phytoliths and weedy pasture grasses are absent from plot soil cores, in contrast to permanent pre-Columbian settlement areas along the Rio Chagres several kilometres away (D. Piperno, pers. comm.). However, radiocarbon dating of cores indicate that from 500 A.D. until 545 years ago, small temporary clearings were occasionally made in the forest, probably for seasonal hunting camps. Thus the forest has been essentially undisturbed by man for the past 500 years or more.

Slide 34.   Slide 35.

[SLIDE 35] My colleague also told me about another recent experiment in which British researchers identified and counted each tree in a tropical rain forest. About 250,000 trees were enumerated altogether. I imagine a typical computer will execute something like that number of instructions every second, so my specification of exactly one computer second seems to be reasonable in scale.

Here are some of the questions I would like to ask about randomly captured seconds of computation: [SLIDE 36]

- Are the programs correct or erroneous? (I have to report reluctantly that nearly every program I have examined closely during the past thirty years has contained at least one bug.)

- Do the programs make use of any nontrivial theoretical results?

○ **Are the programs correct?**

○ **Do they use existing theory?**

○ **Would existing theory help?**

○ **Would new theory help?**

Slide 36.

- Would the programs be substantially better if they made more use of known theory? Here I am thinking about theories of compiler optimization as well as theories of data structures, algorithms, protocols, distributed computation, and so on.

- Can you devise new theoretical results that would significantly improve the performance of the programs during the second in question?

In a sense, I'm asking questions something like the botanists considered. I'm asking to what extent computer programs have been "fertilized" by theory, and to what extent such fertilization and cross-pollination might be expected to improve our present situation. I hope many of you will be inspired to look into questions like this.

[SLIDE 37] In conclusion, let me encourage all of you to strive for a healthy balance between theory and practice in your own lives. If you find that you're spending almost all your time on theory, start turning some attention to practical things; it will improve your theories. If you find that you're spending almost all your time on practice, start turning some attention to theoretical things; it will improve your practice.

The theme of this year's IFIP Congress is Better Tools for Professionals. I believe that the best way to improve our tools is to improve the ways we blend Theory with Practice. Thank you for listening.

Acknowledgment

I wish to thank Jill Knuth for her help in preparing the slides. I am pleased to dedicate the text of this address to the memory of Andrei Ershov, whose own life was such a fine blend of theory and practice.

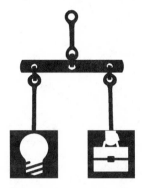

BETTER TOOLS FOR PROFESSIONALS

Slide 37.

References

[1] Pacific Bell SMART Yellow Pages for Palo Alto, Redwood City and Menlo Park, May 1989–1990, page A47.

[2] C. F. Gauss's *Werke*, volumes 10^1 and 12.

[3] Franklin Mark Liang, "Word hy-phen-a-tion by com-put-er," Ph.D. dissertation, Stanford University, August 1983.

[4] John Douglas Hobby, "Digitized brush trajectories," Ph.D. dissertation, Stanford University, September 1985.

[5] Donald E. Knuth, *Computers & Typesetting*, five volumes (Reading, Massachusetts: Addison–Wesley, 1986).

[6] Richard J. Hobbs, S. L. Gulmon, V. J. Hobbs, and H. A. Mooney, "Effects of fertilizer addition and subsequent gopher disturbance on a serpentine annual grassland community," *Œcologia* **75** (1988), 291–295.

[7] Stephen P. Hubbell and Robin B. Foster, "Canopy gaps and the dynamics of a neotropical forest," in *Plant Ecology*, ed. by Michael J. Crawley (Blackwell Scientific, 1986).

The preparation of this report was supported in part by the National Science Foundation. 'TEX' is a trademark of the American Mathematical Society. 'METAFONT' is a trademark of Addison–Wesley Publishing Company.

Chapter 10

Are Toy Problems Useful?

*[Originally published in Popular Computing **5**, 1 (January 1977), 1–10; **5**, 2 (February 1977), 3–7.]*

The instructive "Dialogue" between Fred Gruenberger and Richard Hamming in [6] raises several interesting questions. Hamming makes the following observations, among others:

> "I strongly feel that the entertainment approach to computers produces bad, long term results. ...Don't publish made up problems whose only point seems to be that it takes a machine to find the answer. ...Computing capacity is a wealth, and I deny that the ability to pay for machine time will always justify the expenditure of it even if you want to do it. ...A pied piper like you has not the right to lead children where they love going; you have some obligations to society for their time, attitudes, and the machine time you nominally control. ...A lot of your problems do not appear to be useful to anyone. I would have you pick problems that would appear to be useful to someone."

Gruenberger responds that he learned computing

> "slowly and painfully. I'm trying to shortcut the pain and time lapse for the youngsters. Just what would you have me feed them? Three-dimensional heat transfer problems? ...How to penetrate the time-sharing system so as to be able to wipe out everybody's files? ...I *don't* lead children where they love going, as you put it — far from it. If I let my kiddies alone, they'd play Star Trek all day, or write Tic-Tac-Toe programs. ...I think that computing per se is a useful thing; learning it is difficult for most people, but ... there is no reason why the task cannot be made mildly entertaining and fun."

169

These are important issues. Although I am by no means a competent philosopher, perhaps I will be able to make a few related remarks that may be useful to someone.

To set the scene, let's suppose a nationwide survey has just revealed that 95 percent of all computer time is being spent in playing games like Star Trek, Space War, or chess, or in watching Conway's "Game of Life." Would this necessarily be a bad thing? (Suppose further that 4 of the remaining 5 percent is being used by C.I.A. agents, doing what they consider to be "useful.") I suppose most people would be shocked only by the first statistic, since game-playing is usually considered a waste of time and money. Perhaps this is a vestige of Puritanism: We are admonished that it is immoral to have fun when other people are suffering. We should rather be doing something, something useful, so that ... so that ... well, so that we can have some enjoyment in future years when we retire.

Jeremy Bentham, the nineteenth-century founder of utilitarianism, did not hold any such views; he asked rather, "To what shall the character of utility be ascribed, if not to that which is a source of pleasure?" [2] Furthermore, our present culture massively accepts the value of recreational pastimes, at least in their "proper place"; people rarely question whether or not the quarterback of a pro football team has a useful occupation, although his function is merely to help win a game. Crossword puzzles and jigsaw puzzles are as popular as ever, and computer-controlled ping-pong games have swept the country. Since 50 million people can't be wrong, fun must be a Good Thing.

Yet Hamming, and many other people who do not condemn football players for pursuing a useless career, would insist that *computing* must also be useful in a stronger sense; it should not be merely entertaining. Why this double standard? I don't believe the cost of computer time is the real reason, since so much money is spent on pure entertainment. I think the real reason is that computer scientists have discovered a better way to enjoy themselves with the machines, a Higher kind of fun, so it is distressing for them to see people wasting their time with lesser amusements. A person who discovers high quality music or literature doesn't want to see masses of people listening to or reading trivial things, and the same holds for high quality computing. Thus, Hamming's point is that useful programs are more satisfying than useless ones.

Of course, we can't expect everybody to agree on what is useful or interesting or beautiful. An amusing instance of this occurs in the recent mathematics literature: Let $s(n)$ be the sum of all divisors of n less than n, so that n is a *perfect* number if and only if $n = s(n)$; two numbers m and n are called *amicable* when $s(m) = n$ and $s(n) = m$. In general one might study sequences such as $n, s(n), s(s(n)), s(s(s(n)))$, etc.; and Richard Guy and Mike Williams of the University of Calgary began their article [7] about such sequences as follows:

> "Bombieri [3] has commented on the interest of various problems in number theory, including those concerned with the iteration of arithmetic functions."

Few people are aware of the joke they are making here; for Bombieri's actual comment [3] was that these problems hold no interest at all!

Professor Guy was presumably interested enough in the subject to spend considerable time preparing his paper; and as editor of the Research Problems department of the *American Mathematical Monthly* he is unlikely to be completely off the track. Yet Bombieri, one of the world's foremost number theorists, holds a completely different view. I don't think it's easy to decide who is more correct. From a historical standpoint, one must conclude that perfect numbers (at least) are interesting, since it was the study of perfect numbers that led to the extensive theory of Mersenne primes, and Mersenne primes have recently proved to be useful in computer arithmetic. On the other hand, I am inclined to feel that most of the interesting properties of $s(n)$ have already been found, and the remaining problems are of interest only insofar as they might encourage people to sharpen certain computational and analytical tools. At any rate Guy will probably never convince Bombieri that aliquot sequences are interesting, and Bombieri will probably never convince Guy of the opposite.

Granting that tastes differ, what sorts of problems should young people be given in order to help them discover the higher levels of computer programming enjoyment? The Gruenberger–Hamming dialogue made me think back to how I learned programming. I had the disadvantage (?) of growing up before computing was taught in college, so I had to make up my own problems. I remember my first machine-language program quite well: It was to find the prime factors of a 10-digit number entered onto the computer console. As I recall, the first draft of that program involved about 50 instructions, but during a period of two weeks (while sitting at the console all night) I found and removed roughly 100 bugs. The final program, which I still have on file, was 137 words long.

My second program was radix conversion, taking a decimal number and converting it to another base $b < 10$, yet displaying the answer in the lights of our decimal computer. I don't recall much about that program, so I guess it wasn't especially interesting. Another not-very-memorable program was written in an interpretive system, over 300 lines of numeric three-address code. It found the roots of fifth degree polynomials, by finding one real root and then plugging into a quartic formula that I had found in a book. That program didn't excite me because it worked correctly the first time I ran it. (At least I thought it did.)

The next program I wrote is the one I remember most of all, since I spent two months writing and debugging it. Richard Hamming probably will say that I learned programming in *spite* of this experience, because I chose to work on one of the few things he especially denounced! Yes, my fourth program played Tic-Tac-Toe.

It did this in three different ways: (a) by following a predetermined built-in forcing strategy, (b) by examining all possible moves and choosing the best, and (c) by using past experience to learn what was good and what was bad. I was especially excited by the task of designing the program so that (c) could play against (a), (b) or (c). Incidentally, when (c) played (c) it was like blind leading the blind; after about 350 games the two sides learned to draw against each other by playing safely.

Well, I don't think I wasted computer time that summer, since I learned a lot. After the Tic-Tac-Toe experience I began to read other people's programs, especially Stan Poley's assembler and Alan Perlis's compiler, and I got hooked on software. This turned out to be even more fun, but I wouldn't have believed it when I first started. The toy problems were instrumental in helping me to think algorithmically.

That was 19 years ago. By now I have learned somewhat more about programming, but for some reason I haven't lost all interest in toy problems. I'd like to discuss two of them that recently caught my fancy, since these specific examples may shed light on the general question of problem design.

The first problem is one that Bob Floyd posed to the first-year students in our Ph.D. program at Stanford during the fall of 1972:

"The numbers $\sqrt{1}, \sqrt{2}, \ldots, \sqrt{50}$ are to be partitioned into two parts whose sum is nearly equal; find the best such partition you can, using less than 10 seconds of computer time."

For example, it turns out to be possible to find the best partition of the smaller set of numbers $\sqrt{1}, \sqrt{2}, \ldots, \sqrt{30}$ after only about one second of computer time; the answer is

$$\sqrt{2} + \sqrt{6} + \sqrt{9} + \sqrt{11} + \sqrt{12} + \sqrt{13} + \sqrt{14}$$
$$+ \sqrt{21} + \sqrt{23} + \sqrt{24} + \sqrt{25} + \sqrt{26} + \sqrt{27} + \sqrt{30}$$

$$\approx 56.04142\,25880\,73351\,85163\,20826\,;$$

$$\sqrt{1} + \sqrt{3} + \sqrt{4} + \sqrt{5} + \sqrt{7} + \sqrt{8} + \sqrt{10} + \sqrt{15}$$
$$+ \sqrt{16} + \sqrt{17} + \sqrt{18} + \sqrt{19} + \sqrt{20} + \sqrt{22} + \sqrt{28} + \sqrt{29}$$

$$\approx 56.04142\,26276\,19557\,30332\,11496\,.$$

Notice that the two sums agree to nine significant digits. The problem with 50 instead of 30 is much more difficult, and it appears hopeless to find an absolutely optimum partition in only 10 seconds. This is one of the beautiful features of Floyd's problem, since it allows for a friendly competition between the members of the class (with a tie score very unlikely), and especially because it makes the problem typical of real life situations. We are often confronted with problems that cannot be solved exactly at reasonable cost, so we must do the best we can under finite limitations. I have tried to explain in [11] why such limitations are valuable. The time restriction encourages us to think, not merely to compute!

While solving Floyd's problem, students develop a variety of important skills. They must deal with questions of how to handle large quantities of data and how to estimate computation time. The fact that square roots of numbers are involved is actually of little relevance, compared to these other issues that are of such fundamental importance in computer science. Floyd's problem is simply stated, so that a student will not get bogged down in the sea of minutiae that often is present in real-life situations; the paradigms of computer science are learned more easily when a problem is not cluttered up by extraneous details. On the other hand, the fact that square roots are involved does add just enough anomalies to keep students from confining themselves to approaches that are "too pure." For example, one thing that might be considered when solving Floyd's problem is the fact that $\sqrt{3} + \sqrt{12} = \sqrt{27}$.

For these reasons, I believe that Floyd's problem is excellent, even though it fails Hamming's criterion of "appearing to be useful to someone." The best bipartition of $\{\sqrt{1}, \sqrt{2}, \ldots, \sqrt{50}\,\}$ is hardly likely to be of any use whatever to anybody, yet one learns important skills by looking for it. After all, the purpose of computing is insight, not numbers, and one good way to demonstrate this is to take a situation where the numbers are clearly less important than the insights gained. It will not be especially interesting to know the exact value of the best partition; it is much more interesting to devise a way to compute a good approximation in less than 10 seconds.

I suggest that the reader of this article will find it very instructive to spend an hour thinking about how to solve Floyd's problem. Since I greatly enjoyed working on it, I can't restrain myself from writing down my own solution; but it would spoil your fun if I explained it now, so I have asked the editor to save that part of my article for the next issue of *Popular Computing*.

The second problem I would like to mention is perhaps most interesting because it was condemned by the great G. H. Hardy. In his fascinating little booklet, *A Mathematician's Apology* [8], Hardy explains the difference between what he calls "real" mathematics and "trivial" mathematics, and points out that this distinction is better than the conventional dichotomy between "pure" and "applied." (Hardy's "real" mathematics — the kind that has permanent aesthetic value — does however tend to be mostly pure, and what he calls "trivial" mathematics — the kind that is usually taught in schools — tends to be mostly applied.) He closes with some autobiographical remarks:

> "I have never done anything 'useful'. No discovery of mine has made, or is likely to make, directly or indirectly, for good or ill, the least difference to the amenity of the world. ... I have just one chance, ... that I may be judged to have created something worth creating."

Thus we get some idea of his philosophy.

In Section 15 of Hardy's book he begins to explain what a "serious" or "significant" mathematical theorem is, by giving two examples of insignificant ones. His second example is the fact that there are just four numbers (greater than 1) equal to the sums of the cubes of their digits, namely

$$153 = 1^3 + 5^3 + 3^3, \qquad 371 = 3^3 + 7^3 + 1^3,$$
$$370 = 3^3 + 7^3 + 0^3, \qquad 407 = 4^3 + 0^3 + 7^3.$$

He calls this an odd fact, "very suitable for puzzle columns and likely to amuse amateurs, ... [but the proof is] neither difficult nor interesting — merely a little tiresome."

In other words, Hardy considered this problem to be *worse* than useless. Yet I recently devoted a fair amount of time to discovering such odd facts as these (cf. [12]):

$$94204591914 = 9^{11} + 4^{11} + 2^{11} + 0^{11} + 4^{11}$$
$$+ 5^{11} + 9^{11} + 1^{11} + 9^{11} + 1^{11} + 4^{11};$$
$$564240140138 = 5^{13} + 6^{13} + 4^{13} + 2^{13} + 4^{13}$$
$$+ 0^{13} + 1^{13} + 4^{13} + 0^{13} + 1^{13} + 3^{13} + 8^{13}.$$

There are no solutions with exponent 12, and the unique solution for exponent 10 is 4679307774; there are eight solutions with exponent 11. Although I completely agree with Hardy that the results are mathematically trivial, I cannot agree that the proof (in this case, by computer of course) was uninteresting; in order to avoid considering a large number of cases I had to devise a technique that might be called "double backtracking." Thus I found the problem quite instructive, although I certainly don't consider it the most important thing I have ever done.

Hardy himself made the following remarks in another part of [8]:

> "One rather curious conclusion emerges, that pure mathematics is distinctly more useful than applied. ... For what is useful above all is *technique*, and mathematical technique is taught mainly through pure mathematics."

And that is precisely why I liked this useless problem: Computational technique is taught mainly through pure computer science.

Most of the exercises in calculus books are strictly academic, without any indication of how they might connect to the real world; and my point is that there is good reason for this, because actual applications are usually full of exceptions to the rules and other things that distract from the main principles a student is presently learning. Furthermore it is usually necessary to have a fair amount of background knowledge in a particular application area before a "useful" problem can properly be appreciated. With a diverse group of students, suitable real-world applications are rare, but when the students have a common background it may well be that three-dimensional heat transfer problems are the most exciting and instructive.

Of course we should not make the mistake of saying that pure problems are the only good ones. I'm arguing that they have a well-deserved place in a person's education, but an education is woefully inadequate if it is based purely on such problems. We should remember Gibbon's criticism of the Greeks: "The whole of life was spent studying the art of reasoning, and never in actually reasoning." [5]

Thus it is extremely important to learn how to connect theory with practice — to learn that theory builds up our conceptual apparatus but that we rarely actually use a concept in the way we originally learn it. The limitations of a formalism must be understood clearly; I have written elsewhere about some of the more notorious abuses of computer science theory [9].

We need to know how to deal with complicated systems of rules and exceptions. That is why, for example, I have included a detailed description of a real-life elevator system in the first volume of my books on programming, and why I intend to discuss COBOL's "picture clauses" at some length in Volume 5.

One of the most difficult tasks I had to face when writing the third volume [10] was the preparation of Section 5.4.6, "Practical Considerations for Tape Merging"; for it deals with precisely this question of how theory combines with practice, a question that is almost never discussed in the literature. I wanted to explain how real magnetic tape units operate; this led to the complexities of interblock gaps, start/stop time, dual rewind mechanisms, read/write/compute overlap, and the finiteness of tape, besides the problems of allocating an appropriate amount of buffer space and waiting for the computer operator to change reels. I found that most of the literature's "improved" methods, which looked so good on paper, actually performed poorly in practice, compared to the simpler methods of the 1940s. I had to change these "improved" methods drastically before they really represented any improvement. I also found it necessary to bend the theoretical formulas so that they would appropriately model the real-world assumptions without becoming too detailed.

Since I feel that Section 5.4.6 teaches some very important lessons, I guess I'm proud of how it came out, in spite of its imperfections. Therefore I have been disappointed to find that most of my students aren't especially interested in this section. Their reason is that tapes are being replaced by disks nowadays. In other words, my discussion of "practical considerations" has become largely a toy problem, since the technology has changed! Although everybody would have loved this section in 1966, many of the students would rather not read it at all in 1976; they fail to realize that technology will have changed again by 1986, when they will want to apply their education. The important thing for them to learn now is the methodology of combining theory with practice, not the details of 1976 practice. The former will last a lifetime, but the latter will soon be obsolete. I believe Section 5.4.6 should continue to be interesting and relevant even after the last magnetic tape unit has vanished from the earth, but I will probably replace it by something else in the next edition of [10].

Perhaps I can summarize all of these remarks by saying that *methods are more important than facts*. The educational value of a problem given to a student depends mostly on how often the thought processes that are invoked to solve it will be helpful in later situations. It has little to do with how useful the answer to the problem may be.

On the other hand, a good problem must also motivate the students; they should be interested in seeing the answer. Since students differ so greatly, I can't expect everyone to like the problems that please me. Floyd's problem and the powers-of-digits problem will probably leave many people cold, especially those who are not already somewhat fluent in algorithmic thinking, and I don't expect that every student will be excited about tape sorting in spite of my enthusiastic endorsement. A wide variety of problems is certainly needed, but "usefulness" should not be the main consideration.

[Readers should now work on Floyd's problem, and wait one month, before reading on.]

An Approach to Floyd's Problem

Last month I discussed some of the virtues of Floyd's problem, which is to divide the numbers

$$\sqrt{1}, \ \sqrt{2}, \ \ldots, \ \sqrt{50}$$

into two parts whose sums are as equal as you can make them after ten seconds of computer time. Here is the way I decided to approach the subject; perhaps some reader will have a much better idea.

Since $(\sqrt{1} + \sqrt{2} + \cdots + \sqrt{50}\,)/2$ is equal to

$$119.51790\,03017\,60392\,24702\,02231\ldots,$$

we seek the subset of $\{\sqrt{1}, \sqrt{2}, \ldots, \sqrt{50}\,\}$ whose sum least exceeds this value.

In the first place it is helpful to estimate the kind of results that might be expected. Most subsets of the given set have about 25 elements, and in fact the number of subsets with exactly 25 elements is $50!/25!\,25!$; this is about

$$\frac{2^{50}}{\sqrt{25\pi}},$$

according to Stirling's approximation. [The exact number is 126,410, 606,437,752, compared to $2^{50} = 1,125,899,906,842,624$.] All of these subsets have a sum that lies between $\sqrt{1} + \sqrt{2} + \cdots + \sqrt{25} \approx 85.6$ and $\sqrt{26} + \sqrt{27} + \cdots + \sqrt{50} \approx 153.4$, and they tend to cluster about the average value 119.5. So we have more than 10^{14} numbers packed into an interval of length less than 70; therefore $70/10^{14}$ appears to be a conservative estimate for the amount by which the best partitioning exceeds $(\sqrt{1} + \sqrt{2} + \cdots + \sqrt{50}\,)/2$.

But not all of these subsets will give different sums. In the first place, the seven numbers

$$\sqrt{1}, \ \sqrt{4}, \ \ldots, \ \sqrt{49} \ \ = \ \ 1, \ 2, \ \ldots, \ 7$$

will yield only integer values (and it is easy to verify that each integer from 0 to 28 can be represented). Our problem therefore reduces to finding a subset of the 43 numbers

$$\{\sqrt{2}, \ \sqrt{3}, \ \sqrt{5}, \ \sqrt{6}, \ \ldots, \ \sqrt{48}, \ \sqrt{50}\,\}$$

whose sum has a *fraction part* least exceeding

$$0.51790\,03017\,60392\,24702\,.$$

Unless the integer part of the sum is unusually large or small, we will be able to adjust it by adding a suitable subset of $\{1, 2, \ldots, 7\}$, bringing the integer part up to 119.

We now have 2^{43} possibilities to try; but *they* aren't all distinct, either. The values

$$\{\sqrt{2}, \ \sqrt{8}, \ \sqrt{18}, \ \sqrt{32}, \ \sqrt{50}\,\} \ = \ \{\sqrt{2}, \ 2\sqrt{2}, \ 3\sqrt{2}, \ 4\sqrt{2}, \ 5\sqrt{2}\,\}$$

lead to subsets whose sum is restricted to sixteen values

$$0, \ \sqrt{2}, \ 2\sqrt{2}, \ \ldots, \ 15\sqrt{2}\,;$$

so only 16 of the 32 subsets are different. Similarly, there are only eleven essentially different subsets of

$$\{\sqrt{3}, \ \sqrt{12}, \ \sqrt{27}, \ \sqrt{48}\,\}$$

to try. By means of these observations our program can do in 10 seconds what it would take $10 \cdot 32 \cdot 16/(16 \cdot 11) \approx 29$ seconds to do otherwise.

But there are still more than $2^{41} > 10^{12}$ possibilities remaining, and this is far too large; if it takes 100 microseconds for me to test one subset, I have time to test only 10^5 subsets.

One way to gain speed is to divide

$$\{\sqrt{2}, \ \sqrt{3}, \ \sqrt{5}, \ \sqrt{6}, \ \ldots, \ \sqrt{48}, \ \sqrt{50}\,\}$$

into two parts A and B, and to form a table containing all sums of the subsets of A. Then for each subset of B we can look in the table to see if there is an entry with the appropriate leading bits.

That is what I eventually did. Let

$$A = \{\sqrt{2},\ \sqrt{8},\ \sqrt{18},\ \sqrt{32},\ \sqrt{50},\ \sqrt{3},\ \sqrt{12},\ \sqrt{27},\ \sqrt{48},$$
$$\sqrt{5},\ \sqrt{6},\ \sqrt{7},\ \sqrt{10},\ \sqrt{11},\ \sqrt{13},\ \sqrt{14},\ \sqrt{15}\,\},$$

so that the subsets of A take on $\frac{11}{16} \cdot 2^{16}$ different values. I stored the 32 leading bits of these fraction parts into a hash table of size 2^{16}, and in another table of size 2^{16} I stored a bit pattern identifying the corresponding subset. (The hash code was the low order 16 bits of each 32-bit key.) Let $B = \{\sqrt{17}, \sqrt{19}, \sqrt{20}, \ldots, \sqrt{47}\,\}$ be the remaining set of 26 elements; in the machine I used only the 32 leading bits of the fraction parts of each number $\sqrt{k}$. Since my hash table contained $\frac{11}{16} \cdot 2^{16}$ more-or-less random 32-bit numbers, I expected to get a match once out of every $2^{32}/(\frac{11}{16} \cdot 2^{16}) = \frac{16}{11} \cdot 2^{16}$ times I looked up another 32-bit value. Therefore I wanted to have a program that generated 2^{17} or so subsets S of B, looking up the 32 bits corresponding to $(.51790\ldots - \sum S) \bmod 1$ in the hash table. I figured that such a sampling would probably give me two or three matches, and I could choose the best corresponding partition. But I would have only about 75 to 80 microseconds to spend per subset, so I needed a fast way to probe the hash table and to generate the subset sums.

The solution was to use *ordered* hash tables with linear probing; this is a variant of hashing that Ole Amble and I had discovered a few years ago [1]. Such hash tables are especially well suited to cases when searches are unsuccessful, requiring only 2.1 probes per search in this case. For the subset generation, I used Gray code [4], since this meant that only one subset element changed state each time and the subset sum was therefore easy to update. It took about 1.5 seconds to build the hash table. I started the subset generation of B in a random part of its cycle, since I knew that I would be able to look at only a small fraction of its subsets.

The best of the three results I got before 10 seconds expired was actually typed out after only 6 seconds, namely

$$\sqrt{2} + \sqrt{3} + \sqrt{4} + \sqrt{5} + \sqrt{6} + \sqrt{8} + \sqrt{12} + \sqrt{17} + \sqrt{18}$$
$$+ \sqrt{19} + \sqrt{22} + \sqrt{27} + \sqrt{28} + \sqrt{29} + \sqrt{33} + \sqrt{34} + \sqrt{35}$$
$$+ \sqrt{37} + \sqrt{38} + \sqrt{40} + \sqrt{42} + \sqrt{45} + \sqrt{46} + \sqrt{49} + \sqrt{50}$$
$$\approx 119.51790\,03021\,65123\,39726\,54768\,.$$

This sum differs from its complementary sum by approximately $8 \cdot 10^{-10}$. (The optimum partition might well be a thousand times better, as mentioned above; my program could have found it if 10 thousand seconds were available instead of ten!)

I used a fairly large and fast computer, the DECsystem KL-10 at Stanford's Artificial Intelligence Laboratory. If I had used a slower machine, I would have cut down the number of bits in each hash table entry from 32 to something less, one bit per factor of two in speed. If I had used a smaller machine, I would have had to make the hash table smaller.

If I really wanted to get the optimum partition, I think it could be found in about 30 minutes. The best approach I can think of would be to divide the 43 irrational numbers into two subsets having respectively $\frac{11}{16} \cdot 2^{21}$ and $\frac{7}{8} \cdot 2^{21}$ distinct sums. (The factor $\frac{7}{8}$ comes from the seven essentially different subsets of $\{\sqrt{5}, \sqrt{20}, \sqrt{45}\}$.) I would sort each of these files of sums by their fraction parts; since each file contains about two million entries, this would be the time-consuming part of the operation. (Instead of using a general-purpose sort routine I would write a special one, since it is easy to go from the sorted file for set A to the twice-as-long sorted file for $A \cup \{a\}$ by essentially merging the first file with a shifted version of itself. The total time to build the sorted set for A when A has n elements is therefore of order 2^n, while a general-purpose sort routine would take order $n \cdot 2^n$ steps.) Finally, given two large sorted files

$$x_1 \leq \cdots \leq x_m \qquad \text{and} \qquad y_1 \leq \cdots \leq y_n$$

and a number z, there is a nice algorithm that computes

$$\min\{x_i + y_j \mid x_i + y_j \geq z\}.$$

Readers will enjoy discovering this algorithm for themselves. Curiously it is essentially the same as Hamming's "p/q" algorithm in [6], under a logarithmic transformation, with $x_p = \log p$ and $y_q = \log(1/q)$.

I tested my hashing program by trying it first on

$$\{\sqrt{1}, \sqrt{2}, \ldots, \sqrt{30}\}$$

and then on

$$\{\sqrt{1}, \sqrt{2}, \ldots, \sqrt{40}\}.$$

I gave the optimum partition for the former case in the first part of this article; and I think I found the optimum partition also in the latter case:

$$\sqrt{2} + \sqrt{5} + \sqrt{7} + \sqrt{13} + \sqrt{14} + \sqrt{17} + \sqrt{18} + \sqrt{19} + \sqrt{22} + \sqrt{23}$$
$$+ \sqrt{24} + \sqrt{26} + \sqrt{27} + \sqrt{29} + \sqrt{30} + \sqrt{32} + \sqrt{34} + \sqrt{38} + \sqrt{39}$$
$$\approx 85.80789\,40023\,46\,;$$
$$\sqrt{1} + \sqrt{3} + \sqrt{4} + \sqrt{6} + \sqrt{8} + \sqrt{9} + \cdots + \sqrt{40} \approx 85.80789\,40021\,54\,.$$

However, I am not absolutely sure that this is the best, because there is a slight chance that an unusual rounding error might have occurred somewhere in the calculations.

I still think that the 10-second-limited problem is more interesting. According to Hamming's famous aphorism, the purpose of computing is insight, and I believe this problem brings some valuable insights into view.

Postscript: R. L. Graham recently told me about the following sets of nine square roots whose sums agree to 53 decimal places:

$$\sqrt{100000001} + \sqrt{100000025} + \sqrt{100000031} + \sqrt{100000084} + \sqrt{100000087}$$
$$+ \sqrt{100000134} + \sqrt{100000158} + \sqrt{100000182} + \sqrt{100000198}$$
$$= 90000.04499\,99835\,67513\,39873\,55931\,30141\,27033$$
$$05198\,22215\,69856\,20248\,663\ldots\,;$$

$$\sqrt{100000002} + \sqrt{100000018} + \sqrt{100000042} + \sqrt{100000066} + \sqrt{100000113}$$
$$+ \sqrt{100000116} + \sqrt{100000169} + \sqrt{100000175} + \sqrt{100000199}$$
$$= 90000.04499\,99835\,67513\,39873\,55931\,30141\,27033$$
$$05198\,22215\,69856\,20281\,826\ldots\,.$$

To find the secret of his construction, see Hardy and Wright, *An Introduction to the Theory of Numbers*, 4th edition, page 338 (notes on Section 21.10).

References

[1] Ole Amble and Donald E. Knuth, "Ordered hash tables," *The Computer Journal* **17** (May 1974), 135–142.

[2] Jeremy Bentham, *The Rationale of Reward*, Book 3, Chapter 1. (First published in 1811.)

[3] Felix E. Browder, ed., "Problems of present day mathematics," in *Mathematical Developments Arising from Hilbert's Problems, Proceedings of Symposia in Pure Mathematics* **28** (American Mathematical Society, 1976), 35–80, Section 2A.

[4] Martin Gardner, "Mathematical Games," *Scientific American* **227** (August 1972), 106–109. Reprinted in his *Knotted Doughnuts and Other Mathematical Entertainments* (W. H. Freeman, 1986), 11–27.

[5] Edward Gibbon, *Mémoires de l'Académie des Inscriptions* **6** (1729), 151; quoted in Giuseppe Giarrizzo, "Gibbon's other historical interests," *Daedalus* **105** (1976), 49–62.

[6] Fred Gruenberger and Richard Hamming, "Dialogue," *Popular Computing* **4**, 8 (August 1976), 3–7.

[7] Richard K. Guy and M. R. Williams, "Aliquot sequences near 10^{12}," *Proceedings of the Fourth Manitoba Conference on Numerical Mathematics* (1974), 387–406.

[8] G. H. Hardy, *A Mathematician's Apology* (Cambridge University Press, 1940). The 1967 edition of this book includes an informative introduction by C. P. Snow.

[9] Donald E. Knuth, "The dangers of computer science theory," in *Logic, Methodology, and Philosophy of Science* **4**, ed. by P. Suppes et al. (North-Holland, 1973), 189–195.

[10] Donald E. Knuth, *Sorting and Searching*, Vol. 3 of *The Art of Computer Programming* (Reading, Massachusetts: Addison–Wesley, 1973).

[11] Donald E. Knuth, "Computer programming as an art," *Communications of the ACM* **17** (1974), 667–673, especially the section called "Less Facilities: More Enjoyment." Reprinted in *ACM Turing Award Lectures* (New York: ACM Press, 1987), 33–46. [Also reprinted as Chapter 1 of *Literate Programming*.]

[12] Benjamin L. Schwartz, "Self-generating integers," *Mathematics Magazine* **46** (1973), 158–160.

Addendum

While preparing this book for publication, I decided to try Floyd's problem on the computer I now have at home, a vintage 1992 workstation (SPARC 2), in spite of the fact that I claim to be uninterested in the answer. Using a slight improvement of the method sketched above, I found the exact solution after 26 seconds of computation:

$$\sqrt{2} + \sqrt{3} + \sqrt{6} + \sqrt{10} + \sqrt{11} + \sqrt{14} + \sqrt{17} + \sqrt{18} + \sqrt{19}$$
$$+ \sqrt{21} + \sqrt{22} + \sqrt{23} + \sqrt{24} + \sqrt{26} + \sqrt{28} + \sqrt{29} + \sqrt{32}$$
$$+ \sqrt{34} + \sqrt{35} + \sqrt{36} + \sqrt{39} + \sqrt{40} + \sqrt{42} + \sqrt{45} + \sqrt{50}$$
$$\approx 119.51790\,03017\,60463\,73981\,.$$

This sum differs from its complement by approximately 1.4×10^{-13}, so it is more than 5000 times better than the 10-second solution that I found in 1976. The improved procedure avoids storing the two files of $\approx 2^{21}$ numbers in memory; instead, one can use x_i and y_j "on the fly" as they are generated, since the top-level algorithm merely needs to increase i by 1 or decrease j by 1 as it examines each x_i and y_j only once, and since the files can be generated in sorted order by a multiway merge of shifts of shorter files using the "tree of losers" technique [10, Section 5.4.1].

I also confirmed the optimality of the stated result for $\{\sqrt{1}, \sqrt{2}, \ldots,$ $\sqrt{40}\}$, in 1.4 seconds. Here there is a surprising non-solution that brings the fractional parts closer, yet cannot be extended to make the integer parts agree because the subset is so small:

$$\sqrt{7} + \sqrt{10} + \sqrt{11} + \sqrt{12} + \sqrt{17} + \sqrt{18} + \sqrt{20}$$
$$+ \sqrt{30} + \sqrt{32} + \sqrt{37} + \sqrt{38} \approx 48.80789\,40022\,73886\,91674\,.$$

Chapter 11

Ancient Babylonian Algorithms

[Written for the 25th birthday of the Association for Computing Machinery. Originally published in Communications of the ACM **15** *(1972), 671–677;* **19** *(1976), 108.]*

One of the ways to help make computer science respectable is to show that it is deeply rooted in history, not just a short-lived phenomenon. Therefore it is natural to turn to the earliest surviving documents that deal with computation, and to study how people approached the subject nearly 4000 years ago. Archaeological expeditions in the Middle East have unearthed a large number of clay tablets that contain mathematical calculations, and we shall see that these tablets give many interesting clues about the life of early "computer scientists."

Introduction to Babylonian Mathematics

The tablets in question come from the general area of Mesopotamia (present day Iraq), between the Tigris and Euphrates rivers, centered more or less about the ancient city of Babylon near present-day Baghdad. Each tablet is covered with cuneiform (i.e., "wedge-shaped") script, a form of writing that goes back to about 3000 B.C. The tablets of greatest mathematical interest were written about the time of the Hammurabi dynasty, about 1800–1600 B.C., and the following comments are based primarily on texts that date from this so-called Old-Babylonian period.

It is well known that Babylonians worked in a *sexagesimal* (radix 60) number system, and that our present sexagesimal units of hours, minutes, and seconds are vestiges of their system. But it is less widely known that the Babylonians actually worked with *floating-point* sexagesimal numbers, using a rather peculiar notation that did not include

185

any exponent part. Thus, the two-digit number

$$2,20$$

stood for $2 \times 60 + 20 = 140$, and for $2 + 20/60 = 2\frac{1}{3}$, and for $2/60 + 20/3600$, and in general for 140×60^n, where n is any integer.

At first sight this manner of representing numbers may look quite awkward, but in fact it has significant advantages when multiplication and division are involved. We use the same principle today when we do calculations by slide rule, performing the multiplications and divisions without regard to the decimal point location and then supplying the appropriate power of 10 later. A Babylonian mathematician computing with numbers that were meaningful to him could easily keep the appropriate power of 60 in mind, since it is not difficult to estimate the range of a value within a factor of 60. A few instances have been found where addition was performed incorrectly because the radix points were improperly aligned [10, p. 28], but such examples are surprisingly rare.

As an indication of the utility of this floating-point notation, consider the following table of *reciprocals*:

2	30	16	3,45	45	1,20
3	20	18	3,20	48	1,15
4	15	20	3	50	1,12
5	12	24	2,30	54	1,6,40
6	10	25	2,24	1	1
8	7,30	27	2,13,20	1,4	56,15
9	6,40	30	2	1,12	50
10	6	32	1,52,30	1,15	48
12	5	36	1,40	1,20	45
15	4	40	1,30	1,21	44,26,40

Dozens of tablets containing this information have been found, some of which go back as far as the "Ur III dynasty" of about 2250 B.C. There also are many multiplication tables that list the multiples of these numbers; for example, division by $81 = 1,21$ is equivalent to multiplying by 44,26,40, and tables of $44,26,40 \times k$ for $1 \le k \le 20$ and $k = 30, 40, 50$ were commonplace. Over two hundred examples of multiplication tables have been catalogued; they may represent student work.

Babylonian "Programming"

The Babylonian mathematicians were not limited simply to the processes of addition, subtraction, multiplication, and division; they were adept at solving many types of algebraic equations. But they did not have an algebraic notation that is quite as transparent as ours. They represented each formula by a step-by-step list of rules for its evaluation, i.e., by an algorithm for computing that formula. In effect, they worked with a "machine language" representation of formulas instead of a symbolic high-level language.

The flavor of Babylonian mathematics can best be appreciated by studying several examples. The translations below attempt to render the words of the original texts as faithfully as possible into good English, without extensive editorial interpretation. Several remarks have been added in parentheses, to explain some of the things that were originally unstated on the tablets. All numbers are presented Babylonian-style, without exponents; readers are warned that they will have to supply an appropriate scale factor mentally. It is necessary to remember that 1 might mean 60 and 15 might mean $\frac{1}{4}$.

The first example we shall discuss is excerpted from an Old-Babylonian tablet that was originally about $5 \times 8 \times 1$ inches in size. Half of it now appears in the British Museum, about one-fourth appears in the Staatliche Museen, Berlin, and the other fourth has apparently been lost or destroyed over the years. The original text appears in [6, pp. 193–199], [7, Tables 7, 8, 39, 40], and [13, pp. 11–21]; Assyriologists refer to it by the museum accession numbers BM 85200 and VAT 6599.

A (rectangular) cistern.

The height is 3,20, and a volume of 27,46,40 has been excavated.

The length exceeds the width by 50. (The object is to find the length and the width.)

You should take the reciprocal of the height, 3,20, obtaining 18.

Multiply this by the volume, 27,46,40, obtaining 8,20. (This is the length times the width; the problem has been reduced to finding x and y, given that $x - y = 50$ and $xy = 8,20$. A standard procedure for solving such equations, which occurs repeatedly in Babylonian manuscripts, is now used.)

Take half of 50 and square it, obtaining 10,25.

Add 8,20, and you get 8,30,25. (The radix point position always needs to be supplied. In this case, 50 stands for $\frac{5}{6}$ and 8,20 stands for $8\frac{1}{3}$, taking into account the sizes of typical cisterns.)

The square root is 2,55.

Make two copies of this, adding (25) to the one and subtracting from the other.

You find that 3,20 (namely $3\frac{1}{3}$) is the length and 2,30 (namely $2\frac{1}{2}$) is the width.

This is the procedure.

The first step here is to divide 27,46,40 by 3,20; this is reduced to multiplication by the reciprocal. The multiplication may have been done by referring to tables, most likely by manipulating stones or sand in some manner and then writing down the answer. The square root was also probably computed by referring to tables, since we know that many tables of n vs. n^2 existed. In modern notation, the stated rule for computing the values of x and y such that $x - y = d$ and $xy = p$ was to form

$$\sqrt{(d/2)^2 + p} \pm (d/2) \,.$$

The calculations described in Babylonian tablets are not merely the solutions to specific individual problems; they actually are general procedures for solving a whole class of problems. The numbers shown are merely included as an aid to exposition, in order to clarify the general method. This fact is clear because there are numerous instances where a particular case of the general method reduces to multiplying by 1. Such multiplications were explicitly carried out, in order to abide by the general rules. Notice also the stereotyped ending, "This is the procedure," which is commonly found at the end of each section on a tablet. The procedures are genuine algorithms, and we can commend the Babylonians for developing a nice way to explain an algorithm by example as the algorithm itself is being defined.

Here is another excerpt from the same tablet, this time involving only a linear equation:

A cistern.
The length (in cubits) equals the height (in gars, where 1 gar = 12 cubits).
A certain volume of dirt has been excavated.
The cross-sectional area (in square cubits) plus this volume (in cubic cubits) comes to 1,10 (namely $1\frac{1}{6}$).
The length is 30 (namely $\frac{1}{2}$ cubit). What is the width?
You should multiply the length, 30, by 12, obtaining 6; this is the height (in cubits instead of gars).
Add 1 to 6, and you get 7.
The reciprocal of 7 does not exist; what will give 1,10 when multiplied by 7? 10 will. (Hence 10, namely $\frac{1}{6}$, is the cross-sectional area in square cubits.)
Take the reciprocal of 30, obtaining 2.
Multiply 10 by 2, obtaining the width, 20 (namely $\frac{1}{3}$ cubit).
This is the procedure.

Notice the interesting way in which the Babylonians disregarded units, blithely adding area to volume. Similar examples abound, showing that the *numerical* algebra was of primary importance to them, not the physical or geometrical significance of the problems. At the same time they used conventional units of measure (cubits, even "gars" and the understood relation between gars and cubits), in order to set the scale factors for the parameters. And they "applied" their results to practical things like cisterns, perhaps because this would make their work appear to be socially relevant.

In this problem it was necessary to divide by 7, but the reciprocal of 7 didn't appear on the tables because it has no finite reciprocal. (We have no evidence that the Babylonians knew the expansion $1/7 = 8,34,17,8,34,17,\ldots$, which repeats endlessly.) In such cases where the reciprocal table was of no avail, the text always says, in effect, "What shall I multiply by a in order to obtain b?" and then the answer is given. This wording indicates that a multiplication table should be used backwards; for example, the calculation of $11,40 \div 35 = 20$ [6, p. 329] could be read off from a multiplication table. For more difficult divisions, e.g., $43,20 \div 1,26,40 = 30$, a slightly different wording was used (see [6, p. 246] and [8, p. 8]), indicating perhaps that a special division procedure was employed in such cases. At any rate we know that the Babylonians were able to compute

$$7 \div 2,6; \qquad 28,20 \div 17; \qquad 10,12,45 \div 40,51;$$

and similar quotients.

Further Examples

We have noted that general algorithms were usually given, accompanied by a sample calculation. In rare instances such as the following text (again from the British Museum, tablet BM 34568), the style is somewhat different [8, p. 19]:

> The sum of length, width, and diagonal is 1,10 and 7 is the area.
> What are the corresponding length, width, and diagonal?
> The quantities are unknown.
> 1,10 times 1,10 is 1,21,40.
> 7 times 2 is 14.
> Take 14 from 1,21,40 and 1,7,40 remains.
> 1,7,40 times 30 is 33,50.
> By what should 1,10 be multiplied to obtain 33,50?
> 1,10 times 29 is 33,50.
> 29 is the diagonal.

The sum of length, width, and diagonal is 12 and 12 is the area.
What are the corresponding length, width, and diagonal?
The quantities are unknown.
12 times 12 is 2,24.
12 times 2 is 24.
Take 24 from 2,24 and 2 remains.
2 times 30 is 1.
By what should 12 be multiplied to obtain 1?
12 times 5 is 1.
5 is the diagonal.

The sum of length, width, and diagonal is 1 and 5 is the area.
Multiply length, width, and diagonal times length, width, and diagonal.
Multiply the area by 2.
Subtract the products and multiply what is left by one-half.
By what should the sum of length, width, and diagonal be multiplied to obtain this product?
The diagonal is the factor.

This text comes from the considerably later Seleucid period of Babylonian history (see below), which may account for the difference in style. It treats a problem based on the rather remarkable formula

$$d = \tfrac{1}{2}\big((l + w + d)^2 - 2A\big)/(l + w + d),$$

where
$A = lw$ is the area of a rectangle,

$d = \sqrt{(l^2 + w^2)}$ is the length of its diagonals.

There is ample evidence from other texts that the so-called Pythagorean theorem was known already to Old-Babylonian mathematicians, more than 1000 years before the time of Pythagoras. The first two sections quoted above work out the problem for the cases $(l, w, d) = (20, 21, 29)$ and $(3, 4, 5)$ respectively, but without calculating l and w; we know from other tablets that the solution to $x + y = a$, $x^2 + y^2 = b$ was well known in ancient times. The description of the calculation in these two sections is unusually terse, not naming the quantities it is dealing with. On the other hand, the third section gives the *same* procedure entirely *without* numbers. Perhaps the writer was unable to deduce appropriate powers of 60 to attach to the parameters 1 and 5 when it was time to do the subtraction; to a teacher of computer science, this passage is reminiscent of a student's examination paper when an impossible problem has been posed. However, one solution with rational parameters is $l = 15$, $w = 20$, $d = 25$, $l + w + d = 60$, $lw = 5 \cdot 60$. Notice that the second section of the tablet being quoted follows the general procedure as stated in the third section very faithfully, when it comes to dividing 1 by 12, instead of using the reciprocal of 12.

Instances of algorithms without accompanying numbers are very rare. Here is another one, this time an Old-Babylonian text from the Louvre, tablet number AO 6770 ([7, p. 39] and [13, p. 71]):

> Length and width is to be equal to the area.
> You should proceed as follows.
> Make two copies of one parameter.
> Subtract 1.
> Form the reciprocal.
> Multiply by the parameter you copied.
> This gives the width.

In other words, if $x + y = xy$, it is possible to compute y by the procedure $y = (x - 1)^{-1} x$. The fact that no numbers are given made this passage particularly hard to decipher, and it was not properly understood for many years (see [14, pp. 73–74]); hence we can see the advantages of numerical examples.

This procedure reads surprisingly like a program for a "stack machine" like the Burroughs B5500. We are told, as in the very first example that we discussed, to make two copies of some number; this indicates that actual numerical calculations generally destroyed the operands in the process of finding a result. Similarly we find in many texts the instruction to "Keep this number in your head" (e.g., [9, pp. 50–51]), a remarkable parallelism with today's notion that a computer stores numbers in its "memory." In another place we read, in essence, "Replace the sum of length and width by 30 times itself" [6, p. 114], an ancient version of the assignment statement "$x := x/2$".

Conditionals and Iterations

So far we have seen only straight-line calculations, without any branching or decision-making involved. In order to construct algorithms that are really nontrivial from a computer scientist's point of view, we need to have some operations that affect the flow of control.

But alas, there is very little evidence of this in the Babylonian texts. The only thing resembling a conditional branch is implicit in the operation of division, where the calculation usually proceeds a little differently if the reciprocal of the divisor does not appear in the table.

We don't find tests like "Go to step 4 if $x < 0$", because the Babylonians didn't have negative numbers; we don't even find conditional tests like "Go to step 5 if $x = 0$", because they didn't treat zero as a number either. Instead of having such tests, they effectively gave separate algorithms for the different cases. (For example, see [6, pp. 312–314] for a situation in which one algorithm is step-by-step identical to another, but simplified since one of the parameters is zero.)

Nor are there many instances of iteration. The basic operations underlying the multiplication of high-precision sexagesimal numbers obviously involve iteration, and these operations were clearly understood by the Babylonian mathematicians; but the rules were apparently never written down. No examples showing intermediate steps in multiplication have been found.

The following interesting example dealing with compound interest, taken from the Berlin Museum collection (VAT 8528), is one of the few examples of a "DO I=1 TO N" in the Babylonian tablets that have been excavated so far (see [6, pp. 353–365]; [7, Tables 32, 56, 57]; [8, p. 59]; [13, pp. 118–120]):

> I invested 1 maneh of silver, at a rate of 12 shekels per maneh (per year, with interest apparently compounded every five years)
> I received, as capital plus interest, 1 talent and 4 manehs.
> (Here 1 maneh = 60 shekels, and 1 talent = 60 manehs.)
> How many years did this take?
> Let 1 be the initial capital.
> Let 1 maneh earn 12 (shekels) interest in a 6 (=360) day year.
> And let 1,4 be the capital plus interest.
> Compute 12, the interest, per 1 unit of initial capital, giving 12 as the interest rate.
> Multiply 12 by 5 years, giving 1.
> Thus in five years the interest will equal the initial capital.
> Add 1, the five-year interest to 1, the initial capital, obtaining 2.
> Form the reciprocal of 2, obtaining 30.
> Multiply 30 by 1,4, the sum of capital plus interest, obtaining 32.
> Find the inverse of 2, obtaining 1. (The "inverse" here means the logarithm to base 2; in other problems it stands for the value of n such that a given value $f(n)$ appears in some table.)
> Form the reciprocal of 2, obtaining 30.

Multiply 30 by 30 (the latter 30 apparently stands for $32 - 2$, for otherwise the 32 would never be used and the rest of the calculation would make no sense) obtaining 15 (= total interest without initial capital if the investment had been cashed in five years earlier).

Add 1 to 15, obtaining 16.

Find the inverse of 16, obtaining 4.

Add the two inverses 4 and 1, obtaining 5.

Multiply 5 by 5 years, obtaining 25.

Add another 5 years, making 30.

Thus, after the 30th year the initial capital and its interest will be 1,4.

... (Here about 4 lines of the text have broken off. Apparently there is now a question of checking the previous answer.)

... giving 12 as the interest rate.

Multiply 12 by 5 years, giving 1.

Thus in five years the interest will equal the initial capital.

Add 1, the five-year interest, to 1, the initial capital, obtaining 2, the capital and its interest after the fifth year.

Add 5 years to the 5 years, obtaining 10 years.

Double 2, the capital and its interest, obtaining 4, the capital and its interest after the tenth year.

Add 5 years to the 10 years, obtaining 15 years.

Double 4, the capital and its interest, obtaining 8, the capital and its interest after the fifteenth year.

Add 5 years to the 15 years, obtaining 20 years.

Double 8, obtaining 16, the capital and its interest after the twentieth year.

Add 5 years to the 20 years, obtaining 25 years.

Double 16, the capital and its interest, obtaining 32, the capital and its interest after the twenty-fifth year.

Add 5 years to the 25 years, obtaining 30 years.

Double 32, the capital and its interest, obtaining 1,4, the capital and its interest after the thirtieth year.

This long-winded and rather clumsy procedure reads almost like a macro expansion !

A more sophisticated example involving compound interest appears in another section of the Louvre tablet quoted earlier. The same usurious rate of interest (20 percent per annum) occurs, but now compounded annually:

One kur (of grain) has been invested; after how many years will the interest be equal to the initial capital?

You should proceed as follows.

Compound the interest for four years.

The combined total (capital + interest) exceeds 2 kur.

What can the excess of this total over the capital plus interest for three years be multiplied by in order to give the four-year total minus 2?

2,33,20 (months).

From four years, subtract 2,33,20 (months), to obtain the desired number of full years and days.

Translated into decimal notation, the problem is to determine how long it would take to double an investment. Since

$$1.728 = 1.2^3 < 2 < 1.2^4 = 2.0736,$$

the answer lies somewhere between three and four years. The growth is linear in any one year, so the answer is

$$\frac{1.2^4 - 2}{1.2^4 - 1.2^3} \times 12 = 2 + \frac{33}{60} + \frac{20}{3600}$$

months less than four years. This is exactly what was computed [8, p. 63].

Notice that here we have a problem with a nontrivial iteration, like a "**while**" clause: The procedure is to form powers of $1 + r$, where r is the interest rate, until finding the first value of n such that $(1+r)^n \geq 2$; then calculate

$$12((1 + r)^n - 2)/((1 + r)^n - (1 + r)^{n-1}),$$

and the answer is that the original investment will double in n years minus this many months.

This procedure suggests that the Babylonians were familiar with the idea of linear interpolation. Therefore the trigonometric tables in the famous "Plimpton tablet" [9, pp. 38–41] were possibly used to obtain sines and cosines in a similar way.

The Seleucids

Old-Babylonian mathematics has several other interesting aspects, but a more elaborate discussion is beyond the scope of this paper. Very few tablets have been found that were written after 1600 B.C., until approximately 300 B.C. when Mesopotamia became part of the empire of Alexander the Great's successors, the Seleucids. A great number of tablets from the Seleucid era have been found, mostly dealing with astronomy, which was highly developed. A very few pure mathematical texts of this era have also been found; these tablets indicate that the Old-Babylonian mathematical tradition did not die out during the intervening centuries for which archaeological evidence is lacking. Indeed, some noticeable progress was made. For example, a symbol for zero was now used within numbers, instead of the ambiguous blank space that formerly appeared. The following excerpts from tablet AO 6484 in the Louvre Museum ([6, pp. 96–103] and [13, p. 76]) indicate some of the other advances:

> From 1 to 10, sum the powers (literally the "ladder") of 2.
> The last term you add is 8,32 (namely 512).
> Subtract 1 from 8,32, obtaining 8,31.
> Add 8,31 to 8,32, obtaining the answer 17,3.

> The squares from $1 \times 1 = 1$ to $10 \times 10 = 1,40$; what is their sum?
> Multiply 1 by 20, namely by one-third, giving 20.
> Multiply 10 by 40, namely by two thirds, giving 6,40.
> 6,40 plus 20 is 7.
> Multiply 7 by 55 (which is the sum of 1 through 10) obtaining 6,25.
> 6,25 is the desired sum.

Here we have correct formulas for the sum of a geometric series

$$\sum_{k=1}^{n} 2^{k-1} = 2^{n-1} + (2^{n-1} - 1)$$

and for the sum of a quadratic series

$$\sum_{k=1}^{n} k^2 = \left(\tfrac{1}{3} + \tfrac{2}{3}n\right) \sum_{k=1}^{n} k.$$

These formulas have not been found in Old-Babylonian texts.

Moreover, this same Seleucid tablet shows an increased virtuosity in calculation; for example, the roots to complicated equations like

$$xy = 1, \qquad x + y = 2,0,0,33,20$$

(solution: $x = 1,0,45$ and $y = 59,15,33,20$) are computed. Perhaps this problem was designed to demonstrate the use of the new zero symbol.

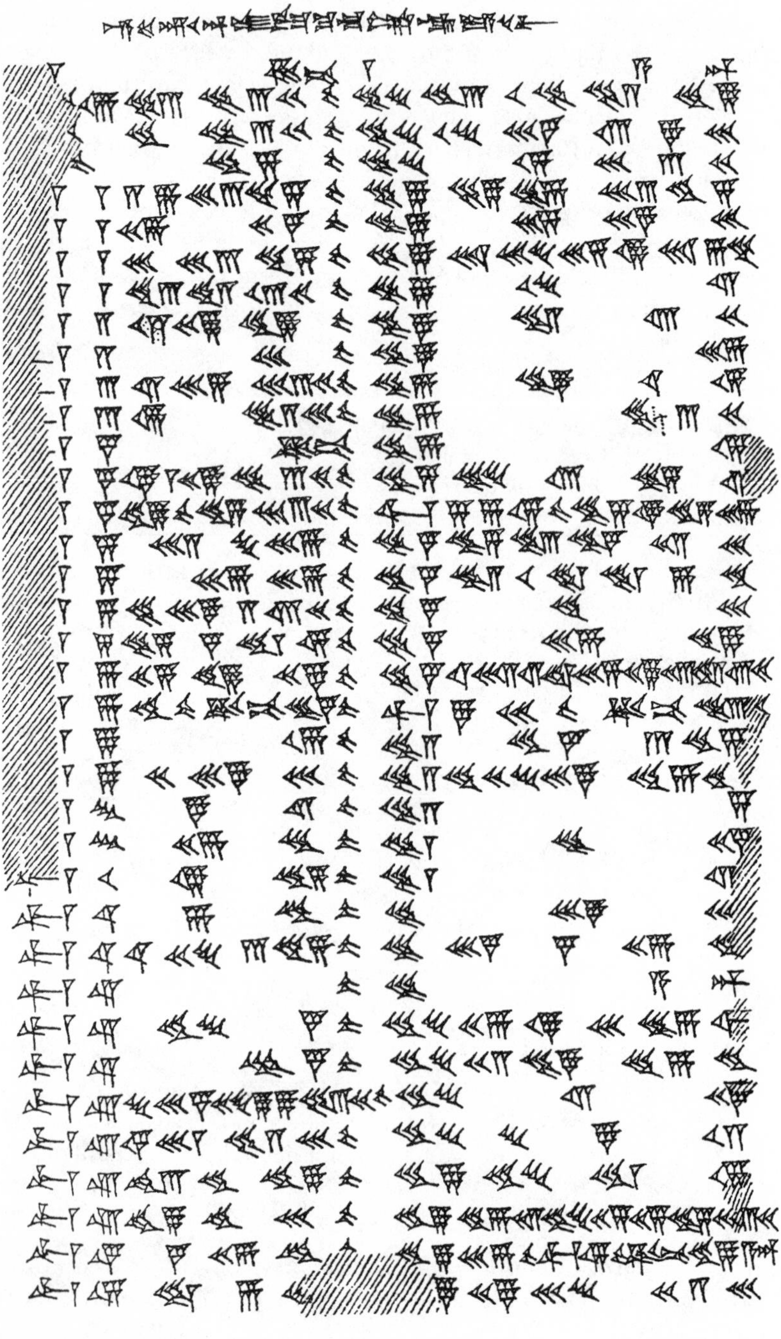

An impressive example of calculating prowess during the Seleucid era appears in Louvre Museum tablet AO 6456 [6, pp. 14–22]. It is a 6-place table of reciprocals, which begins thus:

> By the power of Anu and Antum, whatever I have made with my hands, let it remain intact.

Reciprocal 1	is 1
Reciprocal 1,0,16,53,53,20 .	59,43,10,50,52,48
Reciprocal 1,0,40,53,20	. 59,19,34,13,7,30
Reciprocal 1,0,45	. 59,15,33,20
Reciprocal 1,1,2,6,33,45	. 58,58,56,33,45 (should be 58,58,56,38,24)
Reciprocal 1,1,26,24	. 58,35,37,30
Reciprocal 1,1,30,33,45	. 58,31,39,35,18,31,6,40

The accompanying illustration shows one-fourth of the data on this tablet, namely the left half of the first side, as drawn by F. Thureau-Dangin [12, Plate 55]; the tablet itself is slightly smaller, about 12.5 cm high. The symbol ⟪𒌋 𒐈 that can be seen several times near the upper left corner stands for the sexagesimal digit 53. The tablet continues in this fashion with four columns of reciprocal pairs altogether, two columns on each side. The fourth and final column ends as follows:

Reciprocal 2,46,40	. 21,36
Reciprocal 2,48,45	. 21,20
Reciprocal 2,55,46,52,30	. 20,28,48
Reciprocal 2,57,46,40	. 20,0,15 (should be 20,15)

Reciprocal 3	is 20

First part; results for 1 and 2, incomplete.
Table of Nidintum-Anu, son of Inakibit-Anu, son of Kuzû, priests of
    Anu and Antum in Uruk. Author Inakibit-Anu.

Apparently Inakibit-Anu (whom we shall call Inakibit for short) was the author of this remarkable table; and his son made a less than perfect copy. The table contains 156 reciprocals of numbers that begin with the digits 1 and 2.

There are exactly 144 sexagesimal numbers of six or fewer places that begin with 1 and have a finite reciprocal. (Owen Gingerich has prepared an extensive table of such numbers [4].) The first three columns of Inakibit's table contain 105 of them; this part of the table therefore contains 73% of all six-digit possibilities. The fourth and final column is far less complete; it lists only 31 of the 87 possible entries that begin with leading digit 2, and in fact it contains only 5 of the last 25 such candidates. Evidently the copyist was running out of space, because he omitted even simple cases such as the reciprocal of 2,30 (which is 24) and the reciprocal of 2,40 (which is 22,30).

Inakibit's table includes 20 additional entries for reciprocals of numbers that have more than six sexagesimal places. These appear to have been obtained from other tables, because they include entries like the reciprocal pairs $\{2^{17}, 30^{17}\}$, $\{2^{23}, 30^{23}\}$, $\{3^{11}, 20^{11}\}$, $\{3^{18}, 20^{18}\}$, $\{3^{22}, 20^{22}\}$, and $\{3^{23}, 20^{23}\}$. All instances of $\{2^k, 30^k\}$ and $\{3^k, 20^k\}$ for which one element of the pair has leading digit 1 or 2, and for which the smaller element has at most 6 digits, are given; however, no simple rule is evident that distinguishes the reciprocal pairs that appear from the pairs that do not. For example, 5^{13} is 1,34,11,24,12,5, but Inakibit did not list the pair $\{5^{13}, 12^{13}\}$. The reciprocal of $3^{11}5^5$ appears, but not the reciprocal of its divisor $3^{11}5^3$. The table entries for 20^{22} and 20^{23} are incorrect; most of the errors in 20^{23} can be accounted for, however, if we assume that it was computed from the incorrect value of 20^{22}.

How did Inakibit prepare this table? The simplest procedure would be to start with the pair of numbers (1, 1) and then to go repeatedly from (x, y) to $(2x, 30y)$, $(3x, 20y)$, and $(5x, 12y)$ as long as desired. There is some evidence that this is exactly what he did; for example, several tables are known that start with some pair of reciprocals and then repeatedly apply one of these three operations [9, pp. 13–16].

The complete table of suitable numbers having at most six places requires that 721 pairs (x, y) be generated, and of course it is very laborious to work with such high-precision quantities. (Try it!) The relative completeness of the first three columns indicates that Inakibit prepared a database of roughly 500 pairs (x, y) if he used the stated method.

But even after all those pairs had been computed, the work would be far from finished; it would still be necessary to *sort* them into order! Inakibit's table is the earliest known example of a large file that is in lexicographic order; and this is one of the reasons his work is so impressive, as anyone who has tried to sort 500 cards by hand will attest. To get some idea of the immensity of this task, consider that it takes many hours to sort 500 large numbers by hand nowadays; imagine how difficult it must have been to do this job in ancient times. Yet Inakibit is likely to have done it, since there is no obvious way to generate such a table in order. He probably inserted each new entry into its place in the collection as soon as he had computed it, instead of computing everything first and then sorting. (As we might expect, he made a few mistakes; there are three pairs of lines that should be interchanged to bring the table into perfect order.)

Thus Inakibit may well have been the first person in history to come close to solving a computational problem that takes longer than one second of time on a modern electronic computer.

Another hypothesis, however, has been put forward by E. M. Bruins ([2], [3]), who noted that there is a systematic way to generate all 6-place reciprocals in order without the need for sorting. To understand Bruins's method, let's first consider the simpler but analogous task of listing all 6-digit numbers that have finite reciprocals in the *decimal* system:

100000	163840	320000	524288
102400	200000	327680	625000
125000	204800	390625	640000
128000	250000	400000	655360
131072	256000	409600	781250
156250	262144	500000	800000
160000	312500	512000	819200

We can generate them all by starting with 100000 and multiplying each number x by $1.024 = 2^7 5^{-3}$ and/or by $1.25 = 2^{-2} 5^1$: $100000 \rightarrow \{102400, 125000\}$, $102400 \rightarrow 128000$, $125000 \rightarrow \{128000, 156250\}$, $128000 \rightarrow \{131072, 160000\}$, $131072 \rightarrow 163840$, $156250 \rightarrow 160000$, and so on. More precisely, from $x = 2^a 5^b$ we form $1.024x$ if $b \geq 3$, and $1.25x$ if $a \geq 2$. All the relevant numbers in the range $10^5 < x < 10^6$ are generated. For if $x = 2^a 5^b$, we get x from $x/1.024$ if $a \geq 7$ and from $x/1.25$ if $b \geq 1$; one of these possibilities must exist, otherwise we would have $x \leq 2^6 5^0 = 64$, contradicting the assumption that $x > 10^5$. The numbers are generated almost perfectly in order, although we obtain 156250 before 131072. To generate all 6-digit reciprocal pairs in the decimal system, we can go repeatedly from (x, y) to $(1.024x, .9765625y)$ and/or to $(1.25x, .8y)$.

Similarly, it is possible to obtain all 6-place numbers in the sexagesimal system that have a finite reciprocal, if we begin with $x = 60^5$ and then go from x to αx, βx, and/or γx, where α, β, and γ are suitably scaled versions of the first three entries in Inakibit's table:

$$\alpha = 1,0,16,53,53,20 = 2^{-6} 3^{-5} 5^6,$$
$$\beta = 1,0,40,53,20 = 2^{11} 3^{-4} 5^{-2},$$
$$\gamma = 1,0,45 = 2^{-4} 3^4 5^{-1}.$$

We get to $x = 2^a 3^b 5^c$ from x/α if $c \geq 6$, from x/β if $a \geq 11$, and from x/γ if $b \geq 4$; thus if x is unreachable we have $x \leq 2^{10} 3^3 5^5 = 60^5/9$, a contradiction.

All reciprocals needed for a complete 6-place table can therefore be generated by starting with $(x, y) = (1, 1)$ and then going repeatedly from (x, y) to $(\alpha x, \alpha^{-1} y)$, $(\beta x, \beta^{-1} y)$, and/or $(\gamma x, \gamma^{-1} y)$ by multiplication of medium-large numbers; Babylonian mathematicians knew well how to form such products. The x values are then obtained in perfect lexicographic order, except that $2^8 3^{14} = 1,34,28,42,14,24$ is found before $5^{13} = 1,34,11,24,12,5$. (Neither of the two latter values occurs in Inakibit's table.)

The fact that such a procedure exists does not prove that Babylonian mathematicians used it. Bruins's method, like the more straightforward memory-intensive method discussed earlier, has the advantage of robustness, since it detects errors when an x value is computed from two different predecessors, and since it produces a fairly complete table even when entries are omitted for one reason or another. A Babylonian mathematician who enjoyed playing with numbers would find pleasure in seeing the cancellations that occur when x is multiplied by α, β, or γ.

If Inakibit did use Bruins's sophisticated approach, he or his son failed to copy the entries for $x = 2^5 3^{12} = 1,18,45,55,12$ and $x = 3^{19} = 1,29,40,50,24,27$, because the unique predecessors x/γ of those elements are not present on the Louvre tablet. Similarly, if Inakibit used the approach of going from x to $2x$, $3x$, $5x$, and sorting, he or his son failed to copy entries like $x = 2^{16} 5^1 = 1,31,1,20$, which would be needed to obtain $2^{17} 5^3 = 1,15,51,6,40$ (whose reciprocal does appear). Without additional data we cannot claim to understand his modus operandi with any degree of confidence. Either way, the achievement was notable.

Suggestions for Further Reading

If you have been captivated by Babylonian mathematics, several good books are available that give further interesting details. The short introductory text *Episodes from the Early History of Mathematics* by A. Aaboe [1] can be recommended, as can B. L. van der Waerden's well-known treatise *Science Awakening* [14], although many historians of mathematics discount van der Waerden's more radical claims (cf. [11]). Much of the deciphering of Babylonian mathematical texts was originally due to Otto Neugebauer, who has written an authoritative popular account, *The Exact Sciences in Antiquity* [10]. See especially his fascinating discussion on pages 59–63 and 103–105 of the problems that plague historical researchers in this field.

For more detailed study, it is fun to read the original source material. Neugebauer published the texts of all known mathematical tablets, together with German translations, in a comprehensive series of three volumes during the period 1935–1937 ([6], [7], and [8]). A French edition of the texts [13] was published in 1938 by F. Thureau-Dangin, an eminent Assyriologist. Then in 1945, Neugebauer and A. Sachs published a supplementary volume [9], which includes all mathematical tablets discovered in the meantime, mostly in American museums. The Neugebauer-Sachs volume is written in English, but unfortunately these tablets are not quite as interesting as the ones in Neugebauer's original German series. A list of developments during the period 1945–1957 appears in [10, p. 49].

Most of the Babylonian mathematical tablets have never been translated into English. The translations above have been made by comparing the German of [6], [7], and [8] with the French [13]; but these two versions actually differ in many details. In doubtful cases, the Akkadian and Sumerian vocabularies published in [7], [9], and [13] were consulted in an attempt to give an accurate rendition.

Since only a tiny fraction of the total number of clay tablets has survived the centuries, it is obvious that we cannot pretend to understand the full extent of Babylonian mathematics. Neugebauer points out that the job of discovering what they knew is something like trying to reconstruct all of modern mathematics from a few pages that have been torn at random out of the books in a modern library. We can only place lower bounds on the scope of Babylonian achievements, and speculate about what they did not know.

What about other ancient developments? The Egyptians were not bad at mathematics, and archaeologists have dug up some old papyri that are almost as old as the Babylonian tablets we have discussed. The Egyptian method of multiplication, based essentially in the binary number system, is especially interesting (although their calculations were decimal, using something like Roman numerals); in other respects, however, their use of awkward "unit fractions" left them far behind the Babylonians. Then came the Greeks, with an emphasis on geometry but also on such things as Euclid's algorithm; the latter is the oldest nontrivial algorithm that still is important to computer programmers. (See [10] and [14] for the history of Egyptian mathematics, and [1], [10], [14] for Greek mathematics. A free translation of Euclid's algorithm in his own words, together with his incomplete proof of its correctness, appears in [5, Section 4.5.2].) And then there are the Indians, and the Chinese; it is clear that much more can be told.

References

[1] Asger Aaboe, *Episodes from the Early History of Mathematics* (New York: Random House, 1964), 133 pp.

[2] E. M. Bruins, "Reciprocals and Pythagorean triads," *Physis* **9** (1967), 373–392.

[3] E. M. Bruins, "La construction de la grande table le valeurs réciproques *AO 6456*," *Actes de la XVIIe Rencontre Assyriologique Internationale*, edited by André Finet (Comité belge de recherches en Mésopotamie, 1970), 99–115.

[4] O. Gingerich, "Eleven-digit regular sexagesimals and their reciprocals," *Transactions of the American Philosophical Society* **55**, part 8 (1965), 38 pp.

[5] Donald E. Knuth, *Seminumerical Algorithms* (Reading, Massachusetts: Addison–Wesley, 1971), 624 pp.

[6] O. Neugebauer, "Mathematische Keilschrift-Texte," *Quellen und Studien zur Geschichte der Mathematik Astronomie und Physik* **A3**, part 1 (1935), 516 pp. Reprinted by Springer-Verlag, 1973.

[7] O. Neugebauer, "Mathematische Keilschrift-Texte," *Quellen und Studien zur Geschichte der Mathematik Astronomie und Physik* **A3**, part 2 (1935), 64 pp. plus 69 reproductions of tablets. Reprinted by Springer-Verlag, 1973.

[8] O. Neugebauer, "Mathematische Keilschrift-Texte," *Quellen und Studien zur Geschichte der Mathematik Astronomie und Physik* **A3**, part 3 (1937), 83 pp. plus 6 reproductions of tablets. Reprinted by Springer-Verlag, 1973.

[9] O. Neugebauer and A. Sachs, *Mathematical Cuneiform Texts* (New Haven, Connecticut: American Oriental Society, 1945), 177 pp. plus 49 reproductions of tablets.

[10] O. Neugebauer, *The Exact Sciences in Antiquity*, second edition (Providence, Rhode Island: Brown University Press, 1957), 240 pp. plus 14 photographic plates.

[11] N. Swerdlow, "A lost monument of Indian astronomy" [a review of B. L. van der Waerden, *Das heliozentrische System in der griechischen, persischen und indischen Astronomie* (Zürich, 1970)], *Isis* **64** (1973), 239–243.

[12] F. Thureau-Dangin, *Tablettes d'Uruk*, Musée du Louvre, Textes Cunéiformes, Volume 6 (Paris: Paul Geuthner, 1922), 4 pp. plus 105 plates.

[13] F. Thureau-Dangin, *Textes Mathématiques Babyloniens* (Leiden, The Netherlands: E. J. Brill, 1938), 243 pp.

[14] B. L. van der Waerden, *Science Awakening*, translated by Arnold Dresden (Groningen, The Netherlands: P. Noordhoff, 1954), 306 pp.

The preparation of this paper was supported in part by the National Science Foundation. I wish to thank Professor Abraham Seidenberg for his courtesy in helping me obtain copies of [6] and [13] when I needed them, and Professor E. M. Bruins for helpful correspondence.

Addendum

An excellent survey of what was known about Babylonian mathematics in 1990, prepared by Jöran Friberg, can be found in *Reallexikon der Assyriologie und Vorderasiatischen Archäologie* **7** (Berlin: de Gruyter, 1987–1990), 531–585. Friberg reports that two additional tables of 6-place reciprocals have been discovered since 1960, as well as several fragments of others, containing different sets of reciprocal pairs from those on Inakibit's tablet.

See also Christine Proust's interesting analysis of arithmetical errors that were occasionally made with high-precision numbers: "La multiplication Babylonienne: La part non écrite du calcul," *Revue d'Histoire des Mathématiques* **6** (2000), 293–303.

Chapter 12

Von Neumann's First Computer Program

Abstract

An analysis of the two earliest sets of instruction codes planned for stored program computers, and the earliest extant program for such a computer, gives insight into the thoughts of John von Neumann, the man who designed the instruction sets and wrote the program, and shows how several important aspects of computing have evolved. The paper is based on previously unpublished documents from the files of Herman H. Goldstine.

*[Originally published in Computing Surveys **2** (1970), 247–260.]*

Introduction

A handwritten document now in the possession of Dr. Herman H. Goldstine contains what is probably the earliest extant program for a stored program digital computer. Its author, the remarkably talented mathematician John von Neumann (1903–1957) was in the process of refining the stored program concept as he was writing this code; so his program represents a significant step in the evolution of computer organization as well as of programming techniques. In this paper we will therefore investigate the contents of von Neumann's manuscript in some detail, attempting to relate its ideas to other developments in the early history of high speed computing.

The program we will study is not what we might expect an "ordinary" mathematician to have written; it does not solve a partial differential equation! Instead, it deals with what was generally considered at that time to be the principal example of a nonnumeric application for computers, namely, the problem of sorting data into nondecreasing order.

Von Neumann chose this application for good reason. He had sketched out an order code for a stored program computer, with numerical applications uppermost in his mind; there was no question that his proposed device could do the requisite arithmetic operations. The key question was whether or not the proposed instruction set provided a satisfactory means of logical control for complex processes, and so he felt that a sorting program would be a most instructive test case. Furthermore, the existence of IBM's special purpose machines for sorting gave him a standard against which he could measure the proposed computer's speed.

Before we start to study von Neumann's program, a few disclaimers are in order. In the first place, he probably never intended to have this program published and subjected to such scrutiny; although his manuscript is carefully documented, he probably wanted only to circulate it among a few interested colleagues. So when we find a few errors and a few instances of clumsy coding, we should realize that it was an early effort that was not supposed to represent a polished product.

Second, we should realize that the historical interest of this program is in great measure due to its connection with the development of instruction codes for stored program computers; it is not the earliest instance of a computer program. We have Lady Lovelace's description of a program for calculating Bernoulli numbers that Babbage wrote for his Analytical Engine [1, Note G]; A. M. Turing's construction [16] of his abstract Universal Machine, which involves many important programming concepts; Eckert and Mauchly's first sample program for the ENIAC [4]; and a collection of numerical programs, dating from 1944, written by H. H. Aiken, G. M. Hopper, R. V. D. Campbell, R. M. Bloch, B. J. Lockhart, and others, for the Harvard Mark I [10, Chapters 4 and 6].

A third precaution: The notation used in this paper differs considerably from that used by von Neumann, so that modern readers can more easily understand what he did. Where he would write, for instance,

$$\bar{1}_5) \quad c + (m' - 1)(p + 1) \; \xleftrightarrow{} \; \bar{1}_4 \; \mid p + 2$$

we will use an equivalent assembly-like language form

MOVEIN PIK p+1,BUFFER,[YPTR]

instead. This new notation isn't completely transparent, but it seems to be an improvement, and it doesn't go so far that the machine is obscured. (For further information about von Neumann's original notation, see the section on Storage Allocation and Timing following the program.)

To set the stage for our story, let us consider briefly the developments prior to 1945 when von Neumann wrote his sorting program. Several electromechanical calculators were essentially operational in the late 1930s and early 1940s: those of Stibitz [15] and Aiken [10] in America, and Zuse [3] in Germany. Another machine, which had electronic circuitry for arithmetic although it was slowed down by mechanical memory elements, was also developed in the late 1930s at Iowa State College, by John V. Atanasoff and Clifford E. Berry [see 12]; this machine was designed to solve sets of simultaneous linear equations.

In August 1942, John W. Mauchly of the Moore School of Electrical Engineering in Philadelphia wrote a memorandum to his colleagues summarizing briefly the advantages that could be expected from an electronic high speed computer such as he felt could reasonably be developed. He was familiar with previous American developments in computing, and he was also aware of the extensive calculations needed by the Ballistic Research Laboratory (BRL) in connection with World War II; many of those calculations were currently being done on a Differential Analyzer at the Moore School. It was by no means obvious that a useful electronic computer could be built; but Mauchly and a young electrical engineer named J. P. Eckert, Jr., drew up a tentative technical outline of a suitable machine, and Prof. J. G. Brainerd decided that it was worth the risk of committing the Moore School to a major effort in this direction. A technical proposal was submitted to Col. Leslie E. Simon, Col. Paul N. Gillon, and Lt. Herman H. Goldstine of the BRL in the spring of 1943, and in a remarkably short time the US government entered into a contract with the Moore School for research and development of high speed electronic calculating devices, beginning July 1, 1943. The project, supervised by Brainerd, had Eckert as chief engineer, Mauchly as principal consultant, and Goldstine in charge of technical liaison with BRL. A first machine, the ENIAC (Electronic Numerical Integrator And Computer), was soon designed, and its design was frozen at an early stage so that future efforts could be concentrated on its production and testing; it was dedicated on February 15, 1946. (For further details about the development of the ENIAC, see [6].)

The ENIAC was a highly parallel computer; weighing over 30 tons, it involved more than 19,000 vacuum tubes, 1500 relays, etc. Because of its electronic circuitry, it was considerably faster than any computing machine previously built. But it had only 20 words of internal memory, and it required complicated manual operations for setting up a program on plugboards. Long before ENIAC was completed, it became clear to the designers that they could utilize the equipment more efficiently if they would adopt serial methods instead of so much parallelism; so in January 1944 they sketched out a "magnetic calculating machine" in which successive digits of numbers were transmitted serially from a memory device to central electronic computing circuits and back again. Early in 1944, Eckert and Mauchly invented an acoustic delay-line memory device that made it possible to obtain a fairly large storage capacity with comparatively little hardware; it became evident that great improvements over ENIAC could be made, at considerably less cost. "Therefore, by July, 1944, it was agreed that when work on the ENIAC permitted, the development and construction of such a machine should be undertaken. This machine has come to be known as the EDVAC (Electronic Discrete VAriable Computer)" [5].

In the latter part of 1944, John von Neumann (a consultant to BRL) became a consultant to the EDVAC project. He contributed to many discussions on logical circuitry, and he designed an order code that could be used. In the spring of 1945, he wrote a preliminary report [17] that gives a detailed discussion of arithmetic circuitry and the motivation for various design decisions that were made by the team members as EDVAC evolved. This takes us to the beginning of our story.

The Early EDVAC

Von Neumann's first draft report [17,18] on the EDVAC proposed building a serial computer with three 32-bit registers and 8192 32-bit words of auxiliary memory. The three registers were called i and j (for inputs to the arithmetic circuitry) and o (for output); for convenience in what follows we will denote these registers by the upper-case letters I, J, and A. The EDVAC memory was to be divided into 256 "tanks" of 32 words each, operating in a cyclic fashion. Word 0 of each tank would pass a reading station one bit at a time, then (32 bit-times later) word 1 would be available, ..., finally word 31, then word 0 again. Thus the accessing of information from tanks was essentially the same as we now have from drums or head-per-track disks. A bit-time was to be 1 μsec, so the cycle time for each tank came to $32 \times 32 = 1024$ μsec. The tanks were to be constructed from Eckert and Mauchly's mercury delay lines; this concept was used later in the memory of the UNIVAC I computer (1951). Although von Neumann realized that faster operation could be achieved with a random-access memory, the only known way of building such memories economically was the "iconoscope" (like a TV tube, with light or dark spots created and sensed by an electron beam), and he temporarily rejected it since its reliability was still unproved.

Each 32-bit word was either a number or an instruction code; the first bit was 0 for numbers and 1 for instructions. Von Neumann suggested writing binary numbers in reverse order, with the least significant digits at the left, since binary notation was unfamiliar anyway and since the serial circuitry found it most convenient to process least significant digits first. The last bit of a number, following the most significant bit, was its sign; numbers were represented in two's complement notation. Thus the word

$$b_0 b_1 b_2 b_3 \ldots b_{30} b_{31}, \qquad b_0 = 0,$$

denoted the number

$$2^{-30} b_1 + 2^{-29} b_2 + 2^{-28} b_3 + \cdots + 2^{-1} b_{30} - b_{31},$$

and 30-bit fractions in the range $-1 \leq x < 1$ were representable. For addition, subtraction, and conversion operations, the number could also be regarded as the integer

$$b_1 + 2b_2 + 4b_3 + \cdots + 2^{29} b_{30} - 2^{30} b_{31},$$

so that integers in the range $-2^{30} \leq x < 2^{30}$ were representable. Binary coded decimal integers $(abcdefg)_{10}$ were also allowed, in the form

$$0000 a_1 a_2 a_3 a_4 b_1 b_2 b_3 b_4 \ldots g_1 g_2 g_3 g_4,$$

where $a_1 a_2 a_3 a_4$ was the code for digit a, and $b_1 b_2 b_3 b_4$ was the code for digit b, etc., in reverse binary order. (Thus $0000 = 0$, $1000 = 1$, $0100 = 2$, ..., $0001 = 8$, $1001 = 9$.)

Instruction words were to have the form

$$1 a_0 a_1 a_2 a_3 a_4 b_0 b_1 b_2 0000000000 y_0 y_1 y_2 y_3 y_4 x_0 x_1 x_2 x_3 x_4 x_5 x_6 x_7,$$

where $a = a_0 a_1 a_2 a_3 a_4$ denoted an operation code, $b = b_0 b_1 b_2$ denoted a variant, $y = y_0 + 2y_1 + 4y_2 + 8y_3 + 16y_4$ denoted a word position within a tank, and $x = x_0 + 2x_1 + \cdots + 128 x_7$ denoted a tank number. The following arithmetic operation codes were proposed, affecting the registers I, J, and A:

- AD $(a = 00000)$. Set $A \leftarrow I + J$.
- SB $(a = 00001)$. Set $A \leftarrow I - J$.
- ML $(a = 00010)$. Set $A \leftarrow A + I \times J$ (rounded).
- DV $(a = 00011)$. Set $A \leftarrow I/J$ (rounded).

- SQ ($a = 00100$). Set $A \leftarrow \sqrt{J}$ (rounded).
- II ($a = 00101$). Set $A \leftarrow I$.
- JJ ($a = 00110$). Set $A \leftarrow J$.
- SL ($a = 00111$). If $A \geq 0$, set $A \leftarrow I$; if $A < 0$, set $A \leftarrow J$.
- DB ($a = 01000$). Set $A \leftarrow$ binary equivalent of decimal number I.
- BD ($a = 01001$). Set $A \leftarrow$ decimal equivalent of binary number I.

(As stated in the Introduction, we are changing von Neumann's notation: The mnemonic symbols for these operation codes are ad hoc symbols contrived solely for the purposes of the present paper. Notice that multiplication, division, and square root were supposed to produce *rounded* results. Not all details of these operations were fully specified in von Neumann's memo; for example, division and square root would change the contents of I, but it is not clear whether a valid remainder would be left there. The decimal-to-binary and binary-to-decimal conversions were not worked out. Apparently overflow conditions caused no special action.)

Each of the arithmetic operations above was to be used with one of several variants specified by $b = b_0 b_1 b_2$:

- H ($b = 111$). Do the operation as described above, holding the result in A.
- A ($b = 100$). Do the operation as described above, then set $J \leftarrow I$, $I \leftarrow A$, $A \leftarrow 0$.
- S ($b = 000$). Do the operation as described above, then store the result A in memory location yx and set $A \leftarrow 0$.
- F ($b = 101$). Do the operation as described above, then store the result into the word immediately following this instruction, set $A \leftarrow 0$, and perform the altered instruction.
- N ($b = 110$). Do the operation as described above, then store the result into the word immediately following this instruction, set $A \leftarrow 0$, and *skip* the altered instruction.

Thus, for example, ADS yx would have the effect of setting location yx to $I + J$, and clearing A to zero; JJA would interchange the contents of I and J, and clear A; SLH would set A to either I or J, according as the previous sign of A was 0 or 1. (The memory specification yx was ignored on all variants except S.)

Besides arithmetic operations, the machine could do the following:

- JMP ($a = 11000, b = 000$). Take the next instruction from location yx (then $1 + yx$, etc.).

- LOD ($a = 10000, b = 000$). Set $J \leftarrow I$, then set I to the contents of memory location yx.

Further codes $a = 01010, 01011, 01100, 01101, 01110$, and 01111 were reserved for input and output operations (which were not yet specified) and for stopping the machine.

There was an important exception to the operations as we have described them: Only numbers, not instructions, ever appeared in the registers I, J, and A. When the LOD operations specified a memory address containing an instruction, only the yx part of that instruction was to be loaded into I; the other bits were cleared. Conversely, when storing into memory by means of variants S, F, and N, only the least significant 13 bits of the number in A were to be stored in the yx part, if the memory location contained an instruction word.

Instructions were to be executed from consecutive locations, unless the sequence of control was modified by a JMP order. If the control sequence would come across a number (not an instruction word), the effect would be as if an LOD instruction were performed referring to that number.

Most instructions would be performed in one word-time, so that the machine could keep up with the speed of the long tanks where instructions were stored. But multiplication, division, square root, and radix conversion took 33 word-times (1056 μsec). References to memory, by means of LOD operations and the S variant, would require an additional 1024 μsec unless the memory address was perfectly synchronized to match the following word of instructions. (For multiplication, division, and square root extraction, there was a little more leeway, since those operations actually were completed in about 950 μsec.)

The reader will note that much of the space in instruction words is wasted. Von Neumann realized this, but did not think it important at the time, since [17, p. 96] the programming problems he had considered required only a small fraction of the memory for instruction storage. But we will see that he changed his mind later.

The machine discussed here differs slightly from von Neumann's first description [17], since the modifications stated in his letter [18] have been included. He wrote, from Los Alamos to Philadelphia, "The contents of this letter belong, of course, into the manuscript [17], and I will continue the manuscript and incorporate these things also, after I get it back from you — if possible with comments ... from you, Pres

Eckert, John Mauchly, and the others." But the manuscript was never completed, nor were the modifications inserted when it was typed a month later, presumably because there were so many other things to be done. It is interesting to note that von Neumann's letter [18] also proposed the design of a special typewriter for preparing programs from partially mnemonic input. Pushing a key marked + would cause the bits 100000 to be assembled (the first six bits of an addition instruction); then a key marked H would insert the subsequent bits 111000...00, forming a complete instruction word on a magnetic tape.

The differences between [17] and the machine described here are chiefly concerned with improvements in the logistics of instruction modification. (a) There was no variant N; instead, variant F would not treat the altered word as an instruction if it turned out to be a number. (b) The convention about loading only 13 bits of instruction words was not present (although the convention about storing only 13 bits into instruction words was). (c) Three other variants, like S, A, and F but not clearing register A, were originally included.

The Next EDVAC

Von Neumann's letter [18] says, "I have also worked on sorting questions ... I will write you about the details very soon." He said that he had written an internal sorting program requiring about 130 words of instructions; it could sort 500 p-word items on a one-word key in about $1 + .425\ (p - 1)$ minutes. "I suspect that these arrangements, which represent only a first attempt, could be improved.

"At any rate the moral seems to be that the EDVAC, with the logical controls as planned for 'mathematical' problems, and without any modifications for 'sorting' problems, is definitely faster than the [contemporary IBM sorters, about 400 cards/minute]. ... Since the IBM's are really very good in sorting, and since according to the above sorting can be meshed with the other operations of the EDVAC without human intervention or need for additional equipment, etc., the situation looks reasonably satisfactory to me. ... It is legitimate to conclude already on the basis of the now available evidence, that the EDVAC is very nearly an 'all-purpose' machine, and that the present principles for the logical controls are sound."

But von Neumann's code for this sorting program does not seem to have survived; we can only say that his timing estimates look reasonable, since for large p they come to slightly over 5 milliseconds per pass per word transferred. The program that now is in Dr. Goldstine's files is roughly 80 times faster, due to important improvements in machine organization that von Neumann considered shortly afterwards. This second EDVAC design was apparently never defined in as much detail as the previous one, but a brief summary of its instruction codes appears in [5, p. 76] and we can deduce other properties by studying von Neumann's program. Therefore we can reconstruct the main features of the modified machine.

The chief improvement incorporated into this version of EDVAC was the introduction of "short tanks" whose capacity was one word each; this provided a small fast-access memory that essentially increased the number of registers, and the old I and J disappeared. Block transfer operations between the short and the long tanks made many processes faster. The tentative plans in [5] call for 32 short tanks, and 2048 additional words in 64 long tanks. "Combining this with the almost unlimited memory capacity of the magnetic tape (even though the numbers are not available here so quickly) it seems that very few problems will exceed this capacity" [5, p. 81].

Here are the basic operations allowed by the new EDVAC code, exclusive of multiplication and division. Let $C(s)$ denote the contents of short tank number s.

- PIK s, t, x. Transfer s consecutive words, starting at long tank location x, to s consecutive short tanks, starting at short tank number t. If x is unspecified, the next s words following this instruction are used, and the $(s+1)$st is the next instruction.
- PUT s, t, x. Transfer s consecutive words, starting at short tank number t, to s consecutive memory locations, starting at long tank location x. If x is unspecified, the next s words following this instruction are used, and the $(s+1)$st is the next instruction.
- ADD s, t. Set $A \leftarrow C(s) + C(t)$.
- SUB s, t. Set $A \leftarrow C(s) - C(t)$.
- SEL s, t. If $A \geq 0$, set $A \leftarrow C(s)$; if $A < 0$, set $A \leftarrow C(t)$.
- TRA x. Go to long tank location x (then $x+1$, etc.) for subsequent instructions.
- JMP s. Go to short tank number s (then $s+1$, etc.) for subsequent instructions.
- STO s. Set $C(s) \leftarrow A$.
- SET s, t. Set $C(s) \leftarrow C(t)$.

As before, operations that did not refer to long tank addresses took just one word-time (32 μsec), with the exception of "long" arithmetic operations like multiplication and division. When a long tank location was specified, the machine waited until the desired word was accessible. At least two word-times were needed for the instruction TRA x, due to "long tank switching," if the instruction was executed from a short tank.

A distinction was made, as before, between numbers and instruction words: When STO or SET attempted to store a new value into an instruction word, only the instruction bits that specified a long tank location x were to be affected, and the value in A was regarded as an integer.

Tentative plans for representing the instructions in memory are discussed briefly in [5, pp. 83–86].

The Sorting Program

Now we are ready to discuss von Neumann's program. His manuscript, written in ink, is 23 pages long; the first page still shows traces of the penciled phrase "TOP SECRET," which was subsequently erased. (In 1945, all work on computers was classified, due to its connections with military activities.) A facsimile of page 5, the first page of the program itself, appears as Figure 1.

Von Neumann begins his memo by defining the idea of sorting records into order, and of merging two strings of records that have been sorted separately into a single sorted sequence. Then he states the purpose of the program: "We wish to formulate code instructions for sorting and for meshing [i.e., merging], and to see how much control-capacity they tie up and how much time they require."

He never actually gets around to coding the entire sorting routine in this document; only the merging process is described. For the merging problem, we assume that n records $x_0, x_1, \ldots, x_{n-1}$ are given, consisting of p words each; the first word of each record is called its "key," and we have $\text{key}(x_0) \leq \text{key}(x_1) \leq \cdots \leq \text{key}(x_{n-1})$. An additional m records $y_0,$ $y_1, \ldots, y_{m-1}$ are also given, with $\text{key}(y_0) \leq \text{key}(y_1) \leq \cdots \leq \text{key}(y_{m-1})$; the problem is to put the x's and y's together into the merged sequence $z_0, z_1, \ldots, z_{n+m-1}$, in such a way that $\text{key}(z_0) \leq \text{key}(z_1) \leq \cdots \leq$ $\text{key}(z_{n+m-1})$.

He formulated the merging method as follows (based on a procedure then used with the IBM collator): Assume that we have found the first l records $z_0, \ldots, z_{l-1}$ where $0 \leq l \leq n + m$; and assume further that these l records consist of $x_0, \ldots, x_{n'-1}$ and $y_0, \ldots, y_{m'-1}$ in some order, where $0 \leq n' \leq n$, $0 \leq m' \leq m$, and $n' + m' = l$. There are four cases:

(α) $n' < n$, $m' < m$. There are two subcases:

(α1) $\text{key}(x_{n'}) \leq \text{key}(y_{m'})$. Let $z_l = x_{n'}$, and replace (l, n', m') by $(l + 1, n' + 1, m')$.

(α2) $\text{key}(x_{n'}) > \text{key}(y_{m'})$. Let $z_l = y_{m'}$, and replace (l, n', m') by $(l + 1, n', m' + 1)$.

(β) $n' < n, m' = m$. Same action as (α1).

(γ) $n' = n, m' < m$. Same action as (α2) .

(δ) $n' = n, m' = m$. The process has been completed.

His program is divided up according to cases in this same way, rather like the style of "decision table" programs. In order to make his coding reasonably easy to follow, it is transliterated here into a symbolic assembly language such as people might use with the machine if it existed today. We use the pseudo-operation σ RST k (RST means "reserve short tank") to mean that symbol σ is to refer to the first of k consecutive short tank locations. The first RST in a program reserves short tank number 0, and short tanks are reserved consecutively thereafter. The other notations of our assembly language are more familiar: "EQU" denotes equality, "CON" denotes an integer constant, an asterisk denotes the current location, and "**" denotes an address that will be filled in dynamically as the program runs.

Von Neumann's first step in coding the program was to consider the four-way division into cases; see (A) opposite Figure 1. All numbers manipulated in his program are treated as integers. The code for this COMPARE routine assumes that the short tank locations have been set up appropriately; in particular, location SWITCH must contain a TRA instruction. The instruction in line 22 of (A) sets the address of that TRA to either ALPHA, BETA, GAMMA, or DELTA.

Next comes the code for routines (α), (β), (γ), and (δ); see (B). Here we have a rather awkward piece of coding; von Neumann thought of a tricky way to reduce cases (β) and (γ) to case (α) by giving artificial values 0 and -1 to $\text{key}(y_{m'}) - \text{key}(x_{n'})$. But he didn't realize the far simpler approach of making (β) and (γ) identical, respectively, to (α1) and (α2). Thus, he could have simply changed line 27 to "SEL LBETA,LGAMMA", omitting lines 24, 25, 30, 31, 32, 33, 34, and 35 entirely; then he could have used BETA and GAMMA instead of ALPHA1 and ALPHA2 in the remainder of the program. This would have saved four of the precious short tank locations, and it would have made the calculation slightly faster. Similarly, line 36 is unnecessary, since location EXIT could be stored in LDELTA. Apparently the idea of making equivalent program states identical is not a natural concept, since even von Neumann missed it here.

⑤

(g) We now formulate a set of instructions to effect this 4-way decision between $(\alpha)-(\delta)$. We state again the contents of the short tanks already assigned:

$\overline{1}.)\ N\,n'_{(-30)}$ $\overline{2}.)\ N\,m'_{(-30)}$ $\overline{3}.)\ N\,x^{\circ}_{m'}$ $\overline{4}.)\ N\,y^{\circ}_{m'}$

$\overline{5}.)\ N\,n_{(-30)}$ $\overline{6}.)\ N\,m_{(-30)}$ $\overline{7}.)\ N\,l_{\alpha(-30)}$ $\overline{8}.)\ N\,l_{\beta(-30)}$

$\overline{9}.)\ N\,l_{\gamma(-30)}$ $\overline{10}.)\ N\,l_{\delta(-30)}$ $\overline{11}.)\ \ldots \to \mathcal{C}$

Now let the instructions occupy the (long tank) words $1., 2., \ldots$:

$1.)\ \overline{1}.-\overline{5}.$	$\sigma)\ N\,n'-n_{(-30)}$		
$2.)\ \overline{9}.\ s\ \overline{7}.$	$\sigma)\ N\,l_{\gamma(-30)}$		for $n' \lessgtr n$
$3.)\ \sigma \to \overline{12}.$	$\overline{12}.)\ N\,l_{\gamma(-30)}$		for $n' \gtrless n$
$4.)\ \overline{1}.-\overline{5}.$	$\sigma)\ N\,m'-m_{(-30)}$		
$5.)\ \overline{10}.\ s\ \overline{8}.$	$\sigma)\ N\,l_{\delta(-30)}$		for $m' \lessgtr m$
$6.)\ \sigma \to \overline{13}.$	$\overline{13}.)\ N\,l_{\beta(-30)}$		for $m' \gtrless m$
$7.)\ \overline{2}.-\overline{6}.$	$\sigma)\ N\,m'-m_{(-30)}$		
$8.)\ \overline{13}.\ s\ \overline{a}.$	$\sigma)\ N\,\overline{\overline{a}.)}\ldots$		for $m' \lessgtr m$

i.e.

$\sigma)\ N\,l_{\gamma}\ l_{\delta}\atop l_{\alpha(-30)}$ for $m'=m, n'=n \quad m'=m, n'=n$
   $m' \lessgtr m, n'=n \quad m' \lessgtr m, n' \lessgtr n$

i.e. for $\begin{smallmatrix}(\beta)(\beta)\\(\sigma)(\alpha)\end{smallmatrix}$, respectively.

$9.)\ \sigma \to \overline{11}.$ $\overline{11}.)\ l_{\alpha},l_{\beta},l_{\gamma},l_{\delta} \to \mathcal{C}$ for $(\alpha),(\beta),(\gamma),(\delta)$, respectively.

$10.)\ \overline{11}. \to \mathcal{C}$

~~[struck out line]~~

Now

$\overline{11}.)\ l_{\alpha},l_{\beta},l_{\gamma},l_{\delta} \to \mathcal{C}$ for $(\alpha),(\beta),(\gamma),(\delta)$, respectively.

Thus at the end of this phase $\mathcal{C}$ is at $l_{\alpha},l_{\beta},l_{\gamma},l_{\delta}$, according to which case $(\alpha),(\beta),(\gamma),(\delta)$ holds.

(h) We now pass to the case (α). This has ~~2 subcases~~ 2 subcases (α_1) and (α_2), according to whether $x^{\circ}_{m'} \gtrless$ or $< y^{\circ}_{m'}$. According to which of the 2 subcases holds, $\mathcal{C}$ must be sent to the place where its instructions begin, say the (long tank) words $l_{\alpha_1}, l_{\alpha_2}$. ~~Their~~ Their numbers must ~~[struck out line]~~

FIGURE 1. The original manuscript.

(A)

Line no.	Location	Op	Address(es)	Remarks
1	NPRIME	RST	1	n'
2	MPRIME	RST	1	m'
3	XKEY	RST	1	key$(x_{n'})$
4	YKEY	RST	1	key$(y_{m'})$
5	N	RST	1	n
6	M	RST	1	m
7	LALPHA	RST	1	Location ALPHA
8	LBETA	RST	1	Location BETA
9	LGAMMA	RST	1	Location GAMMA
10	LDELTA	RST	1	Location DELTA
11	SWITCH	RST	1	Instruction TRA **
12	TEMP1	RST	1	Temporary storage
13	TEMP2	RST	1	Temporary storage
14	COMPARE	SUB	NPRIME,N	$A \leftarrow n' - n$.
15		SEL	LGAMMA,LALPHA	$A \leftarrow$ **if** $n' \geq n$ **then** GAMMA **else** ALPHA.
16		STO	TEMP1	TEMP1 $\leftarrow A$.
17		SUB	NPRIME,N	$A \leftarrow n' - n$.
18		SEL	LDELTA,LBETA	$A \leftarrow$ **if** $n' \geq n$ **then** DELTA **else** BETA.
19		STO	TEMP2	TEMP2 $\leftarrow A$.
20		SUB	MPRIME,M	$A \leftarrow m' - m$.
21		SEL	TEMP2,TEMP1	$A \leftarrow$ **if** $m' \geq m$ **then** [TEMP2] **else** [TEMP1].
22		STO	SWITCH	SWITCH $\leftarrow$ TRA $[A]$.
23		JMP	SWITCH	

(B)

Line no.	Location	Op	Address(es)	Remarks
24	LALPHA1	RST	1	Location ALPHA1
25	LALPHA2	RST	1	Location ALPHA2
26	ALPHA	SUB	YKEY,XKEY	$A \leftarrow$ key$(y_{m'})$ − key$(x_{n'})$.
27		SEL	LALPHA1,LALPHA2	**if** $A \geq 0$ **then** $A \leftarrow$ ALPHA1 **else** $A \leftarrow$ ALPHA2.
28		STO	SWITCH	
29		JMP	SWITCH	
30	ZERO	RST	1	0
31	MONE	RST	1	−1
32	BETA	SUB	ZERO,ZERO	$A \leftarrow 0$.
33		TRA	ALPHA+1	Go to ALPHA + 1.
34	GAMMA	SUB	MONE,ZERO	$A \leftarrow -1$.
35		TRA	ALPHA+1	Go to ALPHA + 1.
36	DELTA	TRA	EXIT	Merging is complete.

(Perhaps it is in bad taste to make such detailed criticism of the programming, since von Neumann was not intending to write an optimum program for sorting; he was merely experimenting with a tentative order code. Every great mathematician has a wastebasket full of things he doesn't want people to study carefully! On the other hand, this particular manuscript was not merely a rough sketch; it was evidently put together with some care. So it seems fair to look at it closely in an attempt to discern the aspects of programming that were most difficult in their conception. The idea is not to chortle over the fact that von Neumann's program wasn't perfect; it is rather to realize that the imperfections give some historical insights, because of when the code was written.)

The sorting program continues with the routine for case $(\alpha 1)$: In (C) a block of $p + 1$ words (including the key for the next record) is transferred into short tanks, and p words are moved into the z area. This is a good way to avoid the latency problems of delay-line memories, and it accounts for the considerable increase in speed in this program compared to what was possible with the first EDVAC code.

A slight improvement could be made here if ZPTR were omitted, letting MOVEOUT keep track of the current z location; a short tank would be saved, as well as the instruction in line 47 (and a similar instruction for case $(\alpha 2)$). However this trick would have made the setup somewhat less symmetrical. Line 58 could have been omitted if the code for COMPARE were placed right after line 57. If line 51 were changed to "SUB NPRIME,MONE", another short tank could have been saved. Since von Neumann didn't mention these simplifications, while his work on logic design strongly suggests that he would have thought of them, it is plausible to say that he wasn't especially concerned with saving space in short tanks, although he does mention that the scarcity of short tanks places limits on the record size p. (He says that $p \leq 8$ would be required if there were only 32 short tanks, while $p \leq 40$ if there were 64; perhaps he was purposely wasting short tanks, in order to convince his colleagues that at least 64 short tanks are desirable!)

We need not discuss the code for $(\alpha 2)$, since it is essentially the same as the code for $(\alpha 1)$. All that is left, therefore, is to write an initialization routine that gets everything started properly. For this purpose, von Neumann juggled the short tank locations so that the first six would hold the control values that are set up from outside this routine (namely N, M, XPTR, YPTR, ZPTR, and SIZE); then come two that are somewhat special (namely XKEY and YKEY, which must contain $\mathrm{key}(x_0)$ and $\mathrm{key}(y_0)$); then come 14 that are to be set to certain constant

(C)

Line no.	Location	Op	Address(es)	Remarks
37	XPTR	RST	1	Location of $x_{n'}$
38	YPTR	RST	1	Location of $y_{m'}$
39	ZPTR	RST	1	Location of $z_{n'+m'}$
40	SIZE	RST	1	p
41	MOVEIN	RST	1	Instruction PIK $p+1$, BUFFER,**
42	MOVEOUT	RST	1	Instruction PUT p, BUFFER,**
43	RETURN	RST	1	Instruction TRA BACK1 or TRA BACK2
44	ONE	RST	1	1
45	BUFFER	RST	$p+1$	Place for record being transferred
46	ALPHA1	SET	MOVEIN,XPTR	MOVEIN ← PIK $p+1$, BUFFER,[XPTR].
47		SET	MOVEOUT,ZPTR	MOVEOUT ← PUT p, BUFFER,[ZPTR].
48		PIK	1,RETURN	RETURN ← TRA BACK1.
49		⌈TRA	BACK1	(This line "picked.")
50		JMP	MOVEIN	Execute three commands in short tank.
51	BACK1	ADD	NPRIME,ONE	$A ← n' + 1$.
52		STO	NPRIME	$n' ← A$.
53		SET	XKEY,BUFFER+p	Update key($x_{n'}$).
54		ADD	XPTR,SIZE	$A ← $[XPTR]$+p$.
55		STO	XPTR	Update location of $x_{n'}$.
56		ADD	ZPTR,SIZE	$A ← $[ZPTR]$+p$.
57		STO	ZPTR	Update location of $z_{n'+m'}$.
58		TRA	COMPARE	Return to COMPARE.

values; and then come the remaining "scratch" locations. Figure 2 shows the resulting complete program, including the initialization of the short tanks. (At this point in his discussion, von Neumann apparently forgot about TEMP1 and TEMP2; Figure 2 assigns them to the buffer area.)

Like nearly all programs, this one has a bug: The next-to-last line of Figure 2, "CON 1", actually belongs two lines earlier. If von Neumann had had an EDVAC on which to run his program, he would have discovered debugging!

Storage Allocation and Timing

Although von Neumann didn't use a symbolic language to express his instructions, as done here, his notation wasn't completely numeric either.

He used $\bar{1}_1, \bar{2}_1, \ldots$ for short tanks NPRIME, MPRIME, $\ldots$ in the first piece of code, and later $\bar{1}_2, \bar{2}_2, \ldots$ for the short tanks in the second, etc. Long tank locations were represented by unbarred numbers with subscripts; for example, lines 32 and 33 in his notation were written as follows:

$$1_\beta) \quad \bar{3}_2 - \bar{3}_2 \qquad\qquad \sigma) \quad \mathcal{N}0$$
$$2_\beta) \quad 2_\alpha \to \mathcal{C}$$

This was essentially a "regional" addressing technique, which was used by many programmers in the ensuing decade.

After having written the program, he assigned actual addresses to the subscripted ones. In order to make the code relocatable, for use as a general open subroutine, he let the addresses be relative to an unspecified starting location e. His address assignments are shown in Figure 2 at the right of the instructions.

He made an interesting and rather subtle error of judgment here, regarding latency time. Since the instruction in location ALPHA1+4 (line 50 of the program in the preceding section) jumps into the short tanks to execute three commands and transfer to BACK1, he didn't want BACK1 to occupy location ALPHA1+5 since the long tank wouldn't be ready for that instruction until at least 33 word times after ALPHA1+4. So he intercalated 4 empty words between ALPHA1+4 and BACK1, "in order to avoid a delay of about one long tank." But since the instructions in MOVEIN and MOVEOUT make essentially random references to long tanks, an elementary argument can be given to prove that the average computation time that elapses between the execution of instruction ALPHA1+4 and the execution of instruction BACK1 is $2p + 49.5$ word times, completely *independent* of the location of BACK1! Therefore BACK1 should really have been placed so that its *subsequent* instructions are optimally located, i.e., so that the TRA COMPARE takes the least amount of time. Von Neumann inserted extra blank words into the initialization routine for the same fallacious reason. On the other hand his allocations of ALPHA, BETA, and GAMMA vis-a-vis each other and the COMPARE routine were correctly handled; the instruction in SWITCH is not a random memory reference, so his intuition didn't mislead him here. (ALPHA1 and ALPHA2 were placed badly; this was apparently an oversight.)

Von Neumann discussed the relocatability of this routine by enumerating the nine instructions that are variable (those whose codes depend on p, EXIT, or the relocation factor e). He didn't say exactly how those instructions were to be changed after they have been read in from tape. He apparently did not yet realize that the limited EDVAC code

```
N          RST 1                                 PIK  1,RETURN           e+49
M          RST 1                                ⎡TRA  BACK1              e+50
XPTR       RST 1                                ⎣JMP  MOVEIN             e+51
YPTR       RST 1                      BACK1      ADD  NPRIME,ONE         e+56
ZPTR       RST 1                                 STO  NPRIME             e+57
SIZE       RST 1                                 SET  XKEY,BUFFER+p      e+58
XKEY       RST 1                                 ADD  XPTR,SIZE          e+59
YKEY       RST 1                                 STO  XPTR               e+60
NPRIME     RST 1                                 ADD  ZPTR,SIZE          e+61
MPRIME     RST 1                                 STO  ZPTR               e+62
LALPHA     RST 1                                 TRA  COMPARE            e+63
LBETA      RST 1                      ALPHA2 SET  MOVEIN,YPTR            e+64
LGAMMA     RST 1                                 SET  MOVEOUT,ZPTR       e+65
LDELTA     RST 1                                 PIK  1,RETURN           e+66
SWITCH     RST 1                                ⎡TRA  BACK2              e+67
LALPHA1    RST 1                                ⎣JMP  MOVEIN             e+68
LALPHA2    RST 1                      BACK2      ADD  MPRIME,ONE         e+73
ZERO       RST 1                                 STO  MPRIME             e+74
MONE       RST 1                                 SET  YKEY,BUFFER+p      e+75
ONE        RST 1                                 ADD  YPTR,SIZE          e+76
MOVEIN     RST 1                                 STO  YPTR               e+77
MOVEOUT    RST 1                                 ADD  ZPTR,SIZE          e+78
RETURN     RST 1                                 STO  ZPTR               e+79
BUFFER     RST p+1                                TRA  COMPARE            e+80
TEMP1      EQU BUFFER             BRING      EQU  NPRIME
TEMP2      EQU BUFFER+1           MERGE      PIK  3,BRING            e+0
                                             ⎡PIK  1,XKEY,**          e+1
COMPARE    SUB NPRIME,N      e+27  PIK  1,YKEY,**          e+2
           SEL LGAMMA,LALPHA e+28 ⎣TRA  BACK3              e+3
           STO TEMP1         e+29  SET  BRING,XPTR         e+4
           SUB NPRIME,N      e+30  SET  BRING+1,YPTR       e+5
           SEL LDELTA,LBETA  e+31  JMP  BRING              e+6
           STO TEMP2         e+32 BACK3      PIK  14,NPRIME          e+11
           SUB MPRIME,M      e+33 ⎡CON  0                 e+12
           SEL TEMP2,TEMP1   e+34  CON  0                 e+13
           STO SWITCH        e+35  CON  ALPHA             e+14
           JMP SWITCH        e+36  CON  BETA              e+15
ALPHA      SUB YKEY,XKEY     e+43  CON  GAMMA             e+16
           SEL LALPHA1,LALPHA2 e+44 CON  DELTA             e+17
           STO SWITCH        e+45  TRA  **                e+18
           JMP SWITCH        e+46  CON  ALPHA1            e+19
BETA       SUB ZERO,ZERO     e+39  CON  ALPHA2            e+20
           TRA ALPHA+1       e+40  CON  0                 e+21
GAMMA      SUB MONE,ZERO     e+41  CON  -1                e+22
           TRA ALPHA+1       e+42  PIK  p+1,BUFFER,**     e+23
DELTA      TRA EXIT          e+81  PUT  p,BUFFER,**       e+24
ALPHA1     SET MOVEIN,XPTR   e+47 ⎣CON  1                 e+25
           SET MOVEOUT,ZPTR  e+48  TRA  COMPARE           e+26
```

FIGURE 2. The complete program for merging.

he had proposed (with no shift instructions, for example) made it difficult or perhaps even impossible to insert p into the "PIK" and "PUT" instructions, since the machine could change instruction words only in the address field.

It is perhaps significant that he thought of this program as an open subroutine, not closed, since he did not regard EXIT as a parameter on a par with n, m, location(x_0), etc.

He concludes his memorandum with an analysis of the running time, leading to a total time of $2.60 + (n + m)(p/16 + 2.61)$ milliseconds. (His actual figure was 1.61 instead of 2.61, due to a slip in arithmetic.) Some errors in the calculation of latency times, related to his misunderstanding cited above, make this analysis slightly invalid; the reader may verify that the actual running time (averaged over all possible placements of x_0, y_0, and z_0 in the long tanks) is $3056 + (n + m)(64p + 4016)$ μsec. If we incorporate all of the improvements to the coding that have been mentioned above, the average time decreases to $2576 + (n + m)(64p + 2560)$ μsec.

The Sequel

After World War II came to an end, the original EDVAC group disbanded. Eckert and Mauchly remained in Philadelphia, to form their own company, while Goldstine and von Neumann went to the Institute for Advanced Study in Princeton. The veil of secrecy surrounding electronic computers was lifted when ENIAC was dedicated, and the great potential for high speed computing was gradually realized by more and more people. The principles of EDVAC's design were very strong influences on all of the computers constructed during the next decade (see [14]).

After von Neumann's first two versions of instruction codes had been digested by a number of people, other variations began to be proposed: In November 1945, Calvin N. Mooers devised a three-address code as an alternative to von Neumann's idea; and in August 1946, he lectured at the Moore School about a further development, the use of flagged data for terminating loops [13, Vol. 4, lecture 39]. Another interesting three-address code, due to John Mauchly, was described by Eckert in the same series of lectures [13, Vol. 1, lecture 10]. Meanwhile von Neumann had developed his ideas somewhat further; he and Goldstine, in collaboration with Arthur W. Burks, prepared a monograph that was to be the first widely circulated document about high speed computers, "Preliminary discussion of the logical design of an electronic computing instrument" [2]. By this time, their proposed machine had already changed drastically: It was to have a random-access (iconoscope) memory of 4096 40-bit words. Instructions were 20 bits long, packed two to a word. The operation codes had a different flavor, too, resembling today's IBM 7094 "Clear and add x", etc. Left and right shift operations were included for the first time.

The EDVAC project itself continued at the Moore School until August 1949, when EDVAC was delivered to the BRL. In its final form, the EDVAC had a four-address instruction code (the fourth address specifying the location of the next instruction), devised by Samuel Lubkin. Its memory consisted of 128 long tanks, each containing eight 44-bit words, plus six one-word nonaddressable short tanks, and an auxiliary drum. One of the only things that remained unchanged throughout most of its design was the basic clock rate of one μsec per bit; the completed machine processed one word every 48 μsec, leaving four "blank" bits between words. Further development work on input/output devices was necessary before EDVAC became operational late in 1951. Then it continued steady and inexpensive operation for many years, averaging, for example, 145 hours of useful work per week in 1961 [11]. It was finally retired from service in December 1962.

For the story of von Neumann's other pioneering contributions to computing, see Goldstine's recent account [6]. Goldstine and von Neumann published three important supplements to [2] during the next years; these famous documents [7–9] formed the foundation for computer programming techniques, covering a wide range of topics from flowcharts to numerical analysis to relocatable loading routines. Reference [8, Section 11] deals with sorting and merging in considerable detail; von Neumann here put the finishing touches onto the work he had sketched in 1945.

Acknowledgments

I wish to thank Drs. Goldstine and Mauchly for considerable assistance in checking the historical details presented in this paper, and for several delightfully informative discussions.

References

[1] Augusta Ada, Countess of Lovelace, annotated translation of "Sketch of the Analytical Engine invented by Charles Babbage" by L. F. Menabrea, in *Charles Babbage and his Calculating Engines*, edited by Philip Morrison and Emily Morrison (New York: Dover, 1961), 225–297; see also page 68.

[2] Arthur W. Burks, Herman H. Goldstine, and John von Neumann, *Preliminary Discussion of the Logical Design of an Electronic Computing Instrument* (Princeton, New Jersey: Institute for Advanced Study, 28 June 1946; 2nd edition, 2 September 1947), 42 pp. Reprinted in von Neumann's *Collected Works* **5**, edited by A. H. Taub (New York: Pergamon, 1963), 34–79.

[3] William H. Desmonde and Klaus J. Berkling, "The Zuse Z-3," *Datamation* **12**,9 (September 1966), 30–31.

[4] J. Presper Eckert, Jr., and John W. Mauchly, "Application of analyzer to a set of equations for external ballistics," in *Proposal for an Electronic Difference Analyzer*, edited by J. G. Brainerd (Philadelphia: Moore School of Electrical Engineering, University of Pennsylvania, 10 April 1943), Appendix C, 4 pp. (Originally classified "Confidential.")

[5] J. Presper Eckert, Jr., and John W. Mauchly, *Automatic High-Speed Computing: A Progress Report on the EDVAC* (Philadelphia: Moore School of Electrical Engineering, University of Pennsylvania, 30 September 1945), 111 pp. (Originally classified "Confidential.")

[6] Herman H. Goldstine, "Early electronic computers," in *Computers and Their Role in the Physical Sciences*, edited by S. Fernbach and A. H. Taub (New York: Gordon & Breach, 1970), 51–102.

[7] Herman H. Goldstine and John von Neumann, *Planning and Coding of Problems for an Electronic Computing Instrument* **1** (Princeton, New Jersey: Institute for Advanced Study, 1 April 1947), 69 pp. Reprinted in von Neumann's *Collected Works* **5**, edited by A. H. Taub (New York: Pergamon, 1963), 80–151.

[8] Herman H. Goldstine and John von Neumann, *Planning and Coding of Problems for an Electronic Computing Instrument* **2** (Princeton, New Jersey: Institute for Advanced Study, 15 April 1948), 68 pp. Reprinted in von Neumann's *Collected Works* **5**, edited by A. H. Taub (New York: Pergamon, 1963), 152–214.

[9] Herman H. Goldstine and John von Neumann, *Planning and Coding of Problems for an Electronic Computing Instrument* **3** (Princeton, New Jersey: Institute for Advanced Study, 16 August 1948), 23 pp. Reprinted in von Neumann's *Collected Works* **5**, edited by A. H. Taub (New York: Pergamon, 1963), 215–235.

[10] Harvard University, Staff of the Computation Laboratory, "A manual of operation for the automatic sequence-controlled calculator,"

edited by H. H. Aiken et al., *Annals of the Computation Laboratory* **1** (Cambridge, Massachusetts: Harvard University Press, 1946), 561 pp.

[11] Karl Kempf, *Electronic Computers Within the Ordnance Corps* (Aberdeen, Maryland: Aberdeen Proving Ground, November 1961), 140 pp.

[12] Angeline Pantages, "Computing's early years," *Datamation* **13**, 10 (October 1967), 60–65.

[13] George W. Patterson, editor, *Theory and Techniques for the Design of Electronic Digital Computers* (Philadelphia: Moore School of Electrical Engineering, University of Pennsylvania, 1946), 4 volumes.

[14] Saul Rosen, "Electronic computers: A historical survey," *Computing Surveys* **1** (March 1969), 7–36.

[15] George R. Stibitz, as told to Mrs. Evelyn Loveday, "The relay computers at Bell Labs," *Datamation* **13**, 4 (April 1967), 35–44; **13**, 5 (May 1967), 45–49.

[16] A. M. Turing, "On computable numbers, with an application to the Entscheidungsproblem," *Proceedings of the London Mathematical Society* (2) **42** (1936), 230–265; **43** (1937), 544–546.

[17] John von Neumann, *First Draft of a Report on the EDVAC* (Philadelphia: Moore School of Electrical Engineering, University of Pennsylvania, 30 June 1945), 101 pp. (This draft was written March–April 1945.) Reprinted, with corrections by M. D. Godfrey, in *IEEE Annals of the History of Computing* **15**, 4 (1993), 27–75.

[18] John von Neumann, letter to Herman H. Goldstine dated 8 May 1945.

Chapter 13

The IBM 650: An Appreciation from the Field

[Originally published in Annals of the History of Computing **8** *(1986),
50–55, as part of a special issue devoted to the IBM 650.]*

I suppose it was natural for a person like me to fall in love with his
first computer. But there was something special about the IBM 650,
something that has provided the inspiration for much of my life's work.
Somehow this machine was powerful in spite of its severe limitations.
Somehow it was friendly in spite of its primitive man-machine interface.

I had just turned 19 when I was offered a part-time job helping the
statisticians at Case Institute of Technology. My first task was to draw
graphs; but soon I was given some keypunching duties, and I was taught
how to use the wondrous card sorter. Meanwhile a strange new machine
had been installed across the hall — it was what our student newspaper
called "an IBM 650 Univac," or a "giant brain." I was fascinated to look
through the window and see the lights flashing on its console.

One afternoon George Haynam explained some of the machine's
internal code to a bunch of us freshmen who happened to be in the lab.
It all sounded mysterious to me, but it seemed to make a bit of sense,
so I got ahold of some manuals. My first chance to try the machine
came a few weeks later, when one of the upperclassmen at the fraternity
I was pledging needed to know the five roots of a particular fifth degree
equation. I decided that it would be fun to compute the roots by using
the 650. More precisely, I had been reading the manual of the Bell
Interpretive System [14], and I decided that polynomial root finding
would be a good test case.

A program for the Bell System (as we called it) consisted of 10-digit
numbers like "1 271 314 577," which meant, "Add the (floating-point)
number in location 271 to the (floating-point) number in location 314

227

and put the result in location 577." I found a book that gave formulas for the roots of a general fourth-degree equation; so it was easy to factor a general real polynomial of degree 5 by first doing a simple-minded search for a real root r, then dividing by $x - r$ and plugging the result into the formulas for quartics.

I realize now how lucky I was to have had such a good first encounter with computers. The polynomial problem was well matched to my mathematical knowledge and interests; and I had a chance for hands-on experience, pushing buttons on the machine and seeing it punch the cards containing the answers. Furthermore the Bell language was an easy way to learn the notion of a program that a machine could carry out. I've forgotten the name of the fraternity brother who asked me to solve this particular problem, but I bet he's kicking himself now for not having done it himself.

I often wonder whether it might not still be best to teach programming to novices by starting with a numeric language like that of the Bell interpreter, instead of an algebraic language like BASIC or LOGO. I think a small child can understand machine-like language better than an algebraic language. But I know that such ideas are now considered out of date, and I suppose I'm being an old fogey.

I learned a few years ago that the Bell interpreter had been inspired by John Backus's Speedcoding System for the IBM 701 [1]. During my student days I had never heard of the 701; and this, I think, leads to an important point: The IBM 650 was the first computer to be manufactured in really large quantities. Therefore the number of people in the world who knew about programming increased by an order of magnitude. Most of the world's programmers at that particular time knew only about the 650, and were unaware of the already extensive history of computer developments in other countries and on other machines. We can still see this phenomenon occurring today, as the number of programmers continues to grow rapidly.

When I did finally learn about the existence of the IBM 701, it had been improved to the 709, and it was shortly to become the 7090; but I must confess that I still liked my good old 650 a whole lot better. The 650 had only 44 operation codes [2], while the 709 had more than 200; yet I never enjoyed coding for the 709, because I never seemed to be able to write short and elegant programs for it — the opcodes didn't blend together especially well. By contrast, it was somehow quite easy and pleasant to do complex things on the 650 with very few instructions. Most of the commands in the 650's repertoire accomplished several things at once, and it was frequently possible to make good use of the side effects. For example, the instruction

60   1234   1009

meant, "Load the contents of location 1234 into the upper accumulator and the distributor; set the lower accumulator to zero; and then go to location 1009 for the next instruction." All four of these actions were often useful in the subsequent program steps.

In fact, I usually got by with only 34 of the 44 opcodes, because I seldom had a good application for the ten "branch on distributor digit equal to 8" commands. After 25 years I still can remember the numeric codes for most of the remaining 34 ops; and I'll never forget the fact that addresses 8001, 8002, and 8003 referred to the distributor, lower, and upper accumulator registers.

The 650's "one-plus-one address" code, in which each instruction designated the location of its successor (and branch instructions designated both successors) has been rejected by modern machine designers, for good reasons. But it was in fact extremely effective, because it allowed convenient subroutine linkage and because it became easy to execute instructions from registers. A one-plus-one scheme was important, of course, on a machine without random access memory, because it meant that instructions could be located in "optimum" places on the magnetic drum.

The incredible thing about the 650 was that we could do so many things with it, although it was three orders of magnitude slower than today's computers, and it had three orders of magnitude less memory. The memory consisted of 2000 words, where each word had ten decimal digits plus a sign bit; thus, the total storage capacity was less than 10K bytes. These 2000 words were stored on a magnetic drum that rotated at 12,500 rpm; that's slightly less than 5 milliseconds per revolution. One drum revolution was 50 word times. You could add two numbers in 7 word times (672 microseconds) provided that the addition instruction and its operand and the next instruction were located at just the right places on the drum. But addition would take 106 word times (10.2 milliseconds) if the data was pessimally placed. A division instruction took at least 63 word times plus twice the sum of the digits in the quotient.

In practice, the memory space limitation was more important than anything else during my first year of programming. I had to learn how to pack data and how to use subroutines in order to save space. For example, my first large program was a tic-tac-toe routine that "learned" to play by remembering the relative desirability or undesirability of each position that it had ever encountered. The hardest part was figuring out how to keep one digit of memory for each possible configuration of the board; board positions that were equivalent under rotation or reflection were considered to be identical.

The first program that I ever wrote in machine language still stands out in my mind. It was June, 1957, and my freshman year at Case had just ended. I decided to hang around Cleveland instead of going home, and I was allowed to stay up all night playing with the computer by myself. So I attempted to write a program that would find prime factors. The idea was that a person could set up any 10-digit number in the console switches and start my routine, which would punch the corresponding prime factors on a card and stop; then another number could be set up and factored in the same way, etc. I think my first draft program was about 80 instructions long; but I didn't save it, so I can't be sure. Anyway, I wrote it as a sequence of about 80 decimal numbers, and punched it onto cards — much as I had done with my previous (Bell System) program for root-finding. Then I sat down at the console of the machine and began to learn how to debug, using the "half cycle" switch to step through the instructions slowly, or using the "address stop" switch to discover when the program used particular locations for data or instructions. The 650 console was excellent for online debugging, and nobody else was using the machine at that time of night.

Well, my program was riddled with errors, and I removed them one by one during the next two weeks. Besides the "obvious" mistakes, I hadn't realized at first that a 10-digit number can have as many as 33 prime factors. Only eight numbers could be punched on a card, so the program would sometimes have to punch up to five cards. (My original program was only able to punch a single card.) Then I had to clear the memory between runs so that spurious data from a previous factorization wouldn't appear on the next one, and so on. You know the story; we all make the same mistakes. I was lucky enough to have the opportunity to make lots of mistakes right from the beginning, and to diagnose them all by myself, sitting at the machine. All the facts I needed were available to me, because I was working in machine language and no operating system or other software was interposing itself between me and what I needed to know. Debugging took a long time at first, but I think I had the machine to myself about six hours every night.

Finally I arrived at a program that was satisfactory. I vaguely recall that it took about 11 minutes to determine that the number 9999999967 was prime, although at one point this particular test case had taken 17 minutes.

By this time my program had grown to 140 words long, and I think I had changed each of the instructions at least twice. I had also learned about the SOAP assembly language [12], so my final program was expressed in symbolic form; I had been weaned away from numeric machine language during those two weeks. The success of this program gave me the confidence to try another, which converted a given number on the console switches to a specified radix. Then I was really for tic-tac-toe.

The SOAP language allowed symbols to be up to five letters long, and I recall spending a lot of time trying to come up with suitable names. It was a great moment when I hit on the right term for the program step to be executed when the computer had won at tic-tac-toe by finding three ×'s in a row: I called that step BINGO.

I regret to report that I've just recently looked again at my programs for prime factors and tic-tac-toe, and they are entirely free of any sort of comments or documentation.

Shortly afterwards I encountered the SOAP II manual [11], which impressed me greatly and had an enormous influence on my subsequent career. This manual included the entire listing of SOAP II in its own language, and the program was absolutely beautiful. Reading Poley's code was like listening to a symphony. I wanted to be able to compose programs like that. The SOAP II program also taught me several new techniques, such as hashing. My next project was to write a modification of SOAP II that would have worked on a 650 with only 1000 words of memory. (I had heard that such machines existed, but I never actually saw one.) Then I spent the rest of the summer writing SOAP III [4], which went the other way by adding additional features for enhanced 650s with index registers and/or floating-point hardware.

SOAP III was my introduction to software writing. In particular, I learned about what is now called "creeping featurism," where each of my friends would suggest different things they wanted in an assembler. I probably tried to accommodate them all, since SOAP III had 24 pseudo-operations that were not in SOAP II. I also left 150 memory locations available for user-defined pseudo-operations. And I put liberal comments into the code, having learned that lesson at last.

Our lab received an amazing 650 program from Carnegie Tech during the summer of '57, namely the famous IT compiler by Perlis, Smith, and Van Zoeren [10]. IT took algebraic statements as input, then computed awhile, and punched SOAP programs as output. I had no idea how such a feat would be possible, but I got a copy of the program listing at the end of the summer and read it while vacationing with my parents at a beach resort on Lake Erie. This program was not beautifully written like Poley's, but it accomplished remarkable things. So naturally I had an urge to rewrite everything, in the Poley-like style of 650 coding that I had just learned. Bill Lynch and I began this project late in 1957, under the direction of Fred Way III and George Haynam. We first called our program Compiler III, but it eventually became known as RUNCIBLE ([6] and [13]). The language was a superset of Perlis's IT, and we worked very hard to squeeze in as many new features as we could.

Somehow it was possible to cram a rather complex compiler into the 2000 words of the 650. Yet when we were done, I don't think we could have gotten by with only 1999 words, because we had spent considerable time finding every last bit of space — by using terrible tricks. Small changes to one part of our code would usually cause some apparently unrelated part to blow up. I guess Parkinson's Law applies to programs as well as to organizations; we kept adding features until the space was filled.

RUNCIBLE had four versions called AX, AY, BX, and BY, where X stood for object code that invoked subroutines for floating-point arithmetic while Y stood for object code that used the 650's optional floating-point hardware; A stood for SOAP output, while B stood for directly loadable machine language programs punched five per card (bypassing the need for assembly). It turned out that the X version became a Y version by replacing exactly 95 instructions by 95 others; similarly, the A version became a B by replacing exactly 406 instructions by 406 others. If we discovered a way to save one line of code in, say, the A version, we looked closely at the B version until we had saved a line there too.

We called the A version "two-pass operation" while the B version was called "one-pass." At the end of the summer I hacked together a "zero-pass" version that took one less pass than B, since it loaded machine instructions directly into memory locations instead of punching anything on cards. For this I had to eliminate the matrix feature of IT; that is, doubly subscripted arrays were not permitted in "RUNCIBLE zero." My main goal was to prove that 2000 locations were not too few for a compile-load-and-go system, because somebody (Perlis?) had reportedly said that it would be impossible.

By 1959 our lab had acquired the ultimate in 650 upgrades: We had a full 653 system [3] including index registers, floating-point hardware, and 60 whole new words of core memory! It was heavenly. Besides this, we put our printer online (so that listings didn't have to be made via cards); we acquired a RAMAC disk storage and several tape units.

At this point it was desirable to have a new assembly program so that we could make proper use of the new equipment. I therefore wrote

SuperSoap [5], a major improvement over SOAP III. I'm still pretty proud of SuperSoap, because it introduced some good ways of dealing with programs that would be loaded into the drum but executed from core, and because I had the courage to remove some features of SOAP III that didn't work as well as planned. Furthermore SuperSoap introduced what I think was the best approach to the problem of "optimizing" the drum locations of data and instructions for the 650; it was a combination of machine and hand methods [7].

The name SOAP, by the way, stood for "Symbolic Optimal Assembly Program"; and "optimal" meant that the machine would choose drum locations so that at least one reference to that location would involve no delay. Such optimization was much better than random placement of instructions. I had (for fun) experimented with what I called SHOAP, a "Symbolic Horribly Optimizing Assembly Program" that used the algorithm of SOAP in reverse: At least one SHOAP'd reference to each location would lead to a 49-word-time delay. By adding seven cards to the normal SOAP program deck, you had SHOAP, which produced extremely slow programs. Conversely, it was possible to improve significantly on SOAP's performance by choosing locations carefully by hand and rewriting the program when necessary, as I discuss in [7]. The Bell Interpretive System had been hand-optimized in a particularly beautiful way, which was quite an inspiration to me. In 1958 I wrote HAND SOAP, which permitted me to hand optimize the locations without giving up the advantage of symbolic assembly. We used HAND SOAP to prepare the run-time system for RUNCIBLE. SuperSoap was designed later to incorporate similar ideas into a full-fledged assembler.

All of this software was given away free, of course. I don't believe my cohorts and I ever thought about making a penny from it. We were motivated by the fact that our programs made it easier for people like ourselves to use marvelous machines like the 650 more effectively. Our ultimate thrill was to find a user who appreciated what we did.

Somebody in 1958 or so circulated a joke about a program called RINSO, a "Real Ingenious New Symbolic Optimizer"; we were carried away by acronyms in those days. For some reason there has been an intimate relation between cleaning agents and the software that I've written through the years, even though my programs haven't always been very clean. For example, John McNeley and I devised a system called SOL in 1963 [9]; when I visited Norway a few years later I learned that SOL is the name of a Norwegian laundry detergent. Even more amazing was that my MIXAL assembler language [8] turned out to have the same name as a popular detergent in Yugoslavia — although I had

had no idea that `MIXAL` could possibly be a word in any language! More recently, I have learned that TEX is a brand name for toilet paper in Greece. ... But I am digressing.

My preface to the SuperSoap manual [5] gives a glimpse into the mood that prevailed at IBM 650 sites during the late 50s:

> "Soap 3 was written attempting to get as many features into 2000 memory locations as possible, but SuperSoap was written under a different philosophy; speed was the prime consideration, and storage space was conserved only when speed was not appreciably decreased. A factor of roughly 3:1 in running time over Soap 3 has thus been obtained. ... Some of the pseudo-op rules have become more logical thanks to Carnegie Tech's TASS [a competing assembler, written by Art Evans] ... Once again much gratitude must be given to the Case Computing Center for letting me chew up thousands of cards."

On rereading SuperSoap, I find most of it reasonably similar to today's assemblers except in one significant respect: We assumed in 1959 that the computer lab would be an "open shop" operation in which any student could come in and take personal charge of the machines while running a program. Therefore the error messages in SuperSoap consisted of machine halts, and my manual gave the following advice for error recovery:

> "SuperSoap believes that the best place to catch errors is during assembly, and so it will stop if it finds something amiss. ... The offending card is the fourth-last card out if you clear the read feed. ... To restart, correct the bad card ..., reinsert it in the deck, and hit Program Start."

There was a keypunch right next to the operator's console, so this was probably the most efficient way to get the job done in those days.

Cards, cards, cards; we used tens of thousands each day. The runtime system of RUNCIBLE had a debugging feature whereby you could turn the console knobs and get a card punched for every statement of your program that was being executed; or you could even trace every machine-language operation, with one card per instruction. The IBM 533 Card Read Punch could produce 100 cards per minute, and it often did.

One of the nice things about the 650 and its peripherals was their robustness: Our computing center staff could safely let random students work all of the IBM machines, changing plugboard control panels, clearing the punch hopper, mounting tapes, fixing card jams, etc., without worrying that the machines would be ruined. (This was emphatically *not* the case for the UNIVAC equipment in another part of our laboratory. Those machines had been designed with the assumption that a trained operator would always be in attendance, and I tended to break them accidentally every time I went nearby. If all computers had been like those fragile devices, a lot of people like me would never have gotten a good start on the use of computing machines, because we would never have been allowed to touch them.)

During all my days with the 650 I encountered only two instances where the design could perhaps have been made slightly more foolproof: Once I discovered a special case of the divide operation that put our machine into an infinite loop, restartable only by hitting Power Off. (Later I visited Carnegie Tech and tried it on *their* 650 when nobody was looking; it blew the fuse! Ah yes, those were the joys of student life.) The other time was when one of the tiny console display lights was broken. The glass was gone and two little wires were sticking out. I changed the display so that this particular light was supposed to be off, then tried to pull out the broken bulb by grabbing onto what looked like a dead filament. This gave me quite a jolt, and I was sick for a day or so. Perhaps the machine was trying to fill my brain with advice about how to write better software; or perhaps it was trying to kill me.

By 1959 I had developed a pretty good style of 650 coding, but I must confess also being addicted to tricks. One of the competitions between us students was to do as much as possible with programs that would fit on a single card — which had room for only eight instructions. One of the unsolved problems was to take the 10-digit number on the console and to reverse its digits from left to right, then display the answer and stop; nobody could figure out how to do this on a single card. But one day I proudly marched up to the machine and made a demonstration: I read in a card, then dialled the number 0123456789 on the console, and started the machine. Sure enough, it stopped, displaying the number 9876543210. Everybody applauded. I didn't explain until later that my card would display the number 9876543210 regardless of what number appeared on the console switches.

There's more to the story. Our machine eventually acquired an extra set of console switches, which were called register 8004. (As far as I know, Case's 650 was unique with this particular feature.) It turned out that nine instructions on an extended 650 were sufficient to reverse the digits of a number, and the ninth instruction could be put into one of the two sets of console switches. Therefore I was able to solve the problem without cheating (see the appendix below).

The dirtiest trick I ever discovered for the extended 650 was to use the instruction "shift and count by 9004" in a certain context. It so happened that this one instruction caused four things to happen simultaneously: (a) the upper accumulator was shifted left by four digits; (b) the lower accumulator was set equal to 10; (c) the core memory "timing ring" was set to 9004; and (d) the overflow indicator was turned on. I had an application in which all four of those things were useful.

I wrote a program for basketball statistics in 1958. Case's public relations department got wind of it and put out a news release; the IBM 650 got some free nation-wide publicity as a result [15].

SuperSoap was the last system software I wrote for the 650; I used it to assemble numerous "useful" programs during the following academic year. Then I graduated, and began to tackle other machines. My favorite computer for the next five years became the Burroughs 220, which was another joy to use. But that's another story.

A number of my classmates and coworkers at Case later became leading figures in other computing centers; this includes people like Bill Lynch, Mel Conway, Joe Speroni, Gilbert Steil, Jack Alanen, Mike Harrison, and many others. Our incubation period with the 650 was the foundation of our later work. And the same is true for thousands of other people (e.g., Bob Floyd and Nils Nilsson) who became intimately familiar with 650s at other computer centers.

What was it about the 650 that made our experiences such a good foundation for our later careers? Surely I wouldn't recommend that today's software be produced as we did the job then; we would never advance very far past the rudimentary levels achieved in those days, if we remained rooted in that methodology. But growing up with the 650 gave us valuable intuitions about what is easy for a machine to do and what is hard. It was a great machine on which to learn about machines. We had a computer architecture that was rudimentary but pleasant to use; and we had program masterpieces like the Bell interpreter and Poley's assembler, as examples of excellent style.

We were forced to think and to develop our abilities to make mental abstractions about control structures. These experiences seem to have made us better able to do complex things later, when the task became easier. I'm reminded that Edsger Dijkstra began his programming experience in a similar way (but on a different computer); he and Zonneveld wrote the first Algol 60 compiler in a strictly numeric machine language.

Well, this article about the 650 has turned out to be largely autobiographical. The fact is, it's impossible for me to write about that wonderful machine without writing about myself. We were very close.

(One night I missed a date with my wife-to-be, because I was so engrossed in debugging that I had forgotten all about the time; I'll never live that down.) The 650 provided me with solid instruction in the art of computer programming. It was directly related to the topics of the first two technical articles that I ever submitted for publication ([6] and [7]). Therefore it's not at all surprising that I decided in 1967 to dedicate my books on computer programming

> "to the Type 650 computer once installed at
> Case Institute of Technology,
> in remembrance of many pleasant evenings."

Appendix

NUMBER PERVERTER DEMONSTRATION CARD   (8/15/59)

Instructions for use:

Prepare console as follows:

Storage Entry	70 9000 9001+
Half Cycle	RUN
Address	8000
Control	ADDRESS STOP
Display	UPPER ACCUM

Place Perversion Card in read hopper.
Depress Computer Reset, Program Start.
Depress START and END OF FILE simultaneously
    on card reader.
The program should now be stopped with
    8000 in the Address Lights.
Change Storage Entry switches to 60 8004 9001+
Now the program is satisfactorily initialized.

Set 8004 to any number. Press Program Start. When the machine stops, the number will appear with its digits reading from right to left instead of from left to right.

You may reset 8004 and depress Program Start again as often as you wish.

The card:		
	(9000) 40 9007 8000 NZA	(9004) 00 0000 0010
	(9001) 20 9009 9002 STL	(9005) 10 9009 9006 AUP
	(9002) 65 8003 9003 RAL	(9006) 50 1000 9000 AXA
	(9003) 14 9004 9005 DIV	(9007) 19 9004 9001 MPY

References

[1] J. W. Backus, "The IBM 701 Speedcoding System," *Journal of the Association for Computing Machinery* **1** (1954), 4–6.

[2] International Business Machines Corporation, "IBM 650 Data-Processing System, Manual of Operation," form 22-6060-1 (June 1955), 111 pp. This was described as a "major revision" of forms 22-6060-0 and 22-6149-0, copyright 1953 and 1955.

[3] IBM 650 Data Processing Bulletin, "Immediate access storage, indexing registers, automatic floating-decimal arithmetic, and magnetic tape," form G24-5003-0 (June 1959), 48 pp.

[4] Donald E. Knuth, "Case SOAP III," Case Institute of Technology Computer Center reports, series 4, vol. 1 (February 1958), 28 pp.

[5] Donald E. Knuth, "SuperSoap," Case Institute of Technology Computer Center reports, series 4, vol. 2 (August 1959), 55 pp.

[6] Donald E. Knuth, "RUNCIBLE — Algebraic translation on a limited computer," *Communications of the ACM* **2**, 11 (November 1959), 18–21.

[7] Donald E. Knuth, "Minimizing drum latency time," *Journal of the Association for Computing Machinery* **8** (1961), 119–150.

[8] Donald E. Knuth, *The Art of Computer Programming*, Vol. 1: *Fundamental Algorithms* (Reading, Massachusetts: Addison–Wesley, 1968), xxii + 634 pp.

[9] D. E. Knuth and J. L. McNeley, "SOL — A symbolic language for general-purpose systems simulation," *IEEE Transactions on Electronic Computers* **EC–13** (1964), 401–414.

[10] A. J. Perlis, J. W. Smith, and H. R. Van Zoeren, "A mathematical language compiler," in *Automatic Coding* (Philadelphia: Franklin Institute monograph no. 3), 87–102. For further information see Luis Trabb Pardo and Donald E. Knuth, "The early development of programming languages," in *A History of Computing in the Twentieth Century*, edited by N. Metropolis, J. Howlett, and G.-C. Rota (New York: Academic Press, 1980), 197–273.

[11] Stan Poley, "SOAP II Programmer's Reference Manual," IBM Corporation form 32-7646 (1957), 94 pp.

[12] S. Poley and G. Mitchell, "Symbolic Optimum Assembly Programming (SOAP)," *650 Programming Bulletin* **1**, IBM Corporation form 22-6285-1 (November 1955), 4 pp.

[13] Staff of the computing center, "Runcible I," Case Institute of Technology Computer Center reports, series 5, vol. 1 (March 1959), 67 pp.

[14] V. M. Wolontis, "A complete floating-decimal interpretive system for the IBM 650 magnetic drum calculator," Technical Newsletter No. 11, IBM Applied Science Division (March 1956), 63 + xxi pp.

[15] [anonymous], "What's that about a score card? A computer's the thing," Newsweek (5 January 1959), 63.

The preparation of this paper was supported in part by the National Science Foundation. When I submitted the manuscript to Cuthbert Hurd in 1983 I said, "Tears ran from my eyes as I (sob) wrote the conclusion!"

The author at the console in 1958. The row of switches at the top was Case's "register 8004." (Photo by Case News Service.)

Chapter 14

Artistic Programming

[Originally published in Current Contents®, Physical, Chemical & Earth Sciences 33, 34 (23 August 1993), 8, as "This Week's Citation Classic." At that time the Science Citation Index® indicated that The Art of Computer Programming had been cited in more than 4,345 publications; see [1]. The author was asked to write a commentary about the books, emphasizing the human side of the research — how the project was initiated, whether any obstacles were encountered, and why the work was highly cited.]

On my 24th birthday, a representative of Addison–Wesley asked me whether I'd like to write a book about software creation. At that time (1962) I was a grad student in mathematics at Caltech. I had no idea that a new discipline called computer science would soon begin to spring up at numerous campuses, nor did I realize that "deep-down" I was really a computer scientist, not a mathematician. Computer scientists hadn't discovered each other yet. But I'd been writing computer programs to help support my education, and the book project was immediately appealing.

By the time I reached home that day I had planned the book in my mind, and I quickly jotted down the titles of 12 chapters. But I had almost no time to work on the manuscript until after receiving my PhD in June 1963; I spent the summer of 1962 writing a FORTRAN compiler for UNIVAC. I did take one day off to investigate the statistical properties of "linear probing," an important way to locate data [2], and I happened to discover a trick that made a mathematical analysis possible. This experience profoundly changed my book-writing plans; I decided that a quantitative rather than qualitative approach would be the best way to organize and present the techniques of computing. I also decided to emphasize aesthetics, the creation of programs that are beautiful [3].

241

I worked feverishly during the next years and finally finished the first draft in June 1965. By then I had accumulated 3,000 pages of hand-written manuscript. I typed up chapter 1 and sent it to the publishers as sort of a progress report, and they said, "Whoa, Don! If all 12 chapters are like the first, your book will be more than 2,000 pages long." My estimate of manuscript pages per printed page was off by a factor of three.

After hectic conferences we agreed to change the original book to a series of seven volumes. If I had continued to type the other chapters as they existed in 1965, all seven books would have been published by 1970; but computer science continued its explosive growth, and I decided to try keeping up with current developments. Thus I was lucky to finish volume 3 by 1973. By 1977 I had completed part of volume 4, but the subject of that volume — combinatorial algorithms — had become such a hot topic that more than half of all articles in computer science journals were being devoted to it. So I tried to gain efficiency by taking a year off to develop computer tools for typography. Alas, that project took 11 years [4].

Meanwhile people do seem to like the published volumes [5], for which I received the Turing award in 1974 and the National Medal of Science in 1979. The books have been translated into Russian, Chinese, Japanese, Spanish, Romanian, and Hungarian; more than 475,000 copies have been sold in English. They probably became *Citation Classics*® because they discuss classic principles of computing. I'm now working full time on volumes 4A, 4B, and 4C, which should be completed in 2003.

[1] Eugene Garfield, "The 100 most-cited books in the *CompuMath Citation Index*, 1976–1980," *Essays of an Information Scientist* **7** (1984), 264–269.

[2] Donald E. Knuth, "Algorithms," *Scientific American* **236**, 4 (April 1977), 63–80. [Reprinted as Chapter 3 of the present volume.]

[3] ———, "Computer programming as an art," *Communications of the ACM* **17** (1974), 667–673. Reprinted in *ACM Turing Award Lectures* (New York: ACM Press, 1987), 33–46. [Also reprinted as Chapter 1 of *Literate Programming*.]

[4] ———, "The errors of TEX," *Software — Practice & Experience* **19** (1989), 607–685. [Reprinted with additions as Chapters 10 and 11 of *Literate Programming*.]

[5] Eric A. Weiss, "In the art of programming, Knuth is first; there is no second," *Abacus* **1** (1984), 41–48.

Chapter 15

Speech in St. Petersburg

*[Given at St. Petersburg University, 11 May 1994. Originally published in Programming and Computer Software **20** (1994), 290.]*

It was a wonderful surprise for me to learn that St. Petersburg University would be granting me a doctor's degree. In fact I did not believe it at first, because I first learned the news in an email message; somehow electronic mail does not seem as authoritative as an old-fashioned letter! But the doctorate seems to be real indeed, so I now have the great honor to join the ranks of the many distinguished alumni of this university.

I am especially pleased to accept this honor on behalf of the young field of computer science. The fact that an outstanding Russian university is giving such recognition for the first time to a computer scientist is good news for computer scientists everywhere, because it means that we are slowly growing from scientific childhood to young adulthood. More and more academic people now realize that computer science is not only a branch of knowledge that helps physicists do physics and helps biologists do biology and helps doctors practice medicine and helps mathematicians explore mathematics and helps historians write history and helps musicians write music; computer science also helps computer scientists develop computer science. In other words, computer science is a field that relates strongly to all aspects of human endeavor, yet it also deals with new problems that are interesting for their own sake.

I am also especially pleased to be here in St. Petersburg because so many of the people who have influenced my own life most positively have been closely associated with this city. Above all I am thrilled to be in the place where Leonhard Euler did most of his work, as he revolutionized mathematics during the 18th century. Euler came here in 1727 when he was just 20 years old, shortly after the university was founded — when wolves were still roaming the streets. Mathematics is the science of patterns, and Euler discovered hundreds of the most significant patterns that we know. Nowadays we take most of these fantastic discoveries for

243

granted, but before Euler's time nobody dared to guess that mathematics would turn out to be so rich and exciting. Euler also revolutionized mathematical notations — the symbols we use to describe abstract ideas. He challenged the printers and typesetters of St. Petersburg to produce mathematical books with new high standards of typography. And perhaps even more important were the ways in which Euler revolutionized the teaching and communication of mathematics — he was a master expositor. His collected works, which fill more than sixty volumes, have influenced more great mathematicians than the writings of any other person.

I feel a deep bond to St. Petersburg also because of the work of great musicians like Borodin, Tchaikovsky, and Prokofiev. These composers were themselves masters of mathematical and combinatorial patterns; they have brought me many moments of intense pleasure.

Computer science has its own variety of patterns, complementary to yet distinct from the patterns of mathematics and music. My own work has been largely devoted to the aesthetic aspects of those patterns, to the creation of computer programs that are beautiful as works of art. I believe that computer programs are best regarded as works of literature: to be read by people, not primarily by machines. A computer program can be doubly beautiful, because of the function it performs and because of the graceful way it does the job. In a similar fashion, the Petrovsky room we are in is beautiful both because it provides shelter and structure and because it delights our senses and our intellects. A computer programmer can get double satisfaction from solving an important problem and solving it with elegance.

One of the nicest things about computers is that they are getting better while everything else is getting worse. Even in these times of serious economic inflation, the amount of computation that can be performed per ruble continues to increase. This gives me hope that computers will be a big help in solving the problems that now face our world. The potential is great, but the tasks are enormously difficult. Through greatly improved methods of communication, computer scientists in St. Petersburg are joining forces with computer scientists around the world to meet these challenges.

Chapter 16

George Forsythe and the Development of Computer Science

[Originally published in Communications of the ACM **15** *(1972), 721–726, as part of a special issue dedicated to the memory of G. E. Forsythe.]*

The sudden death of George Forsythe this spring was a serious loss to everyone associated with computing. When we recall the many things he contributed to the field during his lifetime, we consider ourselves fortunate that computer science has had such an able leader.

My purpose in this article is to review George Forsythe's contributions to the establishment of Computer Science as a recognized discipline. It is generally agreed that he, more than any other man, is responsible for the rapid development of computer science in the world's colleges and universities. His foresight, combined with his untiring efforts to spread the gospel of computing, have had a significant and lasting impact; one might almost regard him as the Martin Luther of the Computer Reformation!

Since George's publications express these ideas so well, I believe the best way to summarize his work is to repeat many of the things he said, in his own words. This article consists mainly of the quotations that particularly struck me as I reread his papers recently. Indeed, much of what follows belongs in a computer-science supplement to Bartlett's *Familiar Quotations.*

From Numerical Analysis to Computer Science

George's early training and research in numerical analysis was a good blend of theory and practice:

The fact that the CPC was generally wrong when I knew the answer made me wonder what it was like for someone who didn't know what to expect. [76, p. 5]

Starting in 1948 he worked for the National Bureau of Standards' Institute for Numerical Analysis in Los Angeles, California, where he did extensive programming for the SWAC computer. In 1954 this Institute became part of U.C.L.A., and he put a great deal of energy into the teaching of mathematics and numerical analysis.

He also worked on nonnumerical problems, such as the tabulation of all possible semigroups on four elements; at this time, he considered such combinatorial algorithms to be a part of numerical analysis [46, p. 7], and he regarded automatic programming as another branch [49, p. 655]. He began to foresee the less obvious implications of programming:

The use of practically any computing technique itself raises a number of mathematical problems. There is thus a very considerable impact of computation on mathematics itself, and this may be expected to influence mathematical research to an increasing degree. [46, p. 5]

The automatic computer really forces that precision of thinking which is alleged to be a product of any study of mathematics. [49, p. 655]

He also noticed that the rise of computers was being accompanied by an unprecedented demand for young mathematicians:

The majority of our undergraduate mathematics majors are lured at once into the marketplace, where they are greatly in demand as servants of the fast-multiplying family of fast-multiplying computers. [49, p. 651]

Therefore he began to argue that computers should play a prominent role in undergraduate mathematics education. At this time he felt that only one new course was needed for undergraduates, namely an introduction to programming; he stressed that the best way to teach it would be to combine computer programming with the traditional courses, instead of having separate training in numerical analysis. His paper "The Role of Numerical Analysis in an Undergraduate Program" [49] suggests over 50 good ways to mix computing into other courses. These suggestions ought to be required reading for all teachers today, since they are now perhaps even more relevant than they were in 1959. Indeed, the adaptation of traditional courses has been painfully slow (probably because professors of the older generation have not wanted to dirty their hands with the newfangled machines). In 1970 Forsythe was still strongly urging mathematics teachers to bend a little:

> Compared with most undergraduate subjects, mathematics courses are very easy to prepare for, because they change so slowly. The computing part of it is probably the only part that changes much. Why not devote time to learning that? [80, p. 23]

In 1961 we find him using the term "computer science" for the first time in his writing:

> [Computers] are developing so rapidly that even computer scientists cannot keep up with them. It must be bewildering to most mathematicians and engineers. ... In spite of the diversity of the applications, the methods of attacking the difficult problems with computers show a great unity, and the name of Computer Sciences is being attached to the discipline as it emerges. It must be understood, however, that this is still a young field whose structure is still nebulous. The student will find a great many more problems than answers. [59, p. 177]

He identified the "computer sciences" as the theory of programming, numerical analysis, data processing, and the design of computer systems. He observed that the latter three were better understood than the theory of programming, and more available in courses.

The Establishment of Computer Science

By that time Forsythe knew that numerical analysis was destined to be only a part of the computing milieu; a new discipline was crystallizing, which cried out to be taught. He had come to Stanford as a professor of mathematics in 1957, but now he and Professor John Herriot wanted to hire colleagues interested in programming, artificial intelligence, and similar topics, which are not considered mathematics. Stanford's administration, especially Dean Bowker (who is now Chancellor at Berkeley), also became convinced that computing is important; so George was able to found the Division of Computer Science within the Mathematics Department in 1961.

During that academic year he lectured on "Educational Implications of the Computer Revolution" at Brown University:

> Machine-held strings of binary digits can simulate a great many kinds of things, of which numbers are just one kind. For example, they can simulate automobiles on a freeway, chess pieces, electrons in a box, musical notes, Russian words, patterns on

a paper, human cells, colors, electrical circuits, and so on. To think of a computer as made up essentially of numbers is simply a carry-over from the successful use of mathematical analysis in studying models. ...Enough is known already of the diverse applications of computing for us to recognize the birth of a coherent body of technique, which I call *computer science.* ...Whether computers are used for engineering design, medical data processing, composing music, or other purposes, the structure of computing is much the same. We are extremely short of talented people in this field, and so we need departments, curricula, and research and degree programs in computer science. ...I think of the Computer Science Department as eventually including experts in Programming, Numerical Analysis, Automata Theory, Data Processing, Business Games, Adaptive Systems, Information Theory, Information Retrieval, Recursive Function Theory, Computer Linguistics, etc., as these fields emerge in structure. ...Universities must respond [to the computer revolution] with far-reaching changes in the educational structure. [60]

At this time there were comparatively few graduate computer science programs available in American colleges; and they had other names, like Systems and Communication Sciences (Carnegie), Computer and Information Sciences (University of Pennsylvania), Communication Science (University of Michigan). Forsythe did not invent the term "computer science," which had gradually been working its way into the English language, but his influence was an important factor in the present widespread acceptance of the term.

A brief digression into the history of computer science education seems appropriate at this point. Apparently computing courses got started in universities largely because IBM donated about 100 "free" computers during the 1950s, with the stipulation that programming courses must be taught. This strategy made it possible for computing to get its foot in the academic door. Naturally there were many students and a few members of the faculty who were intrigued and became involved. Engineering departments, especially at schools like M.I.T., Pennsylvania, and Illinois, where computers were being built, also had a head start. Many ideas were exchanged during special summer school sessions at the University of Michigan, and later the Ford Foundation sponsored a project there on the use of computers in engineering education. A good survey of these developments has been given by Howard E. Tompkins [D].

But these early stages hardly represented computer science as it is understood today, nor did many people regard it as the germ of a genuine discipline worthy of study on a par with other subjects. I myself was a graduate student in mathematics who enjoyed programming as a hobby. I had written two compilers, but I had no idea that I would someday be teaching about data structures and relating all this to mathematics. A few people, like George Forsythe and Alan Perlis and Richard Hamming, had no such mental blocks. Louis Fein had also perceived the eventual rise of computer science; he had recommended in 1957 that Stanford establish a Graduate School of Computer Science, analogous to the Harvard Business School (cf. [B]).

George argued the case for computer science long and loud, and he won. At Stanford he was in fact "the producer and director, author, scene designer, and casting manager of this hit show." [A] Several more faculty members were carefully selected, and the Division became a separate academic department in January 1965.

Since this was one of the first such departments, it naturally came under very close scrutiny. Now we realize that eventually every university will have such a department. This development is inevitable in the long run, but it will happen sooner than might be expected largely because George was such an effective spokesman, especially to mathematicians and to people in the government.

Here are some important points he has made, in addition to those quoted earlier:

> The most valuable acquisitions in a scientific or technical education are the general-purpose mental tools which remain serviceable for a lifetime. I rate natural language and mathematics as the most important of these tools, and computer science as a third. ... The learning of mathematics and computer science together has pedagogical advantages, for the basic concepts of each reinforce the learning of the other. [71, pp. 456–457]

> The question "What can be automated?" is one of the most inspiring philosophical and practical questions of contemporary civilization. [75, p. 92]

The last sentence is taken from the introduction to an invited address on Computer Science and Education at the IFIP Congress 1968; I wish I could quote the entire article.

Forsythe frequently stressed the value of *experimental* computer science, as well as the theoretical:

> To a modern mathematician, design seems to be a second-rate intellectual activity. But in the most mathematical of the

sciences, physics, the role of design is highly appreciated. ...If experimental work can win half the laurels in physics, then good experimental work in computer science must be rated very high indeed. [68, p. 4]

Intense Activity

The primary reason George's views have been so influential is that he continually poured so much energy into all aspects of his work. One way to illustrate this is to focus on a randomly-selected period of his life and to look more deeply into his daily activity. Therefore I studied his correspondence file for the months of January and February 1964.

At this time his Division of Computer Science contained two faculty members besides himself (John Herriot and John McCarthy), plus two young "visiting assistant professors" for whom regular appointments were being arranged (Gene Golub and Niklaus Wirth), and an instructor (Harold Van Zoeren). As the correspondence shows, he was actively trying to build up the faculty, and I suspect that every computer scientist in America was approached at least twice during the early 1960s with a potential offer of employment at Stanford! George was also the director of Stanford's Computation Center, and a member of several national advisory panels and committees. In addition, he had just been appointed editor of the Algorithms section of *Communications*.

During this two-month period he wrote a total of 195 letters, which may be grouped as follows:

1. Faculty recruiting, 48 letters (including two addressed to me).
2. Algorithms section, editorial work, 43 letters.
3. Recommendations of policy to outside groups, 36 letters.
4. Departmental correspondence with graduate students, 35 letters.
5. Research interests, 11 letters.
6. Miscellaneous, 22 letters.

Many of these letters were two pages long; some were even longer.

Several letters described the current status of computer science at Stanford:

We are a bit separate from the Mathematics Department, and have responsibility for courses in numerical analysis, programming, artificial intelligence, and any other areas of Computer Science which we can manage. [3 January 1964]

The role of the Computer Science Division is likely to be increasingly divergent from that of Mathematics. It is important to acquire people with strong mathematics backgrounds, who are nevertheless prepared to follow Computer Science into its new directions. [7 January 1964]

We have a master's degree program with about 40 graduate students, and a number of students headed for interdepartmental Ph.D.'s in Computer Science. [8 January 1964]

One thing that enabled computer science to grow was the fact that other universities could point to Stanford's example. Conversely, George was able to make use of other universities' activities; in a memo to the dean on January 30, he said:

I enclose copies of two letters ... which indicate in and between the lines that [the University of Wisconsin in] Madison is putting on a really major effort in Computer Science. They are even calling it Computer Science at last!

On June 5, having been elected president of the ACM, George wrote:

Votes have strange outcomes in California. Goldwater and Forsythe.

By July 2, he was really feeling the increased responsibilities:

The pile of undigested mail on my desk is staggering.

His two years as ACM President were in general a rather happy and prosperous time for that organization. He published regular letters to the members [65] in *Communications*, and these letters are worth rereading today because in them he discussed many of his own feelings, as well as ACM business. His letter in the March 1965 issue contains an excellent account of how he grappled with the problems of a new Computer Science Department:

We must now turn our attention from the battle for recognition to the struggle to recognize the identity of our new discipline. ... One of my personal concerns with our Computer Science Department is to assess the future of numerical analysis. ... The core of Computer Science has become and will remain a field of its own, concerned with the forefront of new ideas. ... I conclude that the computer and information sciences badly need an association of people to study them, improve them, and render them better understood and thus more useful.

But the intended introduction to his President's Letter for September 1965 had to be changed. He had written:

I am delighted that you have voted to change our name to the *Association for Computing and Information Sciences*. ... I think it gives a much clearer picture of who we are and what we do.

A two-thirds majority was necessary for such a name change, and the actual vote was only 3794–2203. I must confess that I was one of the 2203 who opposed making a change; this was one of the few disagreements I ever had with George.

Algorithms

The major thing that distinguishes computer science from other disciplines is its emphasis on algorithms, and in this field George Forsythe made several vital contributions. He inaugurated a new area of scholarly work: refereeing and editing algorithms.

His point of view was nicely expressed in the "Forum on Algorithms" in *Communications*, April 1966:

> There are few problems for which a good algorithm of probable permanent value is known. ...Small details are of the greatest importance. ...The development of excellent algorithms requires a long time, from discovery of a basic idea to the perfection of the method. ...A useful algorithm is a substantial contribution to knowledge. Its publication constitutes an important piece of scholarship. [67]

He was fond of pointing out how much remains to be done, since even the solution to $ax^2 + bx + c = 0$ was at the frontier of well-understood problems:

> Hardly anyone knows how to solve even a quadratic equation on a computer without unnecessarily risking loss of precision or overflow or underflow! [68, p. 4]

As an indication of his behind-the-scenes activities, here are some more excerpts from letters he wrote during January and February 1964:

> The program is really in poor style, and I'm peeved with the referee for not saying so. You use a switch and a mass of **goto**'s where straightforward ALGOL would use conditional expressions. You even **goto** "here" from the line above "here"!! [8 January 1964]

> I am sorry that refereeing increases the time between submittal and publication, but I am confident that the net result of refereeing will be a large gain in the quality of our algorithms. [13 January 1964]

> It is very hard to find matching **begin**s and **end**s, which should be above each other or on the same line. [29 January 1964]

We are punching cards from the galleys and running them as a check. [24 February 1964]

I believe that our algorithms must have enough substantial content to save a programmer at least an hour's thought. [26 February 1964]

At that time approximately 180 algorithms per year were being submitted to *Communications*.

George also contributed to ACM publications in other ways: In 1966 he became the first editor of the Education department of *Communications*. He had been an editor of the *Journal* from 1955 to 1959, and he was chairman of the Editorial Board from 1960 to 1962.

The Permanence of Computer Science

How did George view these developments from a historical perspective? He set down his long-range views in the following memorandum, written at Stanford in 1970 just after Edsger Dijkstra had visited our department and stimulated some thought-provoking discussions:

> My feeling since 1962 has been that, even if Computer Science should turn out to be fully developed and fairly static by 1985, it will have been very important for universities to have created Computer Science Departments in the years 1960–1970. For, given the departmental structure of universities (which I deplore), I don't see how universities could otherwise have got rolling on research in this area. And without this research, much of the quality of computer usage in universities would be frozen at the level of Early FORTRAN.

> I don't mean that I do in fact forecast an end to the development of computer science by 1985. Being the study of computers, Computer Science can't begin to settle down until years after the hardware developments level off. This is not yet in sight.

> However, Dijkstra did set me to thinking about how long Computer Science will last. It may be that its difficult applications (like robotry and problem solving) will move off into various other disciplines. And the difficult problems in the core of Computer Science may get merged into discrete mathematics, as mathematicians get interested in them.

> On the other hand, there is very little evidence at present that mathematicians are taking any interest at all in the important questions of the mathematical theory of computation. (Speed,

optimality, data structures, storage requirements, proofs of correctness, etc., etc.) If they do not, then maybe these core computer scientists may absorb all of discrete mathematics themselves into a still unnamed discipline.

Most of all, I'd like to see universities able to restructure themselves into task forces able to attack new disciplines as they
arise. [14 April 1970]

He also had made another prediction:

In years to come we may expect a department of computer science to mix with departments of pure mathematics, operations
research, statistics, applied mathematics, and so on inside a
school of mathematical sciences. We can hope for some weaken-
ing of the autonomy of individual departments, and a concomi-
tant strengthening of the ability of a university to found and
carry out interdisciplinary programs. [68, p. 6]

Conclusion

I have tried to summarize our debt to George Forsythe by quoting from
the extensive writings in which he expressed important ideas so clearly.
But this is only part of the story. The accompanying article by John
Herriot [C] describes the more personal side of George's life — his selfless
assistance and counsel to his students and colleagues, and the real qual-
ities of leadership for which we are especially grateful.

Since I am not competent to write about numerical analysis, I have
not been able to describe George's respected contributions to research.
A short summary of this aspect of his work is being prepared by A. S.
Householder for publication in the *SIAM Journal on Numerical Analysis*
later this year. George knew that he would have to sacrifice much of the
time he wanted to spend on his main research interests, for the cause of
Computer Science. He quipped:

In the past 15 years many numerical analysts have progressed
from being queer people in mathematics departments to being
queer people in computer science departments! [71, p. 456]

Nevertheless he continued to stress the important connections between
numerical analysis and the other aspects of computer science.

He was a Fellow of both the British Computer Society and the American Association for the Advancement of Science. He was a council
member of the American Mathematical Society, 1960–63, and a Trustee
of the Society for Industrial and Applied Mathematics, 1971–72.

A bibliography of his publications appears below. In addition to these works, he published many shorter book reviews, letters to the editor, etc. He was especially concerned about the need for good books on computer science, so he served as the editor of Prentice–Hall's prestigious Series in Automatic Computation, encompassing more than 75 titles. This is a "fifteen-foot-shelf" to be compared with the books he listed in [26].

He took notes at every lecture he attended and kept them in beautifully organized files. This material, together with his correspondence, has been deposited in the Stanford University archives for the use of future historians.

Acknowledgments. Many people helped me prepare this article, especially John Herriot, Allen Newell, Alan Perlis, Guynn Perry, and Alexandra I. Forsythe. I also wish to thank the Mathematical Association of America, John Wiley and Sons, Ginn and Co., and the American Society for Engineering Education, for permission to reprint copyrighted remarks from George Forsythe's publications.

References

[A] Edward A. Feigenbaum, "A word entr'acte," Stanford University Computation Center newsletter, Autumn quarter, 1965.

[B] Louis Fein, "The computer-related sciences (Synnoetics) at a university in the year 1975," *American Scientist* **49** (1961), 149–168.

[C] John G. Herriot, "In memory of George E. Forsythe," *Communications of the ACM* **15** (1972), 719–720.

[D] Howard E. Tompkins, "Computer education," *Advances in Computers* **4** (New York: Academic Press, 1963), 135–168.

Bibliography of George Elmer Forsythe

BOOKS

Dynamic Meteorology (with Jörgen Holmboe and William Gustin). John Wiley, New York, 1945, 378 pp.

Bibliography of Russian Mathematics Books. Chelsea, New York, 1956, 106 pp.

Finite-Difference Methods for Partial Differential Equations (with Wolfgang Wasow). John Wiley, New York, 1960, 444 pp. Translations into Russian (1963) and Japanese (1968).

Computer Solution of Linear Algebraic Systems (with Cleve B. Moler). Prentice–Hall, Englewood Cliffs, New Jersey, 1967, 153 pp. Translations into Russian (1969), Japanese (1969), German (1971).

Computer Methods for Mathematical Computations (with Michael A. Malcolm and Cleve B. Moler). Prentice–Hall, Englewood Cliffs, New Jersey, 1977, 259 pp.

CLASS NOTES

Copies of the following typescripts exist in the Stanford University Libraries:

Theory of Selected Methods of Finite Matrix Inversion and Decomposition. Notes by Donald G. Aronson and Kenneth E. Iverson. UCLA Summer Session, 1951, 93 pp.

Numerical Methods for Elliptic Partial Differential Equations. Notes prepared with the help of Edwin Blue. UCLA Spring Quarter, 1955, 104 pp.

Computational Aspects of Linear Problems. Notes for a seminar. UCLA Spring Quarter, 1956, 130 pp.

ARTICLES

1. Riesz summability methods of order r, for $R(r) < 0$. *Duke Mathematical Journal* **8** (1941), 346–349.

2. Remarks on regularity of methods of summation (with A. C. Schaeffer). *Bulletin of the American Mathematical Society* **48** (1942), 863–865.

3. Cesàro summability of random variables. *Duke Mathematical Journal* **10** (1943), 397–428.

4. Note on equivalent-potential temperature. *Bulletin of the American Meteorological Society* **25** (1944), 149–151.

5. Remarks on the above paper by Neamtan. *Bulletin of the American Meteorological Society* **25** (1944), 228–229.

6. Determination of absolute height and wind for aircraft operations. Headquarters Army Air Forces Weather Division Report 708 (June 1944), 69 pp. [author's name omitted]

7. A generalization of the thermal wind equation to arbitrary horizontal flow. *Bulletin of the American Meteorological Society* **26** (1945), 371–375.

8. Universal tables for reduction of pressure to sea level. Headquarters Army Air Forces Weather Division Report 972 (June 1945), 22 pp. [author's name omitted]

9. Aircraft weather reconnaissance (with R. B. Doremus). Headquarters Army Air Forces Weather Service Report 105-128-1 (September 1945), 218 pp. [authors' names omitted]

10. War-time developments in aircraft weather reconnaissance. *Bulletin of the American Meteorological Society* **27** (1946), 160–163.

11. Discussion of E. V. Ashburn and L. L. Weiss's article on Vorticity. *Transactions of the American Geophysical Union* **27** (1946), 279–282.

12. Maximum density-altitude in the continental United States (with Morris S. Hendrickson). *Bulletin of the American Meteorological Society* **27** (1946), 576–579.

13. Speed of propagation of atmospheric waves with changing shape. *Journal of Meteorology* **4** (1947), 67–69.

14. On Nörlund summability of random variables to zero. *Bulletin of the American Mathematical Society* **53** (1947), 302–313.

15. Exact particle trajectories for nonviscous flow in a plane with a constant Coriolis parameter. *Journal of Meteorology* **6** (1949), 337–346.

16. Solution of the telegrapher's equation with boundary conditions on only one characteristic. *Journal of Research of the National Bureau of Standards* **44** (1950), 89–102.

17. Matrix inversion by a Monte Carlo method (with Richard A. Leibler). *Mathematical Tables and Other Aids to Computation* **4** (1950), 127–129. Errata, *Mathematical Tables and Other Aids to Computation* **5** (1951), 55.

18. Gauss to Gerling on Relaxation. *Mathematical Tables and Other Aids to Computation* **5** (1951), 255–258. (Translation, with notes, of a letter by Gauss.)

19. New matrix transformations for obtaining characteristic vectors (with William Feller). *Quarterly of Applied Mathematics* **8** (1951), 325–331. [Presented at the International Congress of Mathematicians, 1950.]

20. Second order determinants of Legendre polynomials. *Duke Mathematical Journal* **18** (1951), 361–371.

21. Generation and testing of random digits at the National Bureau of Standards, Los Angeles. *National Bureau of Standards Applied Mathematics Series* **12** (1951), 34–35.

22. Summary of John von Neumann's lecture, "Various techniques used in connection with random digits." *National Bureau of Standards Applied Mathematics Series* **12** (1951), 36–38. Reprinted in von Neumann's *Collected Works* **5**, 768–770.

23. Theory of selected methods of finite matrix inversion and decomposition. Institute for Numerical Analysis Report 52-5 (Los Angeles: National Bureau of Standards, 1951), 93 pp.

24. An extension of Gauss' transformation for improving the condition of systems of linear equations (with Theodore S. Motzkin). *Mathematical Tables and Other Aids to Computation* **6** (1952), 9–17.

25. Bibliographical survey of Russian mathematical monographs, 1930–1951. National Bureau of Standards Report 1628 (25 March 1952), 64 pp. Supplement, Report 1628A (12 December 1952), 17 pp.

26. A numerical analyst's fifteen-foot shelf. *Mathematical Tables and Other Aids to Computation* **7** (1953), 221–228.

27. Tentative classification of methods and bibliography on solving systems of linear equations. *National Bureau of Standards Applied Mathematics Series* **29** (1953), 1–28.

28. Punched-card experiments with accelerated gradient methods for linear equations (with A. I. Forsythe). *National Bureau of Standards Applied Mathematics Series* **39** (1954), 55–69.

29. Alternative derivations of Fox's escalator formulae for latent roots. *Quarterly Journal of Mechanics and Applied Mathematics* **5** (1952), 191–195.

30. Solving linear algebraic equations can be interesting. *Bulletin of the American Mathematical Society* **59** (1953), 299–329.

31. Asymptotic lower bounds for the frequencies of polygonal membranes. *Pacific Journal of Mathematics* **4** (1954), 467–480.

32. Review of A. S. Householder, *Principles of Numerical Analysis*. *Bulletin of the American Mathematical Society* **60** (1954), 488–491.

33. Asymptotic lower bounds for the fundamental frequency of convex membranes. *Pacific Journal of Mathematics* **5** (1955), 691–702.

34. What are relaxation methods? In *Modern Mathematics for the Engineer*, edited by E. F. Beckenbach (New York: McGraw–Hill, 1956), 428–447.

35. On best conditioned matrices (with E. G. Straus). *Proceedings of the American Mathematical Society* **6** (1955), 340–345. [Presented at the International Congress of Mathematicians, Amsterdam, 1954.]

36. SWAC computes 126 distinct semigroups of order 4. *Proceedings of the American Mathematical Society* **6** (1955), 443–447.

37. The Souriau-Frame characteristic equation algorithm on a digital computer (with Louise W. Straus). *Journal of Mathematical Physics* **34** (1955), 152–156.

38. Computing constrained minima with Lagrange multipliers. *Journal of the Society for Industrial and Applied Mathematics* **3** (1955), 173–178.

39. Relaxation methods. In *Mathematical Theory of Elasticity*, 2nd edition, Section 125, edited by I. S. Sokolnikoff (New York: McGraw–Hill, 1956), 454–465.

40. Difference methods on a digital computer for Laplacian boundary value and eigenvalue problems. *Communications on Pure and Applied Mathematics* **9** (1956), 425–434.

41. Selected references on use of high-speed computers for scientific computation. *Mathematical Tables and Other Aids to Computation* **10** (1956), 25–27.

42. Generation and use of orthogonal polynomials for data fitting with a digital computer. *Journal of the Society for Industrial and Applied Mathematics* **5** (1957), 74–88.

43. The educational program in numerical analysis of the Department of Mathematics, U.C.L.A. In *The Computing Laboratory in the University*, edited by Preston C. Hammer (University of Wisconsin Press, 1957), 145–151.

44. Suggestions to students on talking about mathematics papers. *American Mathematical Monthly* **64** (1957), 16–18.

45. The role of computers in high school science education. *Computers and Automation* **6**, 8 (August 1957), 15–16.

46. Contemporary state of numerical analysis. In *Numerical Analysis and Partial Differential Equations* (with Paul C. Rosenbloom), *Surveys in Applied Mathematics* **5** (New York: John Wiley, 1958), 1–42.

47. SWAC experiments on the use of orthogonal polynomials for data fitting (with Marcia Ascher). *Journal of the Association for Computing Machinery* **5** (1958), 9–21.

48. Singularity and near singularity in numerical analysis. *American Mathematical Monthly* **65** (1958), 229–240.

49. The role of numerical analysis in an undergraduate program. *American Mathematical Monthly* **66** (1959), 651–662.

50. Numerical methods for high-speed computers — a survey. *Proceedings of the Western Joint Computer Conference* **15** (Institute for Radio Engineers, March 1959), 249–254.

51. Bibliography on high school mathematics education. *Computers and Automation* **8**, 5 (May 1959), 17–19.

52. Reprint of a note on rounding-off errors. *SIAM Review* **1** (1959), 66–67.

53. The cyclic Jacobi method for computing the principal values of a complex matrix (with P. Henrici). *Transactions of the American Mathematical Society* **94** (1960), 1–23.

54. Solution to problem E1398 (with G. Szegő). *American Mathematical Monthly* **67** (1960), 696–697.

55. Review of John L. Selfridge, *On Finite Semigroups*. *Mathematics of Computation* **14** (1960), 204–207.

56. Remark on Algorithm 15 (with John G. Herriot). *Communications of the ACM* **3** (1960), 602.

57. Crout with pivoting in ALGOL 60. *Communications of the ACM* **3** (1960), 507–508.

58. Vectorcardiographic diagnosis with the aid of ALGOL (with J. von der Groeben and J. G. Toole). *Communications of the ACM* **5** (1962), 118–122.

59. Engineering students must learn both computing and mathematics. *Journal of Engineering Education* **52** (1961), 177–188.

60. Educational implications of the computer revolution. *Applications of Digital Computers*, edited by W. F. Freiberger and William Prager (Boston: Ginn, 1963), 166–178.

61. Tests of Parlett's ALGOL eigenvalue procedure *Eig 3*. *Mathematics of Computation* **18** (1964), 486–487.

62. Automatic grading programs (with Niklaus Wirth). *Communications of the ACM* **8** (1965), 275–278.

63. On the stationary values of a second-degree polynomial on the unit sphere (with Gene H. Golub). *Journal of the Society for Industrial and Applied Mathematics* **13** (1965), 1050–1068.

64. An undergraduate curriculum in numerical analysis. *Communications of the ACM* **7** (1964), 214–215.

65. President's Letters to the ACM Membership. *Communications of the ACM* **7** (1964), 448, 507, 558, 633–634, 697; **8** (1965), 3, 143–144, 422–423, 541, 591, 727; **9** (1966), 1, 244, 325.

66. Solution to Problem 5334. *American Mathematical Monthly* **72** (1965), 1030.

67. Algorithms for scientific computation. *Communications of the ACM* **9** (1966), 255–256.

68. A university's educational program in Computer Science. *Communications of the ACM* **10** (1967), 3–11.

69. Today's computational methods of linear algebra. *SIAM Review* **9** (1967), 489–515. Reprinted in *Studies in Numerical Analysis* **1** (Philadelphia: Society for Industrial and Applied Mathematics, 1968).

70. On the asymptotic directions of the *s*-dimensional optimum gradient method. *Numerische Mathematik* **11** (1968), 57–76.

71. What to do till the computer scientist comes. *American Mathematical Monthly* **75** (1968), 454–462. [Winner of the Lester R. Ford Award, 1969.]

72. Solving a quadratic equation on a computer. In *The Mathematical Sciences*, edited by COSRIMS and George Boehm (Cambridge, Massachusetts: MIT Press, 1969), 138–152.

73. Remarks on the paper by Dekker. In *Constructive Aspects of the Fundamental Theorem of Algebra*, edited by Bruno Dejon and Peter Henrici (New York: Wiley-Interscience, 1969), 49–51.

74. What is a satisfactory quadratic equation solver? In *Constructive Aspects of the Fundamental Theorem of Algebra*, edited by Bruno Dejon and Peter Henrici (New York: Wiley-Interscience, 1969), 53–61.

75. Computer science and education. *Information Processing 68*, edited by A. J. H. Morrell, **2** (Amsterdam: North-Holland, 1969), 1025–1039.

76. Design — then and now. *Digest Record of the ACM–SIAM–IEEE 1969 Joint Conference on Mathematical and Computer Aids to Design* (ACM, 1969), 2–10.

77. Let's not discriminate against good work in design or experimentation. *Proceedings of the Spring Joint Computer Conference* **34** (Montvale, New Jersey: AFIPS Press, 1969), 538–539.

78. Pitfalls in computation, or why a math book isn't enough. *American Mathematical Monthly* **77** (1970), 931–956. [Winner of the Lester R. Ford Award, 1971.]

79. The maximum and minimum of a positive definite quadratic polynomial on a sphere are convex functions of the radius. *SIAM Journal of Applied Mathematics* **19** (1970), 551–554.

80. Computer science and mathematics. *SIGCSE Bulletin* **2**, 4 (September/October 1970), 20–23.

81. Recent references on solving elliptic partial differential equations by finite differences or finite elements. *SIGNUM Newsletter* **6**, 1 (January 1971), 32–56.

82. Variational study of nonlinear spline curves (with E. H. Lee). *SIAM Review* **15** (1973), 120–133.

83. von Neumann's comparison method for random sampling from the normal and other distributions. *Mathematics of Computation* **26** (1972), 817–826.

Ph.D. Students

(A) Ph.D. in Mathematics with specialty in Numerical Analysis
(B) Interdepartmental Ph.D.
(C) Ph.D. in Computer Science

Eldon Hansen (Forsythe, 1960). On Jacobi methods and block-Jacobi methods for computing matrix eigenvalues. (A)

James Ortega (Forsythe, 1962). An error analysis of Householder's method for the symmetric eigenvalue problem. (A)

Betty Jane Stone (Forsythe, 1962). 1. Best possible ratios of certain matrix norms. 2. Lower bounds for the eigenvalues of a fixed membrane. (A)

Beresford Parlett (Forsythe, 1962). Applications of Laguerre's method to the matrix eigenvalue problem. (A)

Donald Fisher (Forsythe and Gilbarg, 1962). Calculation of subsonic cavities with sonic free streamlines. (A)

Ramon E. Moore (Forsythe and McGregor, 1963). Interval arithmetic and automatic error analysis in digital computing. (A)

Robert Causey (Forsythe, 1964). On closest normal matrices. (A)

Cleve B. Moler (Forsythe, 1965). Finite difference methods for the eigenvalues of Laplace's operator. (A)

James Daniel (Forsythe and Schiffer, 1965). The conjugate gradient method for linear and nonlinear operator equations. (A)

Donald W. Grace (Forsythe and Pólya, 1965). Computer search for nonisomorphic convex polyhedra. (B)

James M. Varah (Forsythe, 1966). The computation of bounds for the invariant subspaces of a general matrix operator. (A)

Roger W. Hockney (Buneman, Forsythe, and Golub, 1966). The computer simulation of anomalous plasma diffusion and the numerical solution of Poisson's equation. (B)

Paul Richman (Forsythe and Herriot, 1968). 1. ε-Calculus. 2. Transonic fluid flow and the approximation of the iterated integrals of a singular function. (C)

J. Alan George (Forsythe and Dorr, 1971). Computer implementation of the finite element method. (C)

Richard P. Brent (Forsythe, Dorr, and Moler, 1971). Algorithms for finding zeros and extrema of functions without calculating derivatives. (C)

David R. Stoutemyer (Forsythe, 1972). Numerical implementation of the Schwarz alternating procedure for elliptic partial differential equations. (C)

George Forsythe in 1971

Index